The Illustrated
Reference Book of
The Earth

Picture Credits

The Illustrated Reference Book of The Earth
This edition published in 1982 by
WINDWARD
an imprint owned by W. H. Smith & Son Limited
Registered No. 237811 England Trading as WHS Distributors St John's House East Street Leicester LE1 6NE

© Mitchell Beazley Encyclopaedias Limited 1980, 1982

Pages 2-139 © Mitchell Beazley Encyclopaedias Limited 1976 and 1977
Artwork © Mitchell Beazley Publishers Limited 1970, 1971, 1972, 1973, 1974, 1975 and 1976
© International Visual Resource 1972
© Mitchell Beazley Encyclopaedias Limited 1976

Previously published as *Anatomy of the Earth*

ISBN 0 7112 0232 X

Phototypeset in Great Britain by Filmtype Services Limited, Scarborough
Printed in Yugoslavia by Mladinska Knjiga

The Joy of Knowledge
GENERAL EDITOR: JAMES MITCHELL

The Illustrated Reference Book of The Earth

WINDWARD

Preface

How to use this book

The Earth is one complete section of the *Joy of Knowledge*. It contains all the general knowledge my editors and I think most interesting about the earth's structure. It has been our intention to present the mass of available information on this important subject in such a way that it will make sense to you, and tell a logical, relevant and coherent story.

The spread system

Every topic in the *Joy of Knowledge* takes the form of an article that occupies two facing pages of text and pictures; what we call a "spread". Each two-page spread in the book is organized in the same way. It is the heart of our approach to explaining things.

The spread system is a strict discipline but once you get used to it we hope you'll find the structure to be systematic and reassuring. You should start to feel at home in all sorts of unlikely areas of knowledge with the spread system to guide you. It works like this.

Each two-page spread in *The Earth,* as throughout the *Joy of Knowledge,* tells a self-contained story. It explains all the essential facts you need to know about its subject in as efficient a manner as possible. We believe that the discipline of having to get all the essential and relevant facts on a subject in this comparatively small space actually makes for better results than a rambling essay could achieve – text that gets straight to the point, pictures and diagrams that illustrate the salient points in a clear and comprehensible fashion, and captions that really work and explain the relevance of the illustrations.

The spreads are, in a sense, the building blocks of knowledge. Like the various circuits and components that go to make up a computer, they are also systematically "programmed" to help the reader to find out things more easily and remember them better. Each spread, for example, has a main article of about 850 words summarising the subject. This article is illustrated by an average of ten pictures and diagrams, the captions of which both complement and supplement the basic information in the main article. Each spread, too, has a "key" picture or diagram in the top right-hand corner. The purpose of this picture is twofold: it summarises visually the story of the spread and is intended to act as a memory stimulator to help you to recall all the integrated facts and pictures on a given subject.

Where to start

A good way to begin acquiring knowledge from this particular part of the *Joy of Knowledge* is initially to read the Introduction. The Introduction provides a useful framework for the information contained in the following pages. If, however, you prefer to plunge straight into the book (but don't have much basic general knowledge of the subject) I suggest you look first at the spreads "Anatomy of the earth" beginning on page 2, "Global tectonics" on page 6, "Gravity and the shape of the earth" on page 14, "Shapes and structures of crystals" on page 76 and "Earth's time scale" on page 112. Once you have absorbed the information on these spreads you can build up a more comprehensive general knowledge by exploring the rest of the book.

The Earth is a fascinating book about man's attempts to understand the forces at work in his world. I hope you will enjoy reading it and will find it helpful.

Contents

The Illustrated Reference Book of The Earth

Editor's Introduction

This graphic volume deals with the Earth as a physical whole – what it is made of, what it looks like and the natural influences that have shaped its surface and produced the features that we see around us today. The topics included are geology, meteorology, oceanography, geomorphology, and stratigraphy – in fact, all the subjects that are grouped together under the heading of the earth sciences. These subjects are presented in the various major sections of the book.

The Earth as a whole

An introductory spread describes the composition and structure of the Earth from its core to its crust. The difficulties a geophysicist encounters in collating all this information are revealed by a comparison of the meagre nature of the evidence and the conclusions that can be drawn from it. The Earth's magnetic field and its use in dating geological events and in helping in the search for new deposits of minerals unfolds as a truly fascinating subject.

The Earth in motion

Attention is then focused on the crust of the Earth and the movements that take place there. The crust is not a rigid, stationary shell – it is constantly in motion. Only in the last two decades has the nature of this motion been studied seriously. It has been found that new crust is constantly being created along lines where new material, welling up from the Earth's interior, solidifies. This crust forms plates that move away from their points of origin as they are created. Where plates travelling in opposite directions meet, one slides beneath the other. The continents are carried about on plates like logs embedded in ice, and this movement accounts for the

distribution of oceans and land masses that we see today. New plates are continuously being formed in the ocean ridges, and destroyed in the ocean trenches at the bottoms of the deep oceans.

Following a full description of this process, the book goes on to study the movements of the continents throughout time, and the more spectacular type of motion that manifests itself in earthquakes and volcanic eruptions. All these are looked at in the context of the new study of plate tectonics.

Looking at the Earth

The next section of this fact-filled book studies the surface of the Earth and could be regarded as an examination of the results of plate tectonics. It begins with an explanation of surveying techniques and describes the various ways in which the three-dimensional surface features of the Earth can be recorded and displayed on a flat map. This is followed by descriptions of all the continents, using physical maps and a selection of the best satellite photographs taken during NASA's Apollo and Skylab missions. In this way the strange, almost abstract, shapes on maps are brought to life and seen to be actual coastlines, mountain ranges, deserts, rivers and oceans.

The Earth's canopy

The atmosphere is examined next, from its physical and chemical make-up to the way in which it affects us directly in the form of weather. This section explains how convection currents produce circulation of the winds all round the Earth and establish the various climatic belts. There is also a spread describing the techniques employed in forecasting the day-to-day fluctuations of this climatic pattern. These fluctuations constitute the weather of a particular place.

The oceans

The waters that cover more than 70 per cent of the Earth's surface are then dealt with in a number of spreads. Starting with the chemistry and physics of seawater, the book describes the movement and circulation of seawater in the form of the great ocean currents and their influence on climate. Next, there is a section on the large-scale movements of the waters in the form of the tides, and their small-scale movements as waves. Then comes the seabed – its geographic features and the sediments that cover it. Each ocean is illustrated individually in a series of relief maps that depict the oceanic ridges, where new crustal plates are being created, and the trenches, where they are being destroyed. A brief history of oceanographic exploration follows and there is an account of the developments in technology that have made such exploration possible in recent years.

Minerals

Now the book turns to the materials of the continents. It examines how natural materials form the regular shapes we see as crystals, and progresses to an account of the substances that form such shapes – the minerals, the building blocks of the rocks of the Earth's crust. A spread then looks at the rare and beautiful gems and semi-precious stones that make up such a small but attractive part of the mineral kingdom.

Rocks and their movements

The description of minerals leads naturally to a description of rocks, which are being created and destroyed in a continuous cycle –

the rock cycle. The three different types of rock are: igneous rocks, solidified from hot molten material, sedimentary rocks, formed from sand or other fragments laid down and cemented together, and metamorphic rocks, formed by great heat or pressure. The movements of these rocks produce visible features, such as folds and faults, that help to explain the changing landscape and the creation of mountains.

Landscapes

The section on geomorphology, the study of landscapes, opens with a spread on the movement of water through or over land. This is important because flowing water is one of the most powerful agents of landscape formation. It may dissolve great caverns and gorges in limestone country, or it may form rivers, that cut various types of valleys in high ground and spread the debris so formed over the plains.

Water solidified in the form of ice creates totally different landscapes. These are characterized by extensive erosion producing steep-sided mountains and deep U-shaped valleys; the material gouged out of the valley floors can be carried enormous distances by glaciers.

The vast ice caps – and their changes during the Ice Ages – and the desert landscapes, which do not depend on water for their formation, are fully described as are the coastline features, such as stacks and blow holes, formed as a result of erosion by the sea.

The Earth's history

There are four spreads on the subject of stratigraphy, or historical geology – the study of conditions on the Earth's surface in times past. That part of the rock cycle

dealing with the sedimentary rocks is reiterated and developed. The various sedimentary rocks are formed by different processes and under different conditions. These processes and conditions often leave their marks on the subsequent rocks and give us some idea of what the surface of the Earth was like at the time of the formation of the rocks. For example, sands laid down in a river bed form a totally different type of sandstone from those laid down in a desert, with structures that could be created only by river currents and possibly with fragments of plants that would not grow in a desert. An idealized section through a rocky cliff is shown and the various rocks, structures and fossils found in it indicate the changing conditions at that part of the Earth throughout geological time. All this information can be plotted on maps and the various types of geological map are described. Such maps are valuable as indicators of where to seek mineral deposits, such as oil and coal. Finally, the story of the Earth's surface up to the present day is detailed.

Thus *The Earth* is concerned with the whole panoply of the earth sciences, from our speculations about the Earth's core through the study of the various materials in the crust to our more detailed knowledge of the conditions at the surface. The subject is fascinating in its complexity. This book should provide a valuable introduction and will appeal to anybody wishing to embark on this most interesting aspect of the natural sciences. All the other sciences are also involved in one way or another, and anyone studying any of them is certain to find much relevant information of interest.

Anatomy of the earth

The earth is made up of several concentric shells, like the bulb of an onion. Each shell has its own particular chemical composition and physical properties. These shells are grouped into three main regions: the outermost is called the crust, which surrounds the mantle; the innermost is the core.

The solid crust on which we live is no thicker in relation to the earth than an egg shell, taking up only one-and-a-half per cent of the earth's volume. Scientists have been able to learn a great deal about the uppermost part of the crust by direct observation. Their knowledge of the earth's interior, on the other hand, comes from the study of earthquake wave paths.

Earthquake waves are bent, like light passing through a piece of glass, when they traverse rock boundaries with different densities. If the waves hit the boundary at a low angle, they are reflected instead. Waves from distant earthquakes emerge steeply through the crust while those from earthquakes nearby emerge at shallow angles. By knowing these angles, the velocities at which the waves emerge, their times of arrival and distances travelled, geophysicists have been able to compute the positions and densities of the earth's different shells.

Observing the earth's crust

The chemical composition of the crust [Key] and upper mantle is known from direct observation of rocks at or near the earth's surface [2]. Below the upper mantle, little is certain, although similarities may exist between iron and stony meteorites and the composition of the earth's deep interior.

The upper crust over continental areas is known as "sial" (from the first two letters of its most abundant elements, silicon and aluminium). Over oceanic areas, and underlying the continental sial, is the crust called "sima" (from silicon and magnesium, the most abundant elements found in it) [Key]. The sial has a density of $2.7g/cm^3$; it is lighter than the sima (density $2.9g/cm^3$), and lies above it to form the continents. The oceanic crust is made of sima with a thin veneer of sediments and lavas.

The crust is separated from the mantle by a sudden change of density (2.9 to $3.3g/cm^3$) which shows up as a good reflecting plane for earthquake waves. This plane is known as the Mohorovičić discontinuity (Moho for short) [2], after the Croatian who discovered it in 1909, and is taken to represent the base of the crust. The Moho is at an average depth of 35km (20 miles) under the continents and of a mere 10km (6 miles) below sea-level under the oceans and seas.

Beneath the crust

The upper mantle [1] consists of a thin rigid top layer extending from below the Moho to a depth of about 60–100km (40–60 miles), a pasty layer or asthenosphere down to about 200km (120 miles) and a thick bottom layer between 200 and 700km (120–430 miles). The uppermost layer together with the overlying crust forms the rigid lithosphere which is divided laterally into plates. These plates drift on the asthenosphere where pressure and temperature almost reach melting-point, leading to near-fluidity.

The upper mantle is separated from the lower mantle by another discontinuity, where the rock density again increases (3.3 to 4.3

1 The earth's crust varies in thickness from 40km (25 miles) to 5km (3 miles) under the sea-floor. With the uppermost mantle it forms the rigid lithosphere [1] which overlies a plastic layer, the asthenosphere [2], on which it may drift sideways. The upper mantle [3] goes down to 700km (430 miles) where it overlies the lower mantle [4]. The mantle is made of peridotite which is near melting-point in the asthenosphere. This at least is the explanation for the slowing-down of seismic waves at those depths and it fits the plate tectonics theory. The increase of density in the lower mantle is thought to be due to increased pressure and packing of the atoms, without a change of chemical composition. The mantle is separated from the outer core [6] by another seismic wave discontinuity, the Gutenberg discontinuity [5]. P wave velocity drops from 14km (9 miles) to 8km (5 miles) per second and S waves are not transmitted inside the outer core. These observations indicate that the outer core is in a liquid state. The density jumps from $5.5g/cm^3$ for the lower mantle to $10g/cm^3$ for the outer core where it increases downwards to 12 or $13g/cm^3$. Although the core is only 16% of the earth by volume, it represents 32% of its mass. The core is thought to consist of iron and nickel, a hypothesis that fits the data and is inspired by the iron-nickel meteorites which are thought to be the remnants of another planet. P waves show another discontinuity [7] and increase their speed in the centre of the earth or inner core [8], which is solid.

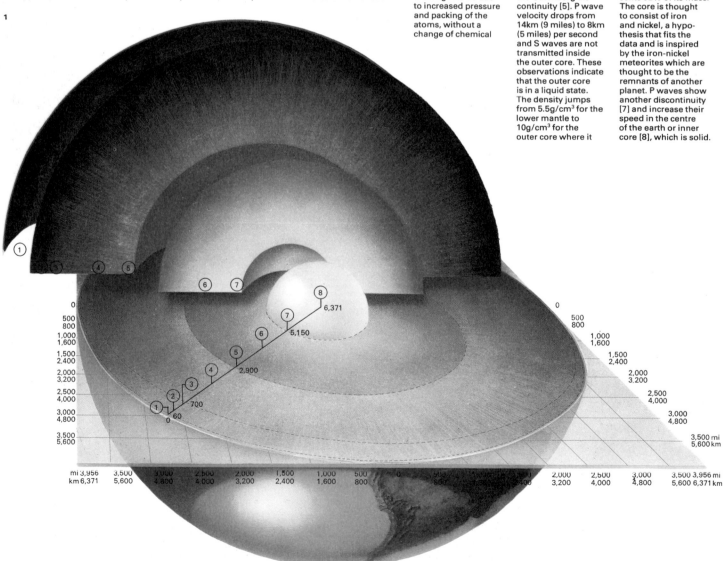

g/cm³). Here, the composition is thought to be chiefly peridotite, plus minerals of higher density, the latter formed as a result of the crushing pressure of the rocks above.

Between the lower mantle and the core lies a further discontinuity at a depth of 2,900km (1,800 miles), at which the density increases from 5.5 to 10g/cm³. This is the Gutenberg discontinuity, discovered in 1914. The core itself is divided at a depth of 5,150km (3,200 miles) into an outer and an inner zone thought to be composed of iron-nickel alloy. The outer zone is believed to be liquid because it stops S waves (shearing earthquake waves), while the inner zone is believed to be solid because P (compressional) waves travel slightly faster there. The density changes from 12.3 to about 13.3g./cm³ at the boundary of outer and inner cores and increases to about 13.6g/cm³ at the centre of the earth, 6, 371km (3,956 miles) down.

Meteorites reaching the earth's surface provide clues as to its composition. Such meteorites are made either of stone or else are made predominantly of iron. The propor-

tion of stony to iron meteorites is more or less equal to the proportion of the mass of the mantle to the core of the earth. Meteorites probably represent the remains of another planet similar to the earth and which broke up at some unknown period [1].

Heat behaviour

The amount of heat reaching the surface from within the earth can be represented on a heat flow profile [2]. From the earth's surface, the temperature rises to about 375°C (710°F), increasing in the upper mantle to 800°C (1,480°F) at 50km (32 miles) and 1,800°C (3,300°F) at 1,000km (625 miles). The estimated temperature for the lower mantle is 2,250°C (4,600°F) at a depth of 2,000km (1,250 miles) and 2,500°C (4,600°F) at the mantlecore boundary – a depth of 2,900km (1,800 miles). The temperature at the centre of the earth is probably about 3,000°C (5,400°F).

Heat is transferred to the surface by convection and conduction. In the solid layers it is probably transferred by conduction; in the liquid layers by convection.

The earth is composed of three main layers – the crust, mantle and core. The crust is subdivided into continental and oceanic material. The upper continental crust is mostly granite, rich in silicon and aluminium (*si*licon and *al*uminium = sial). The oceanic crust is essentially basalt, rich in silicon and magnesium (*si*licon and *ma*gnesium = sima); sima also underlies continental sial. The sial continents, of a lighter material than the sima, tend to float upon it like icebergs in the sea. The mantle consists of rock, rich in magnesium and iron silicates, and the dense core probably consists mainly of iron and nickel oxides in a molten condition.

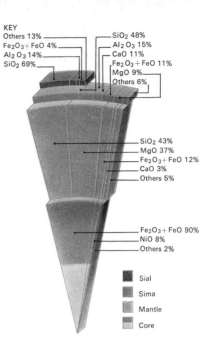

KEY

Others 13%
Fe₂O₃+FeO 4%
Al₂O₃ 14%
SiO₂ 69%

SiO₂ 48%
Al₂O₃ 15%
CaO 11%
Fe₂O₃+FeO 11%
MgO 9%
Others 6%

SiO₂ 43%
MgO 37%
Fe₂O₃+FeO 12%
CaO 3%
Others 5%

Fe₂O₃+FeO 90%
NiO 8%
Others 2%

- Sial
- Sima
- Mantle
- Core

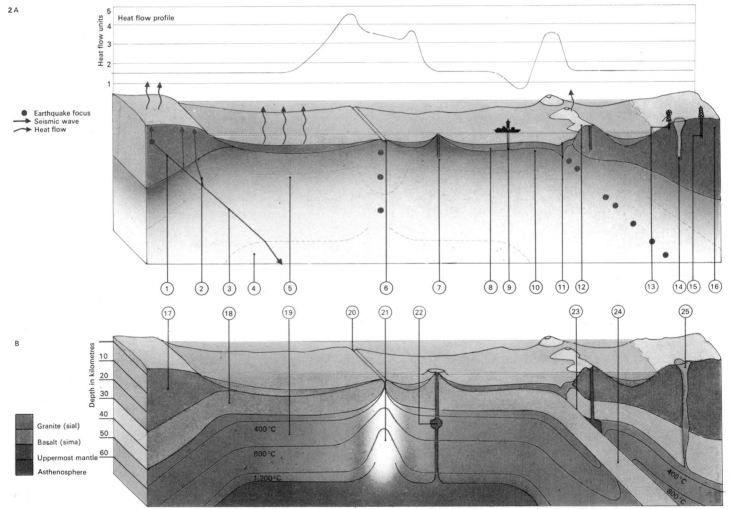

2 A

Heat flow profile

Heat flow units

- ● Earthquake focus
- → Seismic wave
- ⇒ Heat flow

① ② ③ ④ ⑤ ⑥ ⑦ ⑧ ⑨ ⑩ ⑪ ⑫ ⑬ ⑭⑮⑯

⑰ ⑱ ⑲ ⑳ ㉑ ㉒ ㉓ ㉔ ㉕

B

Depth in kilometres

10 20 30 40 50 60

400°C
800°C
1,200°C

400°C
800°C

- Granite (sial)
- Basalt (sima)
- Uppermost mantle
- Asthenosphere

2 The mantle and crust are studied by various means [A]. Heat flow from the earth's interior is high over volcanic areas [7], island arcs [12] and along ocean ridges [6], and low along ocean trenches [11]. The zone of direct observation reaches its limits at [9] the deepest marine drill-hole, 1,300m (4,265ft) below the sea-bed, at [13] the deepest mine, 3,848m (12,600ft), and at [15] the deepest land bore-hole, 9,583m (31,441ft). Earthquake foci occur in particular planes. Earthquake shocks generate seismic waves which travel faster the deeper they go through the crust [1, 2]. Beyond the Mohorovičić discontinuity [5] lies the mantle, where the seismic waves enter a high-velocity zone [3], later slowing down in the underlying low-velocity zone [4]. Marine sediments [8] accumulate on the ocean floor above the oceanic crust [10]. The continental crust [16] lies above the latter. At [14] is a peridotite massif, rich in iron and magnesium, intruded from the earth's interior. All these data are interpreted in [B]. The sea-floor crust [18] is composed of basalt, and the continental one [17] of granite overlying a basaltic layer. The mantle [19] is made of peridotite. High heat flow and low-intensity seisms are associated with oceanic ridges [20] where magma ascends from the mantle [21]. Sometimes magma is temporarily stored in a magma chamber [22] before it is released by eruption. At [24] the cold lithospheric plate is subducted along the Benioff zone [23], diving into the mantle beneath an adjacent plate and melting magma by friction. Peridotic intrusions [25] have risen through deep crustal cracks to the earth's surface.

The earth as a magnet

The earth has a strong magnetic field [Key]. A bar magnet suspended by a thread eventually comes to rest with one end pointing towards the earth's north magnetic pole, the other towards the south magnetic pole. It behaves similarly if another bar magnet, or large coil of wire with electricity flowing through it, is brought near.

Origin of the earth's magnetic field
As the earth spins on its axis the fluid layer of the outer core allows the mantle and solid crust to rotate relatively faster than the inner core. As a result, electrons in the core move relative to those in the mantle and crust. It is this electron movement that constitutes a natural dynamo and as a result produces a magnetic field, similar to that produced by an electric coil [1].

The magnetic axis of the earth is inclined slightly to the earth's geographical axis [Key] by about 11 degrees, and the magnetic poles do not coincide with the geographic north and south poles. The earth's magnetic axis is continually changing its angle in relation to the geographic axis, but over a long time – some tens of thousands of years – an average relative position is established.

A compass needle points to a position some distance away from the geographical north and south poles. The difference, which is known as the declination [3], varies from one geographical location to the next. Small-scale variations in the earth's magnetism are probably caused by minor eddies or swirls in the outer core at the junction between the core and the mantle. Large bodies of magnetized rock and ore in the crust can have a similar effect.

The earth's magnetic field is distorted by electrically charged particles from the sun [5]. These particles flow in the upper atmosphere and create small variations of the magnetic field at ground level. Some variations are regular – such as the diurnal (night and day) variation – and some, such as magnetic storms, are occasional.

The earth's magnetic field in ancient times
The study of the magnetic field of the geological past is called palaeomagnetism. It relies on the fact that rocks may pick up a perma-nent magnetization when they are formed, or when they remelt and cool at some later date. When rocks are heated they lose their magnetization, as an ordinary bar magnet does when heated. Rocks are remagnetized by the earth's field when they cool. This natural remanent magnetization, as it is called, lies parallel to the lines of the earth's magnetic field at the time of rock formation. Rocks magnetized in this way therefore carry a permanent record of the field, and can thus be used to study the geological history of the earth's magnetic field.

There are several ways in which magnetic "clues" to the earth's history can be deposited in the rocks. The technique of palaeomagnetic – literally "old magnetism" – investigation is to drill out a cylinder of rock and then measure its natural remanent magnetism. This gives the palaeomagnetic co-ordinates of the specimen, which allows its original position to be plotted. Magnetic coordinates, expressed in magnetic latitudes [4], are similar to geographical latitudes (but the pole considered is the magnetic pole instead of the rotation pole). Palaeomagnetic

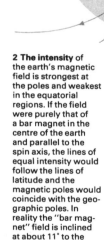

1 The magnetic field originating inside the earth makes up about 90 per cent of the field observed at ground level. The remainder is due to currents of charged particles coming from the sun and to the magnetism of rocks in the crust. The difference in rotation speed between the liquid outer core and the mantle creates a dynamo effect [A], which generates a field similar to that of a coil [B]. In reality the situation is more complex for it involves interaction between two types of magnetic fields and small variations may change the polarity of the earth's field. Irregularities in the magnetic field at the earth's surface are caused by minor eddies of the core liquid. Their displacement in time results in long-term variations of the geomagnetic field, causing gradual changes of direction for magnetic north in given locations.

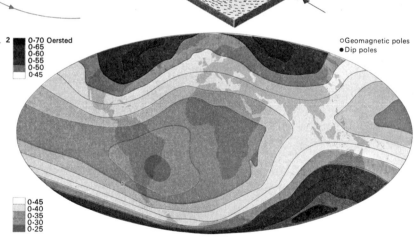

2 The intensity of the earth's magnetic field is strongest at the poles and weakest in the equatorial regions. If the field were purely that of a bar magnet in the centre of the earth and parallel to the spin axis, the lines of equal intensity would follow the lines of latitude and the magnetic poles would coincide with the geographic poles. In reality the "bar magnet" field is inclined at about 11° to the spin axis and so are its geomagnetic poles. Also the real field is not purely that of a bar magnet. The "dip poles", where the field direction is vertical (downwards at the north pole and upwards at the south dip pole), are themselves offset in respect to the geomagnetic poles – each by a different amount so that the S dip pole is not exactly opposite the N dip pole. The poles and the configuration of the field change slowly with time.

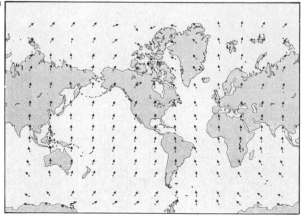

3 The declination is the angle between the direction of a magnetic compass and geographic north. The lines of force radiate from the southern dip pole [S] and converge towards the northern dip pole [N]. The arrows symbolize the direction of the magnetic north in 1955. Declination exists because the earth's field is not exactly like that of a bar magnet lined up along the axis of the earth. Account of this must be taken in navigation.

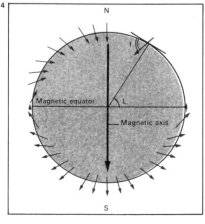

4 The dip or in-clination [I] of the magnetic field at the surface of the earth is related to the magnetic latitude [L], measured relative to the magnetic axis. Assuming that the earth's field averages out like a bar magnet aligned along the geographical axis, this allows the calculation of ancient latitudes of a land using palaeomagnetic data. The inclination is measured with a special compass with a horizontal pivot but does not pose a navigation problem.

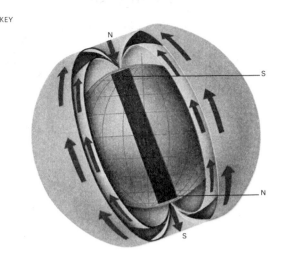

co-ordinates are respective to the apparent magnetic pole at the time the rock was magnetized. Evidence from this type of work reveals that the magnetic poles were not always in the position that they now occupy but have "wandered" over the years.

Polar wandering differs from continent to continent. But the poles for a specific time in geological history can be aligned through the various continents by envisaging the continents in different positions from those they now occupy. It is in this way that the progress of continental drift can be plotted. The results of this technique agree fairly well with other drift indicators such as sea-floor spreading and evidence of ancient climates shown by the rocks and their fossils. Palaeomagnetism is a powerful tool in continental drift research.

Some rocks formed over short time intervals show fossil magnetic polarities 180 degrees apart. This cannot be explained by a 180 degrees rotation of a continent because there was not enough time for that. Thus the earth's field must have undergone a switching of its magnetic polarity, as when the direction

of the current in a coil is reversed [6]. This switching is known as a "reversal". Reversals mark the boundaries of periods of variable length throughout geological time when the magnetic field was of constant polarity. The dating of reversals (by studying the decay of radioactive isotopes in the rocks) provides the geologist with a palaeomagnetic time scale. This can be used to date other rocks by analysing their remanent magnetization. It was the comparison of this palaeomagnetic time scale with the "magnetic anomalies" on the sea floor that supported the sea-floor spreading hypothesis.

Magnetic and electrical prospecting
Many ore bodies and rocks rich in magnetic minerals have a local strong magnetic field [7]. This is utilized by prospectors using sensitive instruments to detect minerals of economic value. Another method utilizes natural electrical currents that are set up between the surface and an ore body by percolating ground water. Its interaction with the magnetic field can be measured and used to locate useful deposits.

The earth's magnetic field is like that of a giant natural bar magnet placed inside the earth with its magnetic

axis inclined at a small angle to the geographical axis. The poles of a compass needle are attracted by the mag-

netic poles of the earth and swing so that one end points to the north magnetic pole and the other to the south.

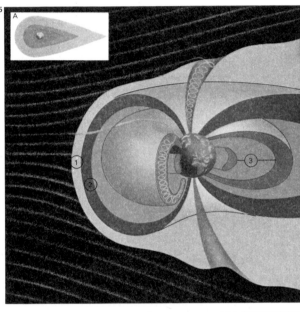

5 **The magnetosphere** is the region in which the earth's magnetic field can be detected. It would be symmetrical were it not for electrically charged particles streaming from the sun [A], which distort it to a teardrop shape. The particles meet the earth's magnetic field at the shock front [1]. Behind this is a region of turbulence and inside the turbulent region is the magnetopause [2], the boundary of the magnetic field. The Van Allen belts [3] are two zones of high radiation in the magnetopause. The inner belt consists of high-energy particles produced by cosmic rays and the outer belt of solar electrons.

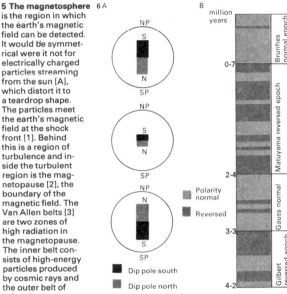

6 A

Polarity normal
Reversed

Dip pole south
Dip pole north

B
million years

Brunhes normal epoch
0.7
Matuyama reversed epoch
2.4
Gauss normal
3.3
Gilbert reversed epoch
4.2

6 **Field reversals** are the changes of polarity (north becoming south and vice versa) which occurred many times during geological history. The polarity of the earth's magnetic field does not flip over; its magnetic strength decreases to zero then slowly increases in the opposite direction [A]. Rocks "fossilize" the magnetic field when they are formed. If a sufficient number of rocks of different ages are dated, and their polarity measured, a worldwide magnetic time scale is obtained. The magnetic time scale featured here [B] shows the significant changes in magnetic polarity over the last 4.2 million years.

7
Gammas
20,000

10,000

2,500
0
-1,000

7 **In mineral prospecting** magnetometers can be used to detect variations in the earth's magnetic field due to ores: [1] regional magnetism of the country rocks; [2] background magnetism due to topsoils; [3] effects of deep-seated ore bodies; [4] effects from near surface ores.

8 **Electrical prospecting** for minerals makes use of natural ground currents [1] related to the magnetic field and influenced by ore bodies [2]. Two electrodes [3], placed in the ground at staked points [4], are connected to a millivoltmeter [5] and the voltages at the points are measured. Variations may indicate the presence of ores.

8
40
20
0
-20
-40
-60
-80
-100
Millivolts

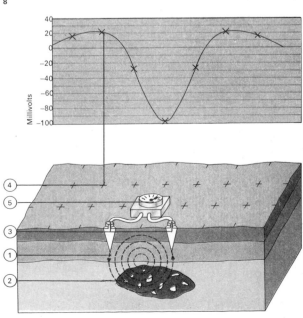

Global tectonics

The theory of plate tectonics was advanced in the late 1960s and has had a revolutionary effect on the earth sciences. It is a unifying, all-embracing theory, offering a plausible and logical explanation for many of the earth's varied structural and geophysical phenomena, ranging from mountain-building to earthquakes and continental drift.

Crustal plates
The theory envisages the crust of the earth together with the upper part of the mantle, which form the lithosphere, as consisting of rigid slabs or plates that are continuously moving their position in relation to each other [1]. Below the lithosphere is the asthenosphere which is thought to be plastic.

The plates are bounded by oceanic ridges, trenches and transform faults. Oceanic ridges are where two plates are moving apart leaving a gap which is continuously filled by magma (molten rock) rising from the asthenosphere. As the magma cools, new crust is created and becomes part of the moving plates. This is the phenomenon of sea-floor spreading. Spreading rates, though

slow, are not negligible. The Atlantic is opening up by 2cm (0.75in) a year. The fastest rate is found at the East Pacific Rise, which creates 10cm (4in) of new crust every year – that is 1,000km (620 miles) in the short geological time of ten million years.

Trenches are formed where two plates converge. One of the plates slides steeply under the other [6] and enters the mantle. Thus trenches are areas where plate edges are destroyed. Since the volume of the earth does not change, the amount of crust created at the ridges is balanced by that destroyed at the trenches.

The leading edges of the colliding plates may be oceanic crust, such as in the Tonga-Kermadec trench north of New Zealand: or one may be oceanic (and will be the sinking plate) while the other is continental, such as at the Peru-Chile trench; or both plates may be continental, such as those of northern India and Tibet. In the last two instances the thick sedimentary covers are crumpled and injected with material melted by the heat generated by the collision, and mountains such as the Himalayas are created [7].

Transform faults form where two plates slide past one another [8]. They offset oceanic ridges and their continuation scars can be followed in places for thousands of kilometres [5]. They sometimes slice through continents, as does the famous San Andreas fault in the south-western United States.

The cause of plate movements
As early as 1927 the British geologist Arthur Holmes suggested that convection currents in the mantle could explain the continental drift theory. Convection currents are generated by heat differences – they can be observed in a saucepan of water placed over a fire. Global tectonics theory suggests that convection currents exist in the asthenosphere and perhaps in the lower mantle. They form convection cells that rise under the ridges and descend under the trenches. This theory is supported by measurements of the heat radiated from the earth which show high values along the ridges and low values along the trenches.

The amazing world pattern of ridges, trenches and faults was discovered in the 1940s and 1950s. Their distribution was seen

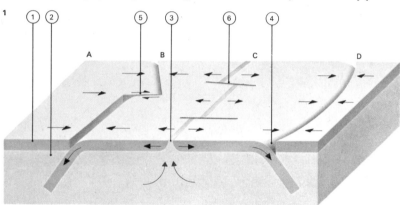

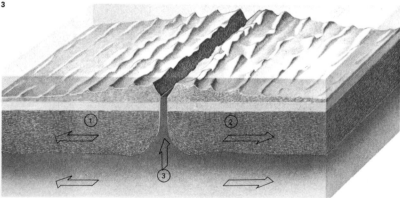

1 The plate tectonics theory envisages the earth's lithosphere [1] as a series of rigid but mobile slabs called plates [A, B, C, D]. The lithosphere floats on a plastic layer called the asthen-osphere [2]. There are three types of boundaries possible. At the oceanic ridges [3], upwelling of mantle material occurs and new sea-floor is formed. A trench [4] is formed where one plate of oceanic crust slides beneath the other, which may be oceanic or continental. The third type of boundary is where two plates slide past one another, creating a transform fault [5, 6]. Trans-form faults link two segments of the same ridge [6], two trenches [5] or a ridge to a trench. Plates move from ridges and travel like conveyor belts towards trenches where they sink.

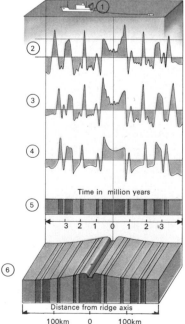

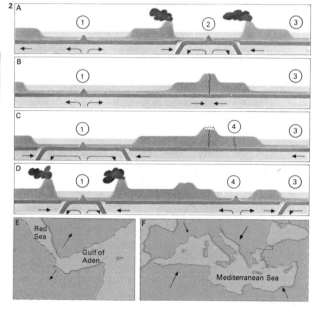

3 Oceanic ridges are found where two plates [1, 2] are moving away from each other. Magma from the mantle [3] continuously wells up from below. As the magma cools, it becomes part of the plates and it is in turn injected by fresh magma. The ridges are thus the newest part of the earth's crust, while the oldest oceanic crust is found where it plunges into the trenches. The dating of cores from the *Glomar Challenger* supports the theory.

4 A magnetic survey from a research ship [1] sailing back and forth over a mid-oceanic ridge gives readings [2, 3, 4] that indicate that the magnetism of the rocks of the sea-bed points alternately north and south in a series of bands parallel to the ridge [6]. The pattern of bands is identical at each side of the axis and corresponds to the pattern of reversals in the earth's magnetic field for the last few million years [5]. The rocks moving away from the axis carry a record of the earth's magnetic field.

2 The birth and death of oceans is a continuous process. In [A] ocean 1 is growing by sea-floor spreading from a mid-ocean ridge while ocean 2 is closing because of the continents forcing the ocean floor down at the trenches. Ocean 3 is young and growing. In [B] ocean 1 has reached maturity, ocean 3 is still growing. Ocean 2 has disappeared with the joining of the continental masses. In [C] oceans 1 and 3 are declining while a new crack appears at 4. [D] shows ocean 1 still declining and ocean 4 growing. [E] shows a widening of the Red Sea and Gulf of Aden while [F] indicates that the Mediterranean Sea has been steadily shrinking.

to fit that of earthquakes and volcanoes. In 1962 the American geologist Harry Hess suggested that these features, as well as continental drift, could be explained by sea-floor spreading, but because of insufficient relevant data could not prove his point.

The proof of a theory

Mysterious zebra patterns of magnetic anomalies were mapped on the ocean floor. In 1963 two Cambridge University graduate students, Frederick Vine and Drummond Matthews, explained these in a way that strongly supported sea-floor spreading. They suggested that material welling up from the mantle along a ridge acquires a remanent magnetization as it cools which is parallel to the then prevailing magnetic field of the earth. The earth's magnetic field is known to have reversed its polarity many times during geological history. Assuming that the newly forming crust at oceanic ridges picked up the prevailing polarity signal of the earth's magnetic field, the result over a long period of time would be strips of ocean floor that were alternately normally and reversely mag-

netized. The correspondence between the patterns on the ocean floor and the known history of the earth's magnetic field is too remarkable to be due to chance [4].

By 1966 the hypothesis of sea-floor spreading had been further established by independent oceanographic data involving microfossils, sediment thickness (thicker on older crust where sediments had more time to accumulate), measures of heat flow from the earth's interior, and palaeomagnetic and seismological studies. The expression "global tectonics" came into use in 1968, to explain the links between spreading ridges, transform faults, sinking trenches, drifting continents and mountain-building. This new theory is undoubtedly the most significant put forward in earth sciences this century.

Also in 1968, the United States commissioned the deep-sea drilling ship *Glomar Challenger* [Key] for a major campaign of oceanographic exploration. Drilled cores have been collected from all the oceans and seas and the sea-floor has been directly dated, proving beyond doubt the validity of the global tectonics theory.

KEY

The *Glomar Challenger* is a purpose-built research vessel for the Deep Sea Drilling Project (DSDP). The vessel is equipped to drill and retrieve cores from the floors of the deep oceans.

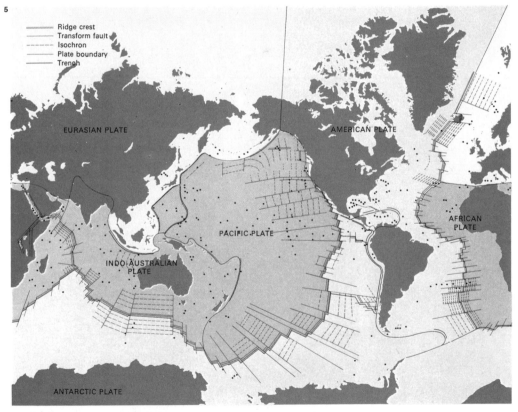

5

Ridge crest
Transform fault
Isochron
Plate boundary
Trench

EURASIAN PLATE

AMERICAN PLATE

AFRICAN PLATE

PACIFIC PLATE

INDO-AUSTRALIAN PLATE

ANTARCTIC PLATE

6

6 Destruction of the oceanic crust takes place where one plate [1] sinks beneath the other [2], forming a trench [3], while the dipping plane forms the sub-

duction zone [4]. Friction along this zone creates localized melting [5] and lava rises to the surface, creating volcanoes [6] forming island arcs [7].

7

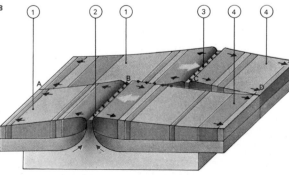

7 Collision zones are where two plates each carrying a continental mass meet. When, in this zone, one of the plates is forced beneath the other, the buoyant

continental material thrusts upwards in a series of high overthrusts and folds, producing great mountain ranges. The Himalayas are the result of such forces.

5 The earth's outer shell is formed of six major mobile plates (the American, Eurasian, African, Indo-Australian, Pacific and Antarctic plates) separated by ridges, transform faults and trenches. These plates contain some smaller plates such as the Arabian and West Indian plates which "absorb" the geometrical discrepancies between the major plates by creating or destroying compensating amounts of crust. The dotted lines

parallel to the ridges are lines of equal age (isochrons) based on magnetic anomalies. The lines closest to the ridges are 10 million years old; each successive line is 10 million years older than its immediate neighbour towards the ridge. Fast rates of spreading are shown by widely spaced isochrons. The age of the crust has been directly verified at most of the DSDP drilling sites [black dots]. The African plate has no trenches

on its border; it is therefore growing in area. Its east-west growth is being compensated for by crust disappearing in the Tonga-Kermadec and Peru-Chile trenches, two and three plates away. Similarly the Antarctic plate is growing northwards, the compensation taking place in the Indonesian, North Pacific and Middle America trenches. Despite spreading along one of their margins, the Pacific and Indo-Australian plates are shrinking overall.

8

8 Transform faults separate two crustal plates [1, 4] where they move apart from one another. A transform fault links two segments of a ridge [2, 3] and the ridge offset gives an apparent motion [blue arrows] opposite to the real movement [black]. The transform fault is active only between the ridge crests [BC] where opposite crustal spreadings occur; it is only a dead scar along [AB] and [CD] where both sides move together.

7

Continents adrift

The idea that the continents were once joined together is by no means a new one: it was held by Francis Bacon (1561–1626) in 1620 and in 1658 R. P. Placet published a book in French whose title, in translation, means "The corruption of the great and little world, where it is shown that before the deluge, America was not separated from the other parts of the world". The first map showing the fit of the continents was published in 1858 by A. Snider-Pelligrini who based his theory on the similarity of the fossil plants which had been found in various parts of Europe and in North America.

Alfred Wegener's hypothesis

The man most closely associated with the theory of continental drift is Alfred Wegener (1880–1930) [2], a German meteorologist. An American, F. B. Taylor, had independently put forward the same ideas a few years before Wegener's first lectures on the subject in 1912. Like others before him, Wegener had been attracted to the idea of drifting continents because of the appearance of the land masses on the world map. He showed

great skill in reconstructing the ancient land masses in arguing his case and brought carefully assembled geological, geodetic, geophysical, palaeontological and palaeoclimatic evidence into his discursions. All of these facets of geology had to be considerably developed before they provided evidence of such a substantial nature that almost all geologists accepted the theory.

It was geologists in the Southern Hemisphere who collected evidence that strongly supported Wegener's own theories. Glaciation during Permo-Carboniferous times was more intense and widespread than that of the more recent Pleistocene ice age. Geological fieldwork revealed evidence of it in South America, Africa, Australia, India, Antarctica and Madagascar. Geologists examining deposits of till (sediment carried and deposited by a glacier) and fossil plants were able to correlate them between the continents. If these land masses had always been fixed in their present positions, it would mean that the ice stretched from the polar regions to the Equator – clearly a preposterous idea. Joining the areas together not only reconciles

the geological facts but also provides evidence of the land mass wandering over the South Pole. This, in turn, allows for an explanation of the other known climatic belts of the world during this period; for example, tropical conditions experienced in northern Europe during the Carboniferous period.

Corresponding structures and fossils

Work in India and in Australia has proved the existence of links between these continents; for example, the basins of Permian age in northwest Australia can be correlated with those of India, and features of eastern Australia match those of Antarctica.

The close links between the geology of West Africa and Brazil provide further proof of their former contact. There is a clear boundary between the 2,000 million-year old rocks of West Africa and the much younger geological province (about 400 million years old) to the east. The boundary between these two is near Accra in Ghana and it heads out into the Atlantic Ocean in a southwesterly direction. The continuation of this boundary in Brazil was found by a geological expedi-

1A

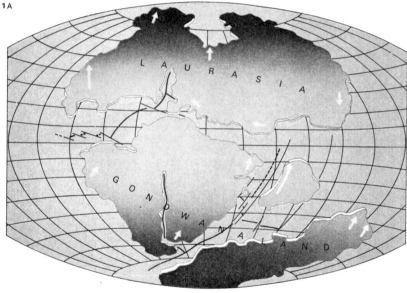

135 million years ago

B
65 million years ago

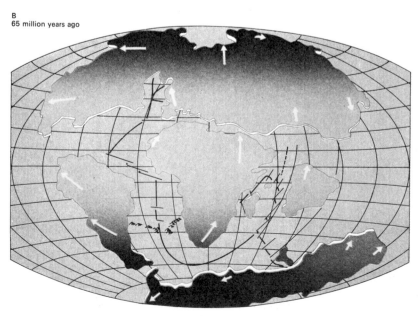

1 A map of Pangaea cannot be accurately constructed. The most suitable fit of the land masses is obtained by matching points midway down the continental slope, about 200m (6,560ft). In reconstructing the appearance of the giant continent, many investigators have used computers. The easiest areas to fit together are Africa and the South American continent. Whereas the fit of the northern lands is possible with a certain degree of accuracy, much remains to be learned of the complex fit of India, Antarctica and Australia with Africa and South America. The break-up of Pangaea began about 200 million years ago. By the end of the Jurassic, about 135 million years ago [A], the North Atlantic and Indian Oceans had become firmly established. The Tethys Sea was being diminished by the Asian land mass rotating in an anticlockwise direction. South America had begun to move away from Africa to form the South Atlantic. By the end of the Cretaceous, c.65 million years ago [B], the South Atlantic had grown, Madagascar had parted from Africa and India had continued northwards. Antarctica was moving away from the central mass, while linked with Australia. The North Atlantic rift forked at the north, thus forming the island of Greenland.

2 Alfred Wegener was born in 1880. Trained as an astronomer, he became interested in meteorology and geophysics. He lectured on continental drift in 1912 and his first paper on the subject was published later the same year. In 1915, his classic exposition, *The Origin of Continents and Oceans*, appeared in print. He died while leading an expedition over the ice cap of Greenland in 1930.

3 Antarctica's tropical past is shown by the existence of coal seams up to 4m (13ft) thick. The study of changes of climate provides evidence confirming continental drift. In the Southern Hemisphere, rocks between 400 million and 180 million years old show marked similarities over now widely separated continents. Plant fossils in coal seams and layering of glacial deposits in one place match those in another, thus providing evidence for the theory.

tion exactly as was predicted, at São Luis.

The drawing together of the now widely separated northern lands (North America, Europe and Asia) has been a little more difficult, but there now exists overwhelming evidence for their once having formed part of a single continent, Laurasia [1]. Geologists have shown that the now widely separated Norwegian, Caledonian, Appalachian and east Greenland mountains were originally formed as a single chain.

Wegener paid considerable attention to the distribution of fossils. When his theory was first put forward, palaeontologists were still postulating land bridges to account for the distribution of some plants and animals in the fossil record. In many cases the land bridges would have to have covered an area equal to that of the continents they joined. It was long assumed that the land bridges disappeared by subsidence. The detailed study of the ocean floors in recent years has ruled out this idea. If, however, the idea of Gondwanaland – the old grouping of the continents of Africa, South America, Antarctica, India and Australia – is accepted [4], it becomes much

easier to explain the distribution of many animals and plants. For example, remains of the reptile *Mesosaurus*, which could not have swum an ocean, have been discovered only in western South Africa and in Brazil.

New developments
Recent investigations, especially the study of palaeomagnetism (the history of the earth's changing magnetic field [6]), have provided data which not only support continental drift but also locate the positions of the various land masses during past geological time. Perhaps the most important impetus to the theory of continental drift has come from the twin theories of sea-floor spreading and plate tectonics which have been so rapidly developed since the 1960s. One of the weakest points in Wegener's original arguments centred on the tremendous forces necessary to drive the continents apart. These new theories, which have been substantially proven, provide an explanation of the necessary motive power, but there is still much to learn about the break-up of Pangaea, the original continent [Key].

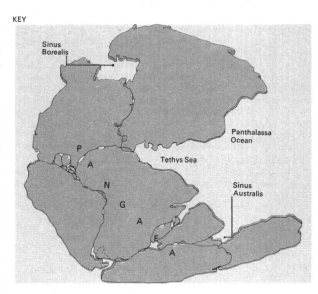

The theory of continental drift proposes a period when all the continents formed one land mass, called Pangaea. The initial break-up made a northern mass, Laurasia, and a southern one, Gondwanaland, called after a province in India.

4 The existence of Gondwanaland is confirmed in many different ways. Constant directions of ice flow in Permo-Carboniferous glaciations; structural trends traced and matched from continent to continent; and fossil distribution form part of the evidence. The distribution of *Mesosaurus*, *Lystrosaurus* and the fossil fern *Glossopteris* suggest the presence of a single land mass in Permian times. Palaeomagnetic techniques – which locate the magnetic pole of any stage in the past – give consistent results on each continent only when the continents are placed in the estimated configuration of Gondwanaland.

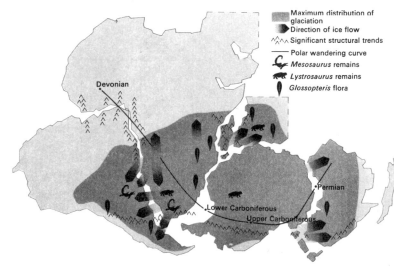

Maximum distribution of glaciation
Direction of ice flow
Significant structural trends
Polar wandering curve
Mesosaurus remains
Lystrosaurus remains
Glossopteris flora

Devonian

Lower Carboniferous
Upper Carboniferous
Permian

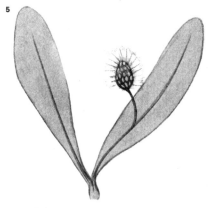

5 Fossil seed ferns (such as the tongue-like *Glossopteris*, shown here, and *Ganganop-teris*) in rocks of the Gondwana series in the southern continents evince support for continental drift theory. They reached their height in Permo-Carboniferous times and the complex nature of their species distribution can only be explained if the now widely separated locations had been in one land mass.

6 Palaeomagnetism – the study of the magnetization of rocks – has developed since the 1950s into a powerful tool for continental drift studies. Rocks record the earth's magnetic field at the time of their formation. Portable drills cut small cylindrical rock cores which are oriented relative to the present north and in a vertical position. In the laboratory a magnetometer determines their original north direction and their original latitude.

7   50 million years ahead

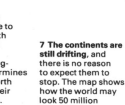

7 The continents are still drifting, and there is no reason to expect them to stop. The map shows how the world may look 50 million years from now if drift is maintained as predicted. The most striking change in the "new world" is the area of new land in the Caribbean, the splitting away from the USA of Baja California and the area west of the San Andreas fault line, the northward drift of Africa almost eliminating the Mediterranean, and the breaking away of that part of the continent east of the present-day rift valley. Australia has continued its journey northwards, but the great continent of Antarctica remains in its present southerly position.

Earthquakes

An earthquake at the earth's surface is the sudden release of energy in the form of vibrations and tremors caused by compressed or stretched rock snapping along a fault in the earth's surface. Rising lava under a volcano can also produce small tremors. It has been estimated that about a million earthquakes occur each year – but most of these are so minor that they pass unnoticed. Really violent earthquakes, which result in widespread destruction, occur about once every two weeks. Fortunately, most of these take place under the oceans, out of harm's way. It is not known what causes deep earthquakes – up to 700km (450 miles) below the surface

Waves and their measurement

Slippage along a fault is initially prevented by friction along the fault plane. This causes energy, which generates movement, to be stored up as elastic strain; a similar effect is created when a bow is drawn. Eventually the strain reaches a critical point, the friction is overcome and the rocks snap past each other releasing the stored-up energy in the form of earthquakes by vibrating back and forth.

Earthquakes can also occur when rock folds that can no longer support the elastic strain break to form a fault.

Seismic (earthquake) waves spread outwards in all directions from the focus – much as sound waves do when a gun is fired [Key, 4]. There are two main types of seismic wave: the compressional wave and the shear wave [2]. Compressional waves cause the rock particles through which they pass to shake back and forth in the direction of the wave. Shear waves make the particles vibrate at right-angles to the direction of their passage. Neither type of seismic wave physically moves the particles: instead it merely travels through them.

Compressional waves, which travel 1.7 times faster than shear waves, are the first ones to be distinguished at an earthquake recording station [3]. Consequently seismologists refer to them as primary (P) waves and to the shear waves as secondary (S) waves. A third wave type is recognized by seismologists – the long (L) or surface wave. It is L waves that produce the most violent shocks. The Richter scale is used to measure the magnitude of earthquakes. The scale of magnitudes is so arranged that each unit on the scale is equivalent to 30 times the energy released by the previous unit. A magnitude of 2 is hardly felt, while a magnitude of 7 is the lower limit of an earthquake that has a devastating effect over a large area.

Tsunamis – giant sea waves

Earthquakes are best known for the havoc they can wreak [1, 9]. The destruction may be the result of ground vibrations or giant tidal waves (*tsunamis*) generated by seismic disturbances on the sea floor. At sea *tsunamis* have wavelengths – the distance between one crest and the next – as great as 200km (120 miles). They can travel at speeds of 800km/h (500mph). When they reach a gently sloping shore they slow down and gather height. As the *tsunami* approaches, the sea withdraws, then rushes back in a series of giant waves that may travel far inland.

In 1755 the city of Lisbon was reduced to rubble in six minutes during one of the most devastating earthquakes ever recorded. The sea withdrew from the harbour and rushed

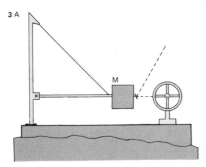

1 Severe surface disturbance ripped apart a road during the 1964 earthquake in Anchorage, Alaska, and minor subsidence left a crack 50cm (20in) wide. Ground waves such as those responsible for the break-up of this highway can disrupt underground services in cities and start fires. Broken water mains may hamper fire-fighting and encourage the spread of epidemics. The Alaskan "quake" affected only a sparsely populated area and 114 lives were lost – a small number considering the magnitude of the shock, which caused a permanent tilting of the land mass along the southern coast of Alaska.

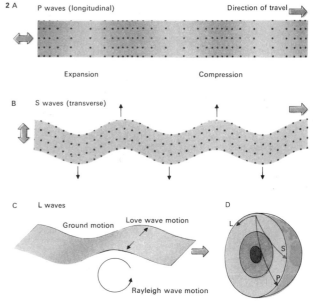

2 Seismic waves are basically of two kinds. Primary (P) waves [A] are compressional and cause the particles of rock to vibrate backwards and forwards like a coil spring. Secondary (S) or shear waves [B] cause the particles to oscillate at right-angles to the wave direction like a vibrating guitar string. When P and S waves reach the surface they are converted into long (L) waves which either [C] travel along the surface vibrating horizontally at right-angles to the wave direction (known as Love waves) or travel like sea waves (Rayleigh waves). Some of the paths followed are shown in D.

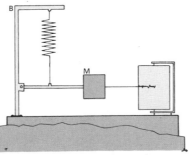

3 Seismographs are instruments that detect and record seismic waves of the three types (P, S and L). Most seismographs contain a sprung mass (M) which, when an earthquake passes, stays still while the rest of the instrument moves. Some seismographs detect horizontal motion [A] while others detect vertical motion [B]. The trace of the waves is recorded by a vibrating pen on a travelling strip of paper [C]. The time interval between the arrival of the P and S waves can be calculated and this interval, applied to a graph (see 5B), gives the distance between station and epicentre.

4 Seismic wave paths vary with the density of the rock, forming curving patterns as they move away from the focus [1]. Primary (P) waves can pass through gases, liquids and solids. The primary waves travel fastest, increasing their velocity as they pass through the mantle [2] but dropping in the outer core [3] and rising in the inner core [4] due to the conditions produced by pressure. Secondary (S) waves travel through solids only and do not penetrate into the dense molten core. As the waves travel down they meet concentric layers of increasing density which bend or refract the waves towards the surface so that these travel along curved paths. The region between 5 and 6 does not receive any direct waves. This area is known as the wave shadow zone. Seismic wave propagation has given invaluable information about the earth's interior.

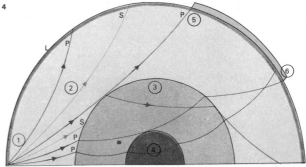

back as a 17m-high (55ft) *tsunami*, drowning hundreds. Smaller aftershocks caused landslides, fires broke out and by nightfall 60,000 people were dead. The shocks from this earthquake were felt over an area nearly 40 times as large as the United Kingdom.

Despite the innate destructive capacity of earthquakes it is possible in some circumstances to take precautions that minimize the hazards. Tall buildings can be constructed on reinforced concrete rafts that literally float during the passage of earthquake waves. Careful planning can ensure that streets are wide in relation to the height of buildings: many of the deaths caused during earthquakes are due to the collapse of tall buildings into narrow streets.

Control and prediction

Recent research indicates that it may now be possible to control earthquakes. In the mid-1960s, the dumping of water-based waste into a well in Denver, Colorado, set up a series of small earthquakes. Thus the idea was born that by drilling deep holes along a fault, and then pumping water down, it might

be possible to relieve strains in a series of small, non-destructive earthquakes instead of allowing them to build up until a major earthquake occurs [8].

Just before an earthquake the ground on either side of a fault suffers elastic deformation that can be measured by triangulation with a theodolite or laser beam. Tilt meters can also be used to discover how much warping of the ground has taken place. Monitoring of large areas has now been introduced. Using artificial satellites, information is transmitted from devices placed in the vicinity of major faults and radioed back to centres where it can be analysed. It is now possible to detect very small movements of the earth's surface and locate areas where strain is building up.

Another recently discovered method involves measuring the amount of water the rocks contain. Under strain, the pores in the rock enlarge, allowing more water to enter. Because of the importance of ground water in producing earthquakes, knowledge of the water level in wells in earthquake-prone areas is extremely valuable.

An earthquake takes place when two parts of the earth's surface move suddenly in relation to each other along a crack called a fault [1]. The point from which this movement originates is called the focus [2] and the point on the surface directly above this is called the epicentre [3]. Shock waves [4] travel outwards from the focus decreasing in intensity the farther they go. These shock waves travel more quickly as they pass through denser material at depth and so the direction of their travel [5] is curved as shown. On the surface the pattern of waves is similar to that of the isoseismal lines connecting points feeling equal shocks.

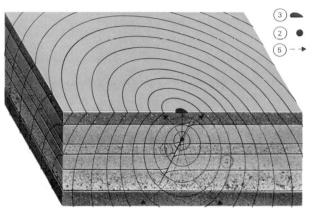

3
2
5

5 **The location of an epicentre** [1] is found by plotting its distance from three recording stations [2]. Each station notes the different arrival times of P and S waves and uses a graph [B] which allows the distance from the epicentre to be measured. The distance is then used as the radius of a circle round each station [A]. The epicentre is located at the intersection of these three circles.

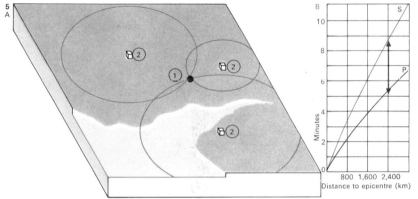

6 **Modified Mercalli scale**
1 Earthquake not felt, except by few.

2 Felt on upper floors by few at rest. Swinging of suspended objects.

3 Quite noticeable indoors, especially on upper floors. Standing automobiles may sway.

4 Felt indoors. Dishes and windows rattle, standing cars rock. Like heavy lorry hitting building.

5 Felt by nearly all, many wakened. Fragile objects broken, plaster cracked, trees and poles disturbed.

6 Felt by all, many run outdoors. Slight damage, heavy furniture moved, some fallen plaster.

7 People run outdoors. Average homes slightly damaged, substandard ones badly damaged. Noticed by car drivers.

8 Well-built structures slightly damaged, others badly damaged. Chimneys and monuments collapse. Car drivers disturbed.

9 Well-designed buildings badly damaged, substantial ones greatly damaged, shifted off foundations. Conspicuous ground cracks.

10 Well-built wood structures destroyed, masonry structures destroyed. Rails bent, ground cracked, landslides. Rivers overflow.

11 Few masonry structures left standing. Bridges and underground pipes destroyed. Broad cracks in ground. Earth slumps.

12 Damage total. Ground waves seem like sea waves. Line of sight disturbed. Objects thrown upwards in the air.

6 **Earthquake intensity** is based on a measure of the damage caused in populated areas. The most common intensity scale used today is the Wood-Neumann or modified Mercalli scale.

7 **Earthquakes** occur in geologically active areas of the earth's crust such as mid-oceanic ridges and mountain-building regions. They can be classified according to the depth of their foci, deep focus earthquakes [black squares] occurring at depths of between 300 and 650km (185–400 miles), intermediate focus [black dots] from 55 to 240km (35–150 miles) and shallow focus [grey areas] from the surface down to 55km (35 miles).

9 **The western Sicily earthquake** of 1968 completely destroyed many buildings in Gibellina and in nearby villages. Dazed survivors picked their way through piles of shattered masonry. Falling masonry is the greatest hazard to human life during a severe earthquake and most injuries are caused outside buildings. Disease often spreads among survivors after the breakdown of essential services. There were 224 deaths in the Sicilian "quake" Some of the most disastrous earthquakes since 1965 have occurred in Peru in 1970 (66,794 deaths), in Guatemala in 1976 (more than 16,000 deaths), and in China, also in 1976 (estimates of up to 100,000 deaths).

8 **Release of the pressure** that could cause a severe earthquake may be achieved by promoting a number of small "quakes" in the fault area. Researchers are investigating the possibility of minimizing the destructive effects of earthquakes in certain regions by regulating their occurrence. Many small earthquakes, for instance, may release as much energy as a single devastating one by lessening the strain built up over a period of time [A]. One method of

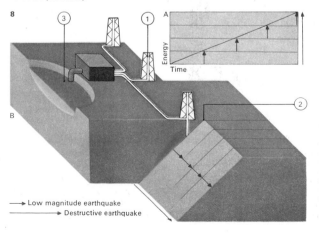

→ Low magnitude earthquake
→ Destructive earthquake

achieving this may be to pump water to act as a lubricant [B]. A number of wells [1] may be set up along a fault line [2] in which stress has been detected. Large quantities of water from a reservoir [3] would then be

pumped into the wells to lessen friction between rocks in the fault and allow them to slip smoothly in a series of gentle tremors. Another method of triggering off small "quakes" may be to explode nuclear devices along a fault plane.

Volcanoes

Volcanoes, the earth's most spectacular displays of energy, are responsible for forming large parts of the earth's crust. They give clues to the earth's history and evolution, and to the nature of the earth's interior. Soils formed by the weathering of volcanic rocks are so exceptionally fertile, that despite the danger large numbers of people often live in the shadow of volcanoes, and eruptions lead to major loss of life. The earth's upper mantle, under the crust, is nearly molten. A slight drop in pressure caused, say, by crustal plates drifting apart, completes the melting process. The molten rock (magma), being lighter than the surrounding rocks, then rises slowly to the surface, often along faults. A small increase in heat, will also melt the rock and it is believed that pockets of radioactive elements generate enough heat to form magma.

Along the mid-ocean ridges, where the crustal plates' drifting apart creates a drop of pressure, magma rises more or less continuously and cools to form new crust. Elsewhere it forms underground reservoirs, which, if they do not cool, can become unstable and produce eruptions. When this happens the flow is speeded up as the drop of pressure allows the gas dissolved in the magma to form bubbles [2]. Many of the gases, such as hydrogen sulphide and carbon monoxide, burn as they reach the air; this increases the temperature at the vent, making the lava even more fluid. If the lava is viscous, trapping the gases, they may escape explosively. The force of such explosions – and of normal eruptions – is increased when water seeps down to the magma and is turned into steam.

The volcanoes formed by escaping magma are characterized by their vent or crater at the summit. They often have side vents as well. Sometimes such large amounts of magma bubble out during an eruption that the chamber below the volcano is more or less emptied. The volcano then collapses into the void, forming a large, steep-sided depression known as a caldera.

Location of volcanoes

Volcanoes are found along the big tensional cracks of the earth's surface – the mid-ocean ridges and their continental continuations – and along the collision edges of crustal plates. The famous "ring of fire" encircling the Pacific is the boundary of the crustal plate that forms the Pacific.

The largest number of volcanoes is under the sea-floor, forming the abyssal hills. Most are probably extinct. They exist because the oceanic crust is very thin and easily pierced by the underlying magma. The Pacific alone is thought to have more than 10,000 volcanoes of above 1,000m (3,300ft) in height. The Hawaiian volcanoes are thought to be due to fixed "plumes" or "hot spots" in the mantle, which give rise to a string of volcanoes as the crust drifts slowly over them.

A few volcanoes that exist on land away from the plate boundaries are perhaps due to localized heating by radioactivity or to a hot spot in the mantle.

Apart from the uncounted abyssal volcanoes, there are about 500 active volcanoes, of which perhaps 20 or 30 erupt in any given year. Between eruptions a volcano is said to be dormant. An active volcano is one that has erupted in historic times. Volcanoes can, however, be dormant for periods longer than

1 **Volcanoes** are fed by molten rock that rises from the earth's mantle. This material, called magma, may rise directly to the surface where it erupts, or be stored in a magma chamber that swells up like a balloon before erupting. The magma rises through a chimney and eventually reaches the surface at the vent. Matter spewed forth as lava or ejecta (bombs and ashes) builds up a volcanic cone or volcano. Vent explosions caused by expanding gases often form craters shaped as inverted cones. The magma does not always reach the surface and often cools at depth forming plutons (large bodies), laccoliths (lens-shaped structures), dykes (that cut through the strata) and sills (injected between two strata). Volcanic regions are also characterized by hot springs, gas vents and, in some areas, by geysers.

1 Rainwater seeps down, is heated by the magma and surfaces as hot springs and geysers, often loaded with dissolved minerals

Fissure eruptions do not form volcanoes but release flows of very fluid lava that can cover areas up to 500km² (200 square miles)

A magma chamber of fluid rock underlies many volcanoes. This is released as ash and lava during eruptions

Lava flows can be released from side vents and gases can issue from crevices in the loose flanks of the volcano

Stratified layers of volcanic rocks build up the main cone. Each eruption adds at least one layer

Pressure in the main vent encourages the opening of side vents as alternative paths to the surface

Geysers are intermittent fountains of water and steam created by the vaporizing of ground waters. They operate like giant safety valves

Active or recent cones often form inside explosion craters or crater-shaped calderas due to the collapse of an empty magma chamber

A laccolith is a giant, lens-shaped intrusion that pushes up the strata above. It is fed from the magma chamber

2 **As the pressure** in rising magma falls, dissolved gases are forced out of it; these form expanding bubbles and drive the magma out of the volcano.

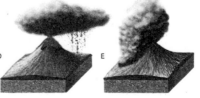

3 **Active volcanoes** mostly occur at crustal plate boundaries. The principal zone of activity is found along a great arc around the Pacific, from Chile to the East Indies.

— Active volcanoes
— Extinct volcanoes

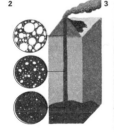

4 **Volcanic eruptions take various forms.** Fissure eruptions [A] release the most basic and runny lava. In Hawaiian eruptions [B] the lava is less fluid and produces a low cone. The Vulcanian type [C] is more violent and ejects solid lava. Strombolian eruptions [D] blow out incandescent material. In the Peléean type [E] a blocked vent is cleared explosively. A Plinian eruption [F] is a continuous gas blast that rises to immense heights.

historic times and "extinct" volcanoes sometimes come back to life, as Helgafell in Heimaey, Iceland did in 1973 [8]. The best-known new volcano on land is Paricutin, in Mexico, which appeared in a field in 1943. The map [3] shows active volcanoes and recent extinct volcanoes, many of which were seen erupting by prehistoric man, such as those in France. The geological record abounds in "fossil" volcanoes (not shown). For instance Scotland's capital, Edinburgh, was a volcano 325 million years ago.

Volcanic products and eruption types

Volcanoes emit gases, liquids and solids. The gases are mainly nitrogen, carbon dioxide, hydrogen chloride, water vapour, carbon monoxide and hydrogen sulphide. Liquid emissions, known as lavas, are either ropy *pahoehoe* [10] or clinker-like *aa* [9], depending on the temperature.

Fluid lava allows calm eruptions; more viscous lava, by preventing the escape of gas before it reaches high pressure, is accompanied by explosions; very viscous magma is thrown out as ash and rubble in huge explosions. Craters at rest are often filled by a lake; an eruption often creates a mud flow which is as destructive as, and even more lethal (owing to its speed) than, a lava flow.

Catastrophic eruptions

Volcanoes are in a sense safety valves in the earth's crust: the tighter the valve the greater the eruption will be. The 1815 eruption of Tambora in Indonesia ranks as the greatest volcanic disaster in history. Ten thousand people were killed outright during the eruption and 82,000 died later of disease and starvation. Again in Indonesia, the uninhabited island of Krakatoa was blown to pieces [Key] in 1883, creating a tidal wave that killed 36,000 people. Evidence on the island of Thera [11] suggests that an even larger explosion occurred there around 1470 BC.

Eruptions cannot be prevented, but they can, in some cases, be predicted. This is done principally by monitoring the small earthquakes created by rising magma, measuring the swelling of the ground with tiltmeters and watching variations in the output of gas and steam vents.

Krakatoa was a small volcanic island in the Sundra Straits of Indonesia that had been inactive since 1680. Two-thirds of the island were destroyed in an eruption in August 1883.

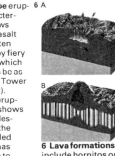
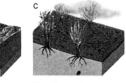
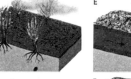

5 Hawaiian-type eruptions are characterized by lava flows consisting of basalt and they are often accompanied by fiery lava fountains which can sometimes be as tall as the Eiffel Tower –300m (1,000ft). The Hawaiian eruption seen here shows how the incandescent lava from the fountain has filled the crater and has then overflown to form a lava flow that is partially chilled on its surface.

6 Lava formations include hornitos or spatter cones, small bursts [A] that form miniature volcanoes on lava flows [B]. Tree moulds [C] form where trees have burned away beneath the cooled lava [D]. Lava tubes occur when the surface flow cools [E] and the hot interior drains away [F].

8 Ash-falls can cause more damage to property and agricultural land than lava flows because they cover greater areas. Volcanic ash is made of fine ejecta of less than 4mm (0.15 in) diameter and is produced by the cubic kilometre. Most is deposited within 10km (6 miles) of the volcano. The picture shows some houses of Heimaey, Iceland, buried by ash from the Helgafell eruption of 1973.

7 Spindle bombs are the product of molten rock pulling apart after ejection. Larger blobs twist in flight and their drawn-out ends curl and give the bomb its characteristic lozenge shape.

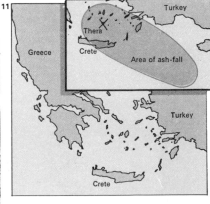

9 The texture of a lava flow depends on the temperature and the velocity of the flow during the eruption and on the composition of the lava. Geologists have borrowed two words from the Hawaiian language, *aa* and *pahoehoe*, to describe two typical surfaces. *Aa* lava has a very rough and clinker-like aspect and is formed by slowly moving or relatively cool outpourings. Seven years after the solidification of this flow, vegetation will gradually return.

10 *Pahoehoe* or ropy lava has a smooth but twisted surface. It is formed by fast-flowing fluid lava, which develops a plastic skin on its surface, by cooling. The skin is dragged into picturesque folds by the still liquid lava running beneath it.

11 In the late Bronze Age the island of Thera experienced an eruption that had a catastrophic effect on the people of Crete and may have been responsible for the fall of the Minoan civilization and the creation of the Atlantis legend.

Gravity and the shape of the earth

Gravity is the mutual attraction of two bodies and its strength depends on the mass of the bodies and their distance apart. The strength of the earth's gravitational field is therefore proportional to the earth's mass and decreases as the distance from the surface of the earth increases.

Gravity is responsible for nearly all major erosion which takes place. Rain falls under gravity; streams, rivers and glaciers move, and sediments compact under gravity.

Rotation, shape and sea-level

The earth's rotation creates a centrifugal force that is greater at the Equator than elsewhere, causing the earth to bulge out slightly at the Equator and to flatten at the poles [1]. This makes the earth's diameter at the Equator greater than that through the poles by about 41km (25 miles).

Mean sea-level is the average sea-level between tides and is taken as the base level when measuring altitudes. It is always perpendicular to the force of gravity. Such a surface, taken all over the earth is known as the "geoid", which is what the earth's true shape is called [2]. The surface of the geoid is irregular because the gravity field varies locally and depends on the type of rocks in the crust. A large òre body or mountain chain will deflect a nearby plumbline away from the centre of the earth and thus the geoid's shape is obtained by directly measuring gravity on land [3] or its variation at sea, where wave motion precludes direct measurement. Perturbations of artificial satellite orbits are now extensively used for broad-scale geoid studies. The shape of the geoid is defined by its departure from a "reference ellipsoid" which fits most closely to the shape of the earth; in this case, the average level of the land and sea is taken as the norm. Mountains are then higher and sea-floors lower than the surface of this ellipsoid. (An ellipsoid is the regular geometric shape obtained by revolving an ellipse round one of its axes.)

The Trigonometrical Survey of India

During the Trigonometrical Survey of India, in the nineteenth century, it was found that some stations, whose positions were determined by astronomical surveying methods, did not coincide with those determined by triangulation, which had not allowed for the sideways attraction of the Himalayas to the north. The mass of the Himalayas was exerting a small gravitational pull on that of the plumbline and introducing discrepancies as large as 91.5m (300ft). As a result, both J. H. Pratt and G. B. Airy (1801–92) proposed that the continents consisted of lighter material floating on a denser substratum [5]. Pratt believed that the different heights of mountains were due to blocks of different densities floating at the same base level, while Airy thought the heights were due to blocks of different thickness and of the same density floating at different depths. Today, Airy's hypothesis is generally accepted.

Another way of putting Airy's hypothesis is that lighter crustal materials "float" in equilibrium on the denser but slightly plastic mantle, like a cork floating on water. If such a cork were covered with an extra load (such as a coin) it would sink a little until the extra immersed volume created enough buoyancy to compensate for the extra load. This is what is observed for the earth's crust: extra loads

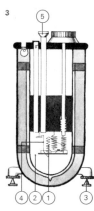

1 The earth's surface is not a true sphere but approximates to an ellipsoid whose equatorial diameter exceeds its polar diameter. The difference is about 41km (25 miles) and may be illustrated by forcing hypothetical wedges [1, 2] through the spaces over the poles; this would not be possible at the Equator [3]. This equatorial bulge is caused by the effect of centrifugal force as the earth rotates on its axis.

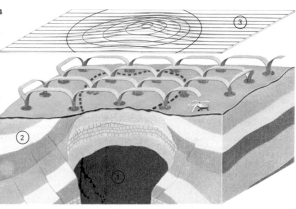

Reference ellipsoid
Geoid

2 The earth's true shape is called the geoid. Because gravity varies locally, the geoid is irregular. Rock masses in mountains [G] attract a plumbline and the assumed direction of the centre of gravity [XC] for the ellipsoid is deflected to the local direction of the centre of gravity [XF]. As XF is perpendicular to the true level [DE] based on the geoid, AB is only the assumed level based on the ellipsoid.

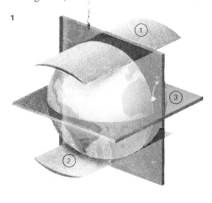

3 A gravimeter is a device used for measuring gravity at a point on the earth's surface by observing the extension of a weighted spring. A quartz spring [1] is housed in a partially evacuated chamber [2] which protects it from pressure changes. Levelling screws [3] keep the meter vertical and the movement of the spring is indicated by the position of the pointer [4] on a scale observed through an eyepiece [5].

4 A negative gravity anomaly – a lower gravity reading than normal – is found over an intrusion of light rock near the surface. A less dense salt dome [1] rises through denser crustal rocks [2] disturbing the local gravitational field. Readings at regular stations on the surface can be plotted on a map [3] and these will show an area of low gravity above the dome. A dense metallic ore body would show a positive anomaly.

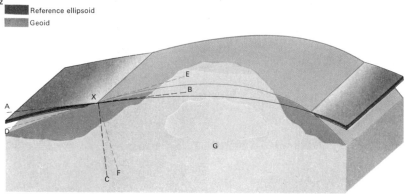

5 In the 1850s Pratt and Airy proposed that the continents consisted of light material floating on a denser substratum. Whereas Pratt suggested that the different heights of mountains were due to blocks of different densities floating at the same base level [A], Airy considered that they were due to blocks of different heights of the same density floating at different depths [B]. Geophysical research has shown Airy's view to be the more likely.

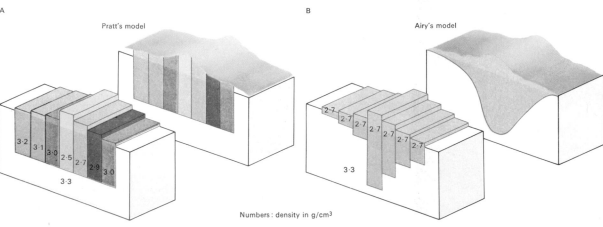

5 A

Pratt's model

3·2 3·1 3·0 2·5 2·7 2·9 3·0

3·3

B

Airy's model

2·7 2·7 2·7 2·7 2·7 2·7

3·3

Numbers : density in g/cm³

cause downwarping of the crust [7]. When the load disappears, for example by the melting of ice or by erosion, the crust bobs up, regaining a new isostatic equilibrium.

Parts of Norway and Sweden are still rising, following the melting of the thick Pleistocene ice caps 10,000 years ago, and it is estimated that the crust there must rise a further 213m (700ft) before equilibrium is restored. However, as Scandinavia rises, the coastlines of The Netherlands and parts of Denmark are sinking [8] because mantle material which is flowing up under Scandinavia is drawn from beneath The Netherlands and parts of Denmark.

Isostatic equilibrium is maintained by variation in the depth of the earth's crust and scientists have shown that every mountain chain floats on a deep root in the mantle. Conversely, below the oceans only a thin layer of crust is found.

Anomalies in the gravitational field

Rock bodies, whose mass differs greatly from that of the surrounding area, cause small variations or anomalies in the local gravita-tional field, making it possible to detect them with sensitive gravimeters [Key]. Gravimeters work on the principle that gravity changes will cause minute variations in a very fine quartz spring [3]. These instruments are sensitive enough to detect minute gravitational changes as small as one ten-millionth of a gramme.

Gravity surveys reveal that large salt domes near the surface (often associated with oil and gas) will show up as a negative anomaly (that is a mass deficit, because salt is lighter than other rocks) [4], while a dense ore body will show up as a positive gravity anomaly (mass excess). Geologists exploring the terrain carry out surveys of the earth's gravity field and the observed values are corrected to eliminate the influence of latitude, height and the mass of material between the observation point and sea-level or the lowest level obtainable. This allowance is called the Bouguer correction and the resulting map is therefore known as a Bouguer anomaly map. Its value to industry lies in its use to determine the possible positions and sizes of economic ores and oil reserves.

Underground rock formations can be detected by measuring the local variations in the pull of gravity on a delicate spring balance called a gravimeter. The lighter the material, the weaker the pull.

1 Normal gravity reading
2 Heavy igneous material near surface giving gravity high
3 Anticline giving gravity high
4 Rift valley where lighter surface material continues to a greater depth giving gravity low
5 Salt dome or
upward emplacement of light material giving gravity low
6 Oceanic trough where lighter crustal material deep in mantle gives gravity low

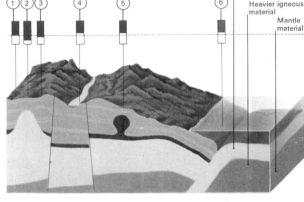

Lighter igneous material
Heavier igneous material
Mantle material

6 A person sitting on a water bed downwarps the surface, causing fluid to flow from beneath him until equilibrium is reached and he no longer sinks. A second person also downwarps the surface and causes the fluid to flow from under her and push up under the first person thus causing him to rise slightly. This is analogous to the floating of mountains on the liquid mantle of the earth.

7 When the earth's surface acquires a heavy load, like an ice sheet, over a period of time the crust downwarps into the mantle. In A the crust is in equilibrium with the mantle below. An ice sheet [B] is heavy and produces a positive gravity anomaly. To compensate for this, the crust downwarps, giving a deficiency in mass and a negative anomaly. The positive and negative anomalies cancel out and the crust remains in equilibrium. When the ice melts [C] the load and positive anomaly are removed leaving a mass deficiency and a negative anomaly. To restore equilibrium [D] the land rises and rivers rejuvenate, cutting deep valleys.

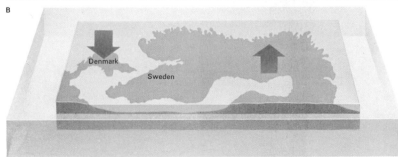

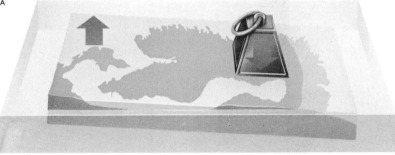

8 Glacial rebound is an example of isostatic activity. During the last ice age Scandinavia was weighed down by ice, causing the north of Europe to tilt [A]. After the ice melted the continent returned to its original attitude [B], buoyed up on upper mantle material flowing from under the sinking areas to under areas of uplift.

9 When the thick ice sheets disappeared from Scandinavia, the land began to rise to restore isostatic equilibrium and is still rising by 100cm (39in) a century. Rivers, rejuvenated by the uprise, have since cut steep-sided valleys in the mountains. The map shows the current rate of uplift in centimetres per century over the Baltic region.

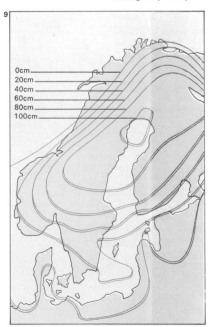

0cm
20cm
40cm
60cm
80cm
100cm

Mapping the earth

Throughout history man has recorded, analysed and communicated information in map form. The oldest map in existence is engraved on a Babylonian clay tablet dating from 3000 BC and like many surviving examples of early mapping it records land tenure. It was not until the fifth century BC, however, that Greek philosophy stimulated attempts to create a map of the world. Unfortunately these were based on philosophical theories rather than the geographical knowledge of the day. Nevertheless, in the following 600 years Greek scholars did develop a more scientific approach to cartography.

Early attempts at cartography
At the end of the first century AD Ptolemy of Alexandria compiled his *Geographia*. In it he discussed the problem of representing the spherical shape of the earth on a plane surface and also introduced the concepts of longitude and latitude [4].

After Ptolemy, cartography entered a period of decline until the Crusades and an expansion of trade revived interest. A cartographic renaissance came in the fifteenth century with the discovery and publication of Ptolemy's work, voyages of exploration like those of Vasco da Gama (*c.* 1469–1525) and Christopher Columbus (1451–1506) and the invention of printing and engraving. In the sixteenth century the work of map-publishing houses in Holland and France, and particularly that of Gerhardus Mercator (1512-94), founded modern map-making.

By the middle of the eighteenth century the French had initiated the first topographic survey. Many special-purpose or thematic maps have been produced since the nineteenth century. Their variety reflects the increasingly specialized demands of modern life, which require such aids as land-use maps, pilot charts and road maps.

Modern surveying
Small areas of the earth can be mapped by plane surveying but larger areas must be done by geodesy which takes into account the earth's curvature. A variety of instruments and techniques is used to determine position, height and extent of features – data essential to the cartographic process. Instruments such as graduated metal rods, chains, tapes and portable radar or radio transmitters are used for measuring distances; the theodolite [Key] is used for measuring angles. Using measured distances and angles further distances and angles are calculated by triangulation [1]. Heights are determined similarly [2].

Perhaps the most dramatic changes in cartography have come with the development of aerial survey techniques. Photographs from satellites or aircraft are used together with data from ground surveys to map accurately large areas of the earth. This technique, called photogrammetry, is particularly useful for mapping remote areas [3], and also for mapping the earth's natural resources using images produced by remote sensing equipment. Almost all topographic mapping today is done from aerial photographs and photomaps are made from the aerial photographs of an area.

Map projections
It is obviously impossible to represent accurately the surface of a sphere on a flat plane without distorting the relationships between

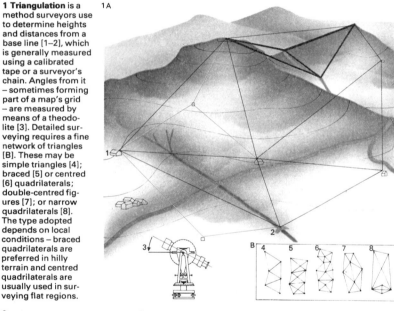

1 Triangulation is a method surveyors use to determine heights and distances from a base line [1–2], which is generally measured using a calibrated tape or a surveyor's chain. Angles from it – sometimes forming part of a map's grid – are measured by means of a theodolite [3]. Detailed surveying requires a fine network of triangles [B]. These may be simple triangles [4]; braced [5] or centred [6] quadrilaterals; double-centred figures [7]; or narrow quadrilaterals [8]. The type adopted depends on local conditions – braced quadrilaterals are preferred in hilly terrain and centred quadrilaterals are usually used in surveying flat regions.

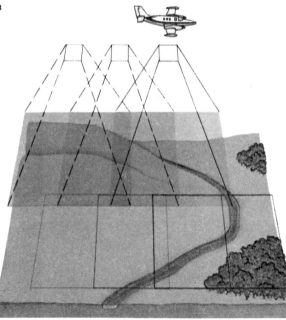

3 Aerial photography is one of the modern techniques that have helped the work of the cartographer. An aircraft flies over the area to be mapped, taking a continuous series of photographs. The area covered by each photograph overlaps by 60% the area of the previous one and so, after processing, any adjacent pair of photographs can be examined stereoscopically and the relief of the area studied directly in three dimensions. By means of an optical instrument the positions of corresponding points on each photograph can be compared and the height of that point calculated. Each "run" of photographs overlaps sideways by 10% the previous run, ensuring total coverage.

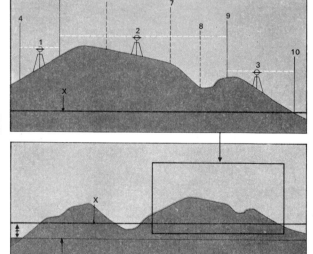

2 Height above sea-level is usually determined by means of a levelling instrument [1, 2, 3] and a measuring rod [4–10] with reference to a known height or bench mark [X]. Level 1 sights on the rod at 4 and then at 5. The instrument is moved to 2 to begin the second stage, sighting first on 5 and then on 6. Finally 10 will be reached using stage 3. Intermediate heights are determined by placing the rod at 8. The heights of the points 4–10 can be related to sea-level [Y] because of the height above sea-level of the bench mark [X] is already known.

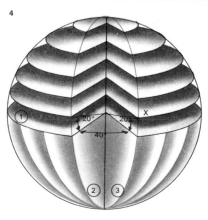

4 Any point on the surface of the earth can be located in terms of longitude and latitude – in degrees, minutes and seconds east or west of a prime meridian or line of longitude, and north or south of the Equator. The latitude of X (the angle between X, the centre of the earth and the plane of the Equator [1]) equals 20° while its longitude (the angle between the plane of the prime meridian [2] and that passing through X and the poles [3]) equals 40°.

features on that surface. A map projection is a device used to plot the earth's features with a minimum of such distortion. There are a number of different types of projection and the choice of one in preference to others depends on the purpose of the map.

If the map is to show relatively small areas of the world, as in a national topographic series that will be used by planners, engineers and the general public, then a projection must be selected that shows distance, angle and shape with the utmost accuracy. For this reason conformal projections are chosen. If on the other hand the map is to show distribution of, say, cultivated land throughout the world, then a projection that shows those areas at their correct relative size must be selected. Such projections are called equivalent or equal area projections.

Conformal projections are not used for world maps except in special circumstances because they exaggerate polar regions to an enormous extent. The Mercator projection, the best known example, is, however, invaluable to navigators as it shows all lines of constant direction as straight lines.

The first essential in making any map is to establish its purpose. The necessary data must then be assembled – this may be in the form of survey data, aerial photography, existing maps and written material – analysed, evaluated and edited before any drafting can begin. Many factors influence the presentation of information in map form, from the size of paper that can be handled in a cockpit or motor car to the visual preconceptions of the probable user. The cartographer has at his disposal all the techniques of graphic communication and the written word and he must carefully consider the possibilities they offer when designing the map. Various forms, symbols, lines and shading may be used. Contours are widely used to represent relief on maps [8] and provide accurate data; however, they give little visual impression of the appearance of the landscape. Cartographers often use layer-colouring for greater clarity and spot heights are marked where an accurate assessment of height or depth is desired, or when a particular crest or low point falls between the contour lines.

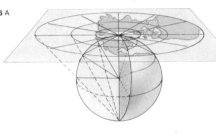

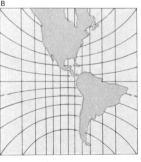

KEY

A theodolite is essentially a tripod-mounted telescope on a base plate that is marked in degrees, minutes and seconds to allow the surveyor to measure horizontal angles. He makes vertical readings from an upright plate at the side.

5 Map projections are mathematical constructions designed to maintain certain selected relationships of the earth's surface. Some projections are purely geometrical and may be thought of as projections of a transparent globe's parallels and meridians on to a cylinder, cone or plane. This illustration shows the construction of cylindrical projections [A] and how, by varying the point of projection, different types are produced: simple cylindrical [B], cylindrical stereographic [C] and cylindrical orthographic [D]. Mercator's [E] and Miller's projection [F] are both constructed mathematically.

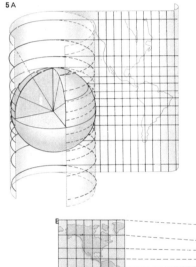

6 Azimuthal or zenithal projections are those produced on plane surfaces [A]. Angles measured from the centre (the point of contact with the globe) are correct. However, distortion of shape and area increases with distance from the centre. The gnomonic projection [B] shows all great circles (circumferences of planes through the centre of the earth) as straight lines. As these are the shortest distances between two points the projection is of importance in navigation. Lambert's azimuthal equal area projection [C] combines usefully the properties of azimuthal projections and equivalence.

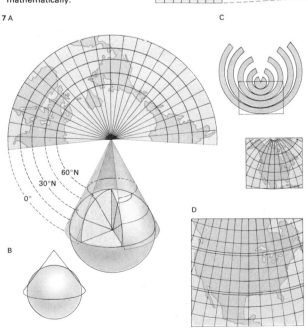

7 The simple conic projection is constructed from a cone tangential to the globe [A]. Scale along the parallel in contact with the globe only – the standard parallel – is correct. Projections constructed from a secant cone [B] have two standard parallels and because scale error increases away from them more of the projection is nearer the correct scale. The polyconic projection [C], mathematically constructed to have all parallels standard, is very accurate over small areas and is therefore used for topographic series. Alber's equal area projection [D] is a modification of the conic projection with two standard parallels [red lines].

60°N
30°N
0°

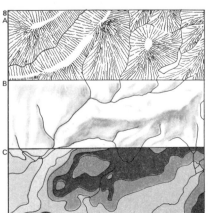

8 Height and slope can be represented on a map in many ways, including hachuring [A] in which fine lines follow the direction of greatest slope. This method can give an excellent impression of the landscape but may obscure other information. Hill shading [B], the representation of a landscape illuminated from one direction, is used alone or with colours. Contours [C] can be separated by colour and intermediate heights given as spot heights.

17

The face of the earth

The earth is the third nearest planet to the sun. It is the heaviest of the stony planets (the gas giants such as Jupiter are heavier) and the densest of all planets. Its orbit, 150 million kilometres (93 million miles) away from the sun, ensures that the planet is neither scorching nor freezing and the presence of water and an atmosphere reduce the temperature extremes, allowing the evolution of life.

From a distance the earth looks one of the most interesting objects in the Solar System. This is largely due to the variable cloud cover which does not prevent a distant observer from seeing the lands and oceans on the surface. Astronaut Neil Armstrong (1930–) said, during the Apollo 11 flight in 1969, that the earth "looks like a beautiful jewel in space". The earth is much brighter than the moon, reflecting about 40 per cent of the light falling on it, compared to the moon's seven per cent. From Mercury, Venus and Mars the earth would look to the naked eye like a brilliant bluish star but from Jupiter and the more distant planets a telescope would be required as the earth would be hidden by the glare of the sun.

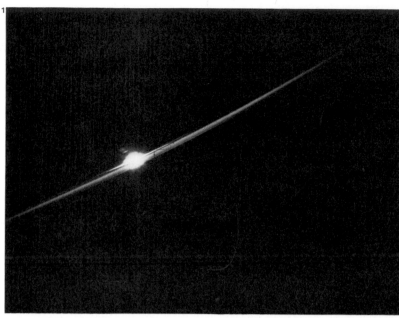

1 This sunset seen from a manned satellite in space shows the diffraction of sunlight by the earth's atmosphere. Only the lower few tens of kilometres are dense enough to produce this effect.

2 A "full earth" was a spectacle unseen by man before the Apollo flights. North and South America and Africa can be seen here but the cloud cover tends to obscure the shapes of continents.

3 These spectacular cloud vortices, photographed from Skylab in 1973, are the result of air being drawn into the pronounced low-pressure area in the lee of Guadalupe Island, off the coast of Baja California, Mexico.

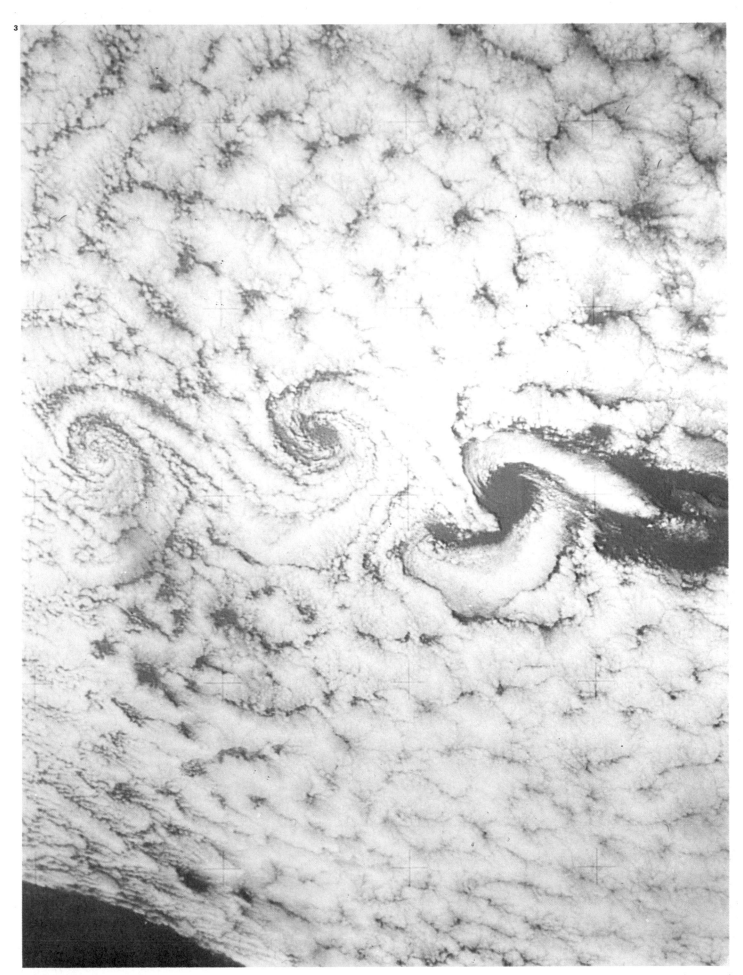

The World

Land Features

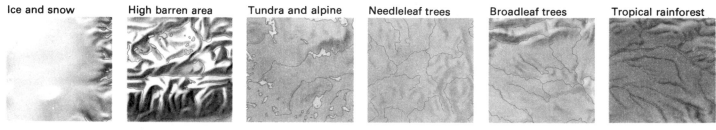

Ice and snow | High barren area | Tundra and alpine | Needleleaf trees | Broadleaf trees | Tropical rainforest

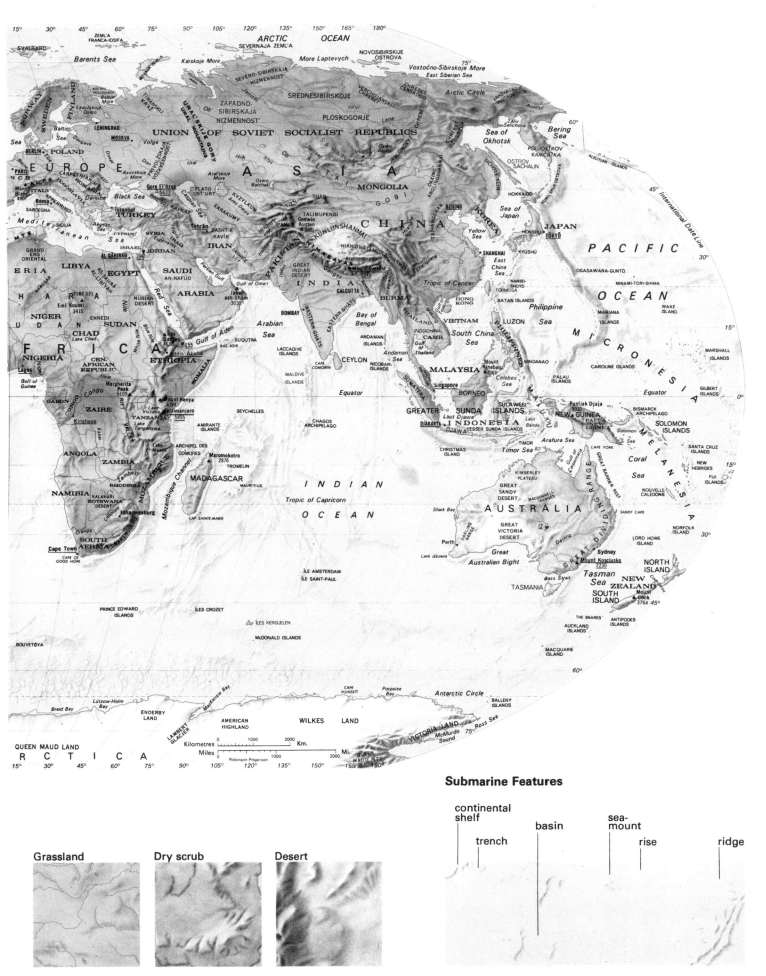

Submarine Features

continental
shelf

trench

basin

sea-
mount

rise

ridge

Grassland

Dry scrub

Desert

Europe and North Africa

Kilometres
0   200   400   600   800
Miles
0   200   400   600   800 Mi.
Lambert Azimuthal Equal-Area Projection

GREENLAND (Den.)

Angmagssalik

Denmark Strait

HORN   Arctic Circle

Norwegian Sea

FONTUR

Reykjavik   ICELAND   Hvannadalshnúkur   2119

CANADA

FAEROE ISLANDS (Den.)

SHETLAND ISLANDS (U.K.)   MAINLAND

ORKNEY ISLANDS

ISLE OF LEWIS
HEBRIDES
KINNAIRD'S HEAD

Trondheim   Glittertind 2470

Bergen   Oslo   Vänern

Stavanger   LINDESNES   Skagerrak   Göteborg

Glasgow   Edinburgh   DENMARK   Kattegat   Malmö   København

Belfast   UNITED KINGDOM   North Sea

Donegal Bay   Irish Sea   Hamburg   Elbe   FED. REP. OF GER.   BERLIN

IRELAND   Dublin   Manchester   Liverpool   Amsterdam   NETH.   GER.   DEM. REP.

Mizen Head   Cork   Saint George's Channel   Birmingham   Rotterdam   Antwerpen   Essen   Leipzig

Cardiff   LONDON   Bruxelles   BEL.   Bonn   Frankfurt   Praha

Plymouth   LAND'S END   Lille   LUX.   Rhine

ATLANTIC   English Channel

Brest   PARIS   Seine   Stuttgart   München   Austria

FRANCE   Loire   Basel   Zürich   SWITZ.   Innsbruck

Nantes   Genève   Trieste

Bay of Biscay   Bordeaux   Lyon   Mont Blanc   MILANO   Venezia   Adriatic

MASSIF CENTRAL   Rhône   Torino   ITALY   APENNINO

OCEAN   La Coruña   Bilbao   PYRENEES   Marseille   Nice   Ligurian Sea

CABO FINISTERRE   CORDILLERA CANTABRICA   Ebro   ANDORRA   Corse CORSICA

CORVO   Porto   Duero   BARCELONA   ROMA

FLORES   SPAIN   SARDEGNA SARDINIA   Vesuvio

GRACIOSA   PORTUGAL   MADRID   ISLAS BALEARES   Napoli 1277

SÃO JORGE   TERCEIRA   Tagus   CABO DE LA NAO   MENORCA

FAIAL   PICO   SÃO MIGUEL   Lisboa   Guadiana   Valencia   Júcar   IBIZA   MALLORCA   Tyrrhenian Sea

AÇORES AZORES (Port.)   SIERRA MORENA   Cagliari   SICILIA SICILY   Palermo

Ponta Delgada   Guadalquivir   Mulhacén 3478   Monte Etna 3390

SANTA MARIA   CABO DE SÃO VICENTE   Strait of Gibraltar   Gibraltar (U.K.)   Alger Algiers   CAP BON   PANTELLERIA (It.)   CAPO PASSERO

Tanger   Oran   Constantine   Tunis   LAMPEDUSA (It.)   MALTA

RIF   Rabat   Fès   Tunisia   Sfax   ÎLES KERKENNA

ARQUIPÉLAGO DA MADEIRA (Port.)   Casablanca   MOYEN ATLAS   Moulouya   Golfe de Gabès   ÎLE DE DJERBA

Funchal   Safi   MOROCCO   ATLAS MOUNTAINS   ATLAS SAHARIEN   TUNISIA   Ţarābulus   Tripoli

Marrakech   Ghardaia   Touggourt

ISLAS CANARIAS CANARY ISLANDS (Sp.)   HAUT ATLAS   TARĀBULUS TRIPOLITANIA

LA PALMA   LANZAROTE   Jbel Toubkal   ANTI ATLAS   Béchar   PLATEAU DU TADEMAIT   PLATEAU DU TINRHERT

TENERIFE   Santa Cruz   FUERTEVENTURA   HAMADA DU DRA   GRAND ERG OCCIDENTAL   GRAND ERG ORIENTAL

GOMERA   Las Palmas   El Aaiún   TASSILI N'AJJER   FAZZAN

HIERRO   GRAN CANARIA   ERG IGUIDI   ALGERIA   L   Marzūq

Tindouf   ERG CHECH   IDEHAN MARZŪQ

Tropic of Cancer   WESTERN SAHARA   EL HANK   TANEZROUFT   Djanet   AHAGGAR

Villa Cisneros   ERG   TASSILI DU   S   A   H   A   R   A

ADRAR   OUARANE   EL DJOUF   AHAGGAR   Tamanrasset

CAP BLANC   Nouadhibou   Atar

MAURITANIA   ADRAR DES IFORAS   AÏR   MONTS BAGZANE   TÉNÉRÉ   GRAND ERG DE BILMA

Nouakchott   AOUKÂR   MALI   Vallée du Tilemsi

SÃO NICOLAU   SAL   CAPE VERDE   Tombouctou   Gao   Vallée de l'Azaouak   Agadez   NIGER

BOA VISTA   Saint-Louis   MACINA   SUDAN

SÃO TIAGO   MAIO   CAP VERT   Mbout   DESERTO

FOGO   Praia   Dakar   SENEGAL

22

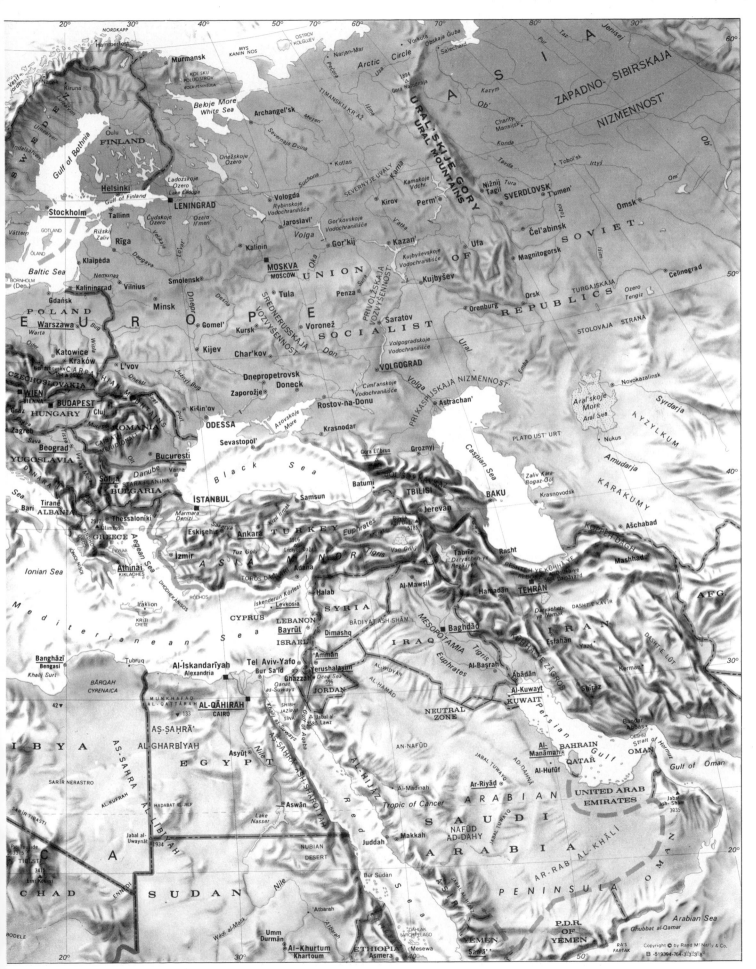

23

Southern Africa

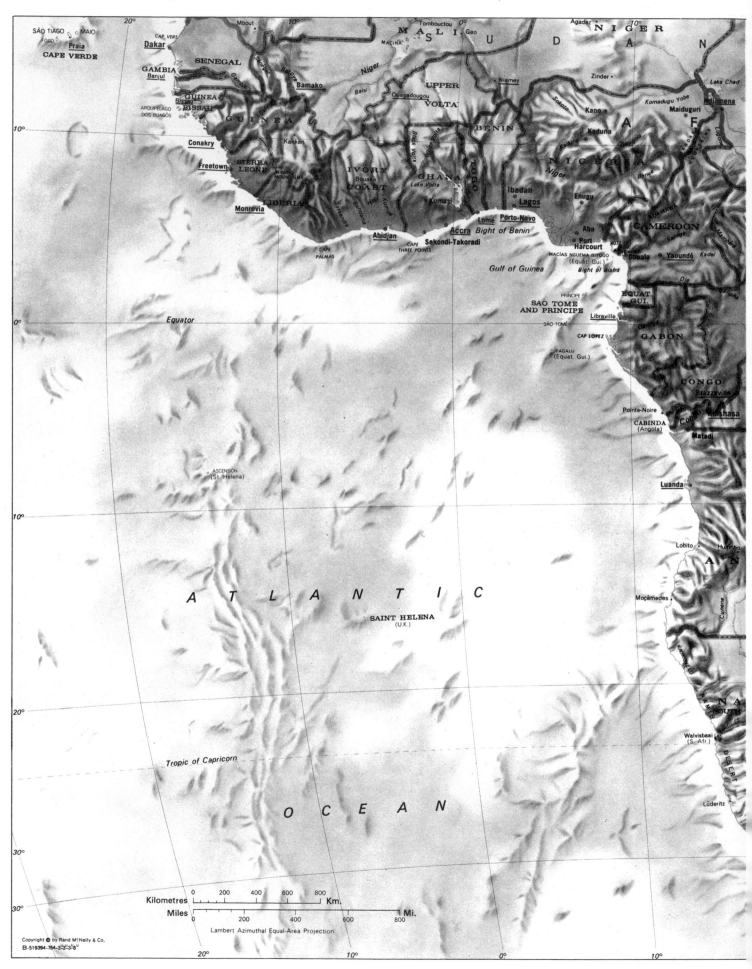

SÃO TIAGO ∘ MAIO
FOGO ∘
Praia
CAPE VERDE

CAP VERT
Dakar
Mbout
MALI
Tombouctou
Gao
Agadez
NIGER
N

SENEGAL
GAMBIA
Banjul
Senegal
Gambia
Bakoye
Bamako
Niger
MACINA
SUDAN
Niamey
Zinder
Lake Chad
Komadugu Yobe
Ndjamena

GUINEA
BISSAU
Bissau
ARQUIPÉLAGO
DOS BIJAGÓS
GUINEA
Bani
UPPER
Ouagadougou
VOLTA
Sokoto
Kano
Kaduna
Maiduguri
A
F

10°
Kankan
BENIN
Black Volta
White Volta
NIGERIA
Niger
Enugu
Benue
Conakry
SIERRA
Freetown
LEONE
NIMBA
MOUNTAINS
IVORY
COAST
Bouaké
GHANA
Lake Volta
TOGO
Ibadan
Lagos
Aba
CAMEROON

Monrovia
LIBERIA
Sassandra
Bandama
Nzi
Komoé
Kumasi
Lomé
Porto-Novo
Port
Harcourt
4070
Yaoundé
Kadei

Abidjan
CAPE
THREE POINTS
Accra Bight of Benin
Sekondi-Takoradi
MACÍAS NGUEMA BIYOGO
(Equat. Gui.)
Douala
Die
CAPE
PALMAS
Gulf of Guinea
Bight of Biafra
EQUAT.
GUI.

PRINCIPE
SAO TOME
AND PRINCIPE
Libreville
GABON

0°
Equator
SÃO TOMÉ
CAP LOPEZ
PAGALU
(Equat. Gui.)

CONGO
Brazzaville
Pointe-Noire
Kinshasa
CABINDA
(Angola)
Matadi

ASCENSION
(St. Helena)

Luanda

10°
Lobito
Huambo
A
N

A T L A N T I C
Moçâmedes
Cunene

SAINT HELENA
(U.K.)

20°
Walvisbaai
(S. Afr.)
NA
SOUTH

Tropic of Capricorn
NAMIB

O C E A N
Lüderitz
DESERT

Kilometres
0 200 400 600 800 Km.

Miles
0   200   400   600   800 Mi.
Lambert Azimuthal Equal-Area Projection

20° 10° 0° 10°

CHAD

SUDAN

Bodele
Abéché
JABAL MARRAH
Al-Fāshir
Al-Ubayyid
Wadi al-Malik
Umm Durmān
Al-Khurtum
Khartoum
DAHLAK ARCHIPELAGO
Mesewa
YEMEN
San'ā
P.D.R. OF YEMEN
Ghubbat al-Qamar
RA'S FARTAK
Arabian Sea
Al-Mukalla
Aden
Gulf of Aden
Alula
'ABD AL-KURI
SUQUTRA
(P.D.R. of Yem.)

CENTRAL AFRICAN REPUBLIC
Bangui
RICA
Sarh
Bahr Aouk
Chari
Ouham
Kotto
Mbari
Uele
Bomu
Uele
Bahr al-'Arab
Boro
Jur
Bahr al-Ghazal
Mountain Nile
Sobat
Blue Nile
White Nile
AL-JAZIRAH
Asmera
Tekeze
Ras Dashen
Gonder
Lake Tana
Atbara
Awash
Berbera
Djibouti
AFARS AND ISSAS
Dire Dawa
Suud Ad
RAS HAFUN
RAS ASIR
CAPE GUARDAFUI

ADDIS ABEBA
ETHIOPIA
Lake Abaya
Genale
Dawa
Shebelle
SOMALIA

Ubangi
CONGO
Congo
Kisangani
Aruwimi
STANLEY FALLS
MURCHISON FALLS
UGANDA
Lake Albert
Lake Kyoga
Margherita Peak
5105
5321
Mount Elgon
Kampala
Lake Edward
RWANDA
Kigali
Lake Kivu
KENYA
Lake Rudolf
5199
Mount Kenya
Nairobi
Juba
Tana
Juba
Shebelle
Mogadisho
Equator

Lac Tumba
BASIN
ZAIRE
Tshuapa
Lac Mai-Ndombe
Lukenie
Lomami
Lualaba
Lake Victoria
Mwanza
Lake Natron
SERENGETI PLAIN
Lake Eyasi
MASAI STEPPE
Kilimanjaro
5895
Pangani
Mombasa
PEMBA ISLAND
Zanzibar
ZANZIBAR
INDIAN
OCEAN
AMIRANTE ISLANDS (Sey.)
SEYCHELLES

Kanganga
Kasai
Kwango
Kwilu
Lukenie
Loange
Kasai
Sankuru
Lomami
Luvua
BURUNDI
Bujumbura
Lake Tanganyika
TANZANIA
Lake Rukwa
Great Ruaha
Ruvu
Dar-es-Salaam
MAFIA ISLAND

GOLA
Cuango
Cuanza
Chicapa
Chiumbe
Cassai
Luena
Kabompo
Lungué Bungo
Zambezi
Kwando
Cuito
Okavango
Cubango
Luapula
KATANGA PLATEAU
Lubumbashi
Ndola
Lake Mweru
Lake Bangweulu
MUCHINGA MOUNTAINS
ZAMBIA
Luangwa
GREAT RIFT VALLEY
Lake Malawi
Lake Chilwa
Zomba
Blantyre
Lilongwe
Luangwa
Lugenda
M'Sali
Lurio
Ruvuma
MOZAMBIQUE
Moçambique
ALDABRA ISLANDS (Sey.)
ASSUMPTION ISLAND
COSMOLEDO GROUP (Sey.)
FARQUHAR GROUP (Sey.)
Mtwara
COMORO ISLANDS
GRANDE COMORE
ANJOUAN
MOHELI
MAYOTTE (Fr.)
Channel
CAP D'AMBRE
Diego-Suarez
2876
Maromokotro

Lusaka
Kafue
Lake Kariba
Livingstone
VICTORIA FALLS
Salisbury
RHODESIA
Bulawayo
Zambezi
Shire
Beira
Mozambique
CAP SAINT-ANDRÉ
Betsiboka
Baie d'Antongil
TROMELIN (Fr.)
Tamatave
Tananarive
MADAGASCAR
MASCARENE ISLANDS
MAURITIUS
RÉUNION (Fr.)

MIBIA
WEST AFRICA
(Afr. Admin.)
Windhoek
Tsumeb
GREAT NAMALAND
Nossob
Nossop
Okavango
Cuito
BOTSWANA
KALAHARI DESERT
Gaborone
KAAP PLATO
Limpopo
Olifants
Changane
Chinde
BASSAS DA INDIA (Fr.)
PONTA SÃO SEBASTIÃO
ILE EUROPA (Fr.)
PONTA DA BARRA FALSA
Manambolo
CAP SAINT-VINCENT
Mangoky
Tulear
CAP SAINTE-MARIE
Fort-Dauphin
Tropic of Capricorn

Pretoria
JOHANNESBURG
Maputo
Mbabane
SWAZILAND
SOUTH AFRICA
Vaal
Orange
Maseru
LESOTHO
Thabana Ntlenyana
3482
Bloemfontein
Durban
GREAT KARROO
Cape Town
CAPE OF GOOD HOPE
CAPE AGULHAS
East London
Port Elizabeth

Earth panorama: Europe

Europe is the second smallest continent. It is bounded by the Arctic Ocean to the north, the Atlantic Ocean to the west and the Mediterranean and Black Seas to the south. It merges into Asia to the east and the conventional boundary from south to north follows the Caucasus mountains, the Caspian Sea and the Ural mountains.

A line following the northern edge of the Pyrenees mountains, the Rhône valley and the northern edge of the Alps and Carpathian mountains separates northern from southern Europe. Northern Europe thus consists of large sedimentary plains, a Precambrian shield and worn-down Palaeozoic highlands. Southern Europe is characterized by Cenozoic mountains (Alps, Pyrenees, Carpathians) surrounding restricted basins.

Apart from a small subarctic fringe in the extreme north, most of Europe is in the temperate zone. The distance from the Atlantic Ocean and the situation of the mountains create a climatic subdivision of Europe into marine areas to the west, Mediterranean areas to the south and continental areas to the east.

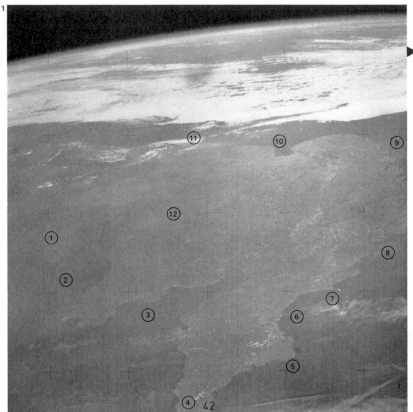

1 Great Britain and Ireland are islands of the European continental shelf and they were part of the mainland during the recent Ice Age. The Irish seashore is indistinct north of Anglesey [1] but Cardigan Bay [2], the Bristol Channel [3], Cornwall [4] and Start Point [5] are clearly visible. All this part of Britain consists of ancient Precambrian and Palaeozoic rocks. East of a line from Lyme Bay [6] to Grimsby [11] the rocks are Mesozoic and Cenozoic. North of Derby [12] the rocks are again Palaeozoic. Other features include Portland Bill [7], the Isle of Wight [8], Orford Ness [9] and the Wash [10].

2 The Dutch coast, from the Schelde and Rhine estuaries [1] to the Frisian islands [2], is seen here with the cities of The Hague [3], Rotterdam [4] and Amsterdam [5] as well as the IJsselmeer [6].

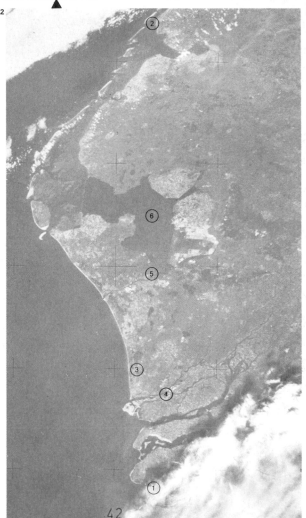

3 The Alps are the highest mountains in western Europe, extending 1,000km (620 miles) from the Mediterranean to Vienna. They are the western limb of a much larger system of mountains which extends to Indonesia through the Balkans and the Himalayas. The highest summit is Mont Blanc [1] at 4,807m (15,771ft). It is part of the inner granite core which has been thrust up in places and uncovered by erosion. Lake Geneva [2], which divides the upper Rhône valley [3] from the lower [4], is in a depression between the Alps and the Jura mountains [5] which were folded, but less severely, as a consequence of the Alpine upheaval. The lakes of Neuchâtel [6] and Thun [7] can also be seen.

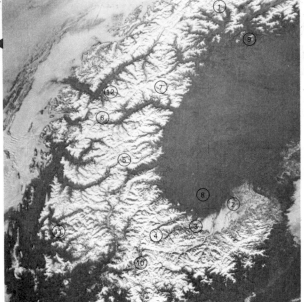

4 The Western Alps extend from the Mediterranean coast [lower right] to the Adula massif [1]. They enclose the Po valley. The following massifs can be seen here: Argentera [2], Monte Viso [3], Mont Pelvoux [4], Vanoise [5], Mont Blanc [6] and Monte Rosa [7]. The major rivers on the Italian side are the Po [8] and the Adda [9], draining through Lake Como; and the Durance [10], Isère [11] and Rhône [12] on the French side.

5 Part of the south coast of France from the Vaccares marshes [1] to Toulon [6] is shown here. The main Rhône outlet [2] is seen near the huge dock area of the modern harbour of Marseille-Fos [3]. Port-de-Bouc docks on the sea side of the canal link the Berre lake [4] with the Mediterranean. The artificial breakwater [5] of the New Harbour of Marseille can also be seen.

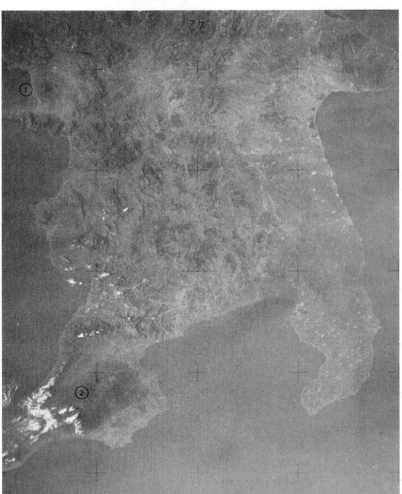

6 The famous boot-shape of southern Italy [A] appears far more squat here because of the camera angle. The western side of the peninsula right down to the "toe" of Calabria has a pronounced relief due to the Apennine range. The Bay of Naples [1] is limited to the north by the island of Ischia and to the south by Capri. Just inland of the bottom of the bay the volcano Mt Vesuvius is conspicuous, as is Botte Donato mountain [2]. The "in-step" between the toe and the heel is the Gulf of Taranto; the heel is terminated by Cape Santa Maria di Leuca. Between the heel and the spur of Gargano (which has some lakes on its north side) is a dry limestone area, Puglia.

The eastern coast of Sicily [B] is seen in this infra-red photograph. Mt Etna, the highest volcano in Europe, is still active as is evidenced by the thin plume of smoke rising from its crater. Etna's height of 3,340m (10,960ft) is approximate because it changes at each eruption. Recent lava flows appear as black in contrast to the older red ones. The numerous small "warts" on the flank of the volcano are cinder cones built by side vents. The town of Catania nestles at the foot of Mt Etna by the sea. Beyond it is a cultivated plain with fields of various colours and a meandering river. The town of Augusta, enclosed by a breakwater, can be seen at bottom left.

Earth panorama: Africa

Africa is the third largest continent and is devoid of any peripheral island arcs. It is entirely surrounded by mid-oceanic ridges (one of them, in the Red Sea, coming right up to its shores) except to the north where it abuts the Mediterranean and the alpine system. The Maghreb (Morocco, Algeria and Tunisia) is the only geologically recent province and it is separated from the Precambrian basement and shield forming the rest of the continent by a big fault running from Agadir to Gabes.

The rolling basement to the south of this fault line forms great basins (Niger, Chad, Congo, Kalahari) surrounded by highlands that dominate the coasts. More than half of the continent lacks drainage towards the sea and the large rivers (Nile, Congo, Niger and Zambezi) have difficult paths to the sea.

The climate is zoned, with a central equatorial band grading the north and the south into tropical lands with a marked dry season, the length of which increases polewards until the desert areas. South Africa has a warm maritime climate, whereas the north coast has a Mediterranean climate.

1 Where the Nile flows, the land is lush and green; where its waters do not reach there is desert. The ribbon oasis along the Nile valley to the south (right) of Cairo [1] spreads out into a rich alluvial delta. The river branches into two, the Rosetta Nile [2] and the Damietta Nile [3]. The front of the delta is marked by large lagoons and infertile desert-sand. Between Alexandria [4] and Cairo there are large fields and modern irrigation projects. The Suez Canal runs from Port Said [5] to Suez [6]. A narrow strip of vegetation links the Nile with Ismailia [7].

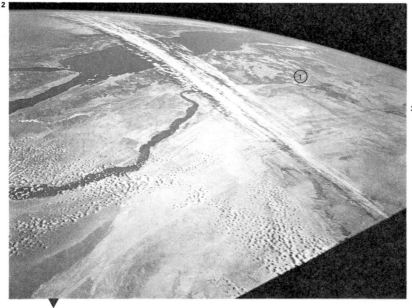

2 The ribbon oasis of the Nile divides the Libyan desert in the foreground from the Arabian desert in the background, beyond which the Red Sea, the gulfs of Suez and Aqaba and the Sinai peninsula can be seen. The Nile's yearly flood used to bring about 55 million tonnes of new fertile silt but much of this is now stopped by the Aswan Dam [1] and it is silting up the artificial reservoir, Lake Nasser. The lake loses water through evaporation, a situation aggravated by a plague of water hyacinths. The reduced flow has increased the salinity of the eastern Mediterranean and seriously affected its plankton population. The local sardine fishing industry has suffered as a result.

3 The Arabian peninsula [1] has moved and rotated away from Africa, opening up the Gulf of Aden [2] and the Red Sea [3]. The Bab el Mandeb strait [4] is a triple junction of three spreading axes: the Gulf of Aden which links up with the Carlsberg Ridge in the Indian Ocean, the Red Sea axis which extends to the Dead Sea, and the Afar Triangle [5] linking up with the East African Rift.

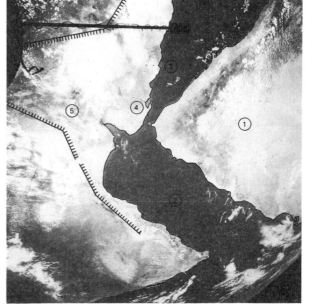

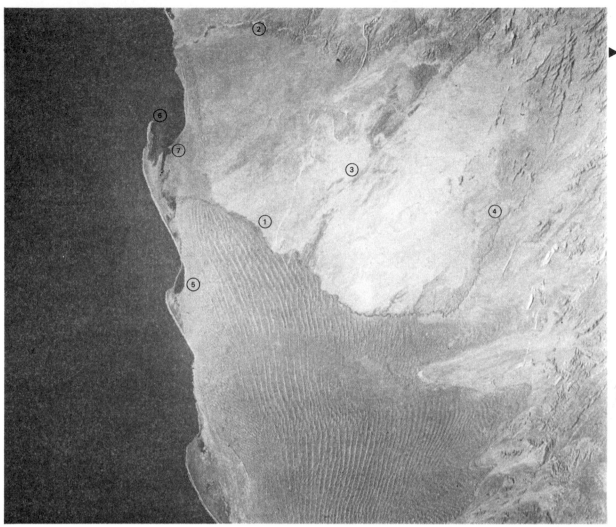

4 The Namib Desert is rocky to the north and sandy to the south. The sand sea or erg is limited to the north by the River Kuiseb [1]. The River Swakop [2] can also be seen. The rocky area is a peneplain exposing the roots of an old Precambrian mountain range; the lineations of the folds can easily be followed. These rocks and folds have a southwesterly trend and they are cut off by the edge of the continental shelf. The missing continuation is found in South America, a clear proof of continental drift. The rocks are granite, gneiss and marble which forms white ridges [3]. A sill of basic rock also shows up [4]; both the sill and marble are rich in minerals. The longshore drift towards the north forms sandspits often enclosing lagoons [5]. A big sandspit encloses Walvis Bay [6]; Walvis Bay town [7] appears as a blue patch.

5 Lake Chad lies across the borders of Chad, Niger, Nigeria and Cameroon. It is the centre for an inland drainage system and has no outlet to the sea. Its main tributary is the 1200km (750 miles) Chari flowing from the south. The intermittent wadi Bahr el Ghazal drains the rare rains from the Saharan north. Because of the high evaporation and the marked seasonal variation of the inflow, the area of the lake varies and therefore precise contours are rarely shown on maps. It is a shallow lake whose average level is dropping at a rate of 1.25cm (0.5in) a year.

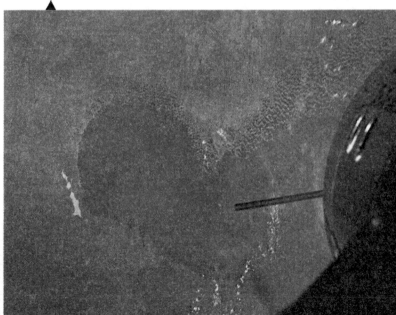

6

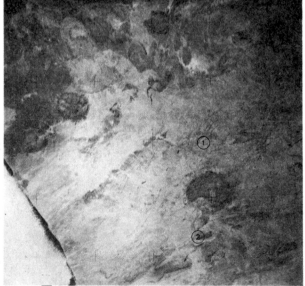

6 This is the bare African shield in southwest Africa – the roots of Precambrian mountains which have been worn down to a peneplain. The area consists mainly of gneiss. The conspicuous circular patches are plugs of granite known as inselbergs. Two intermittent wadis, [1], [2] can be seen. The coastline is underlined by a narrow strip of blue sea; the rest of the sea is clouded over because of the cold Benguela current, which promotes cloud formation.

Northern Asia

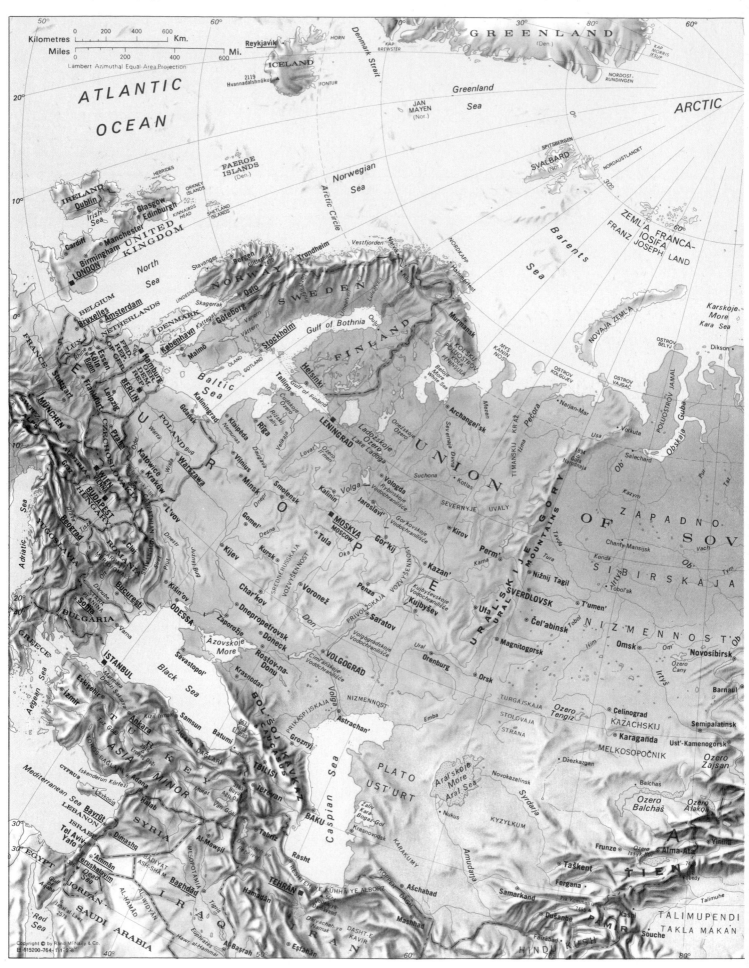

OCEAN

North Pole

120° 150° 80° 160° 70° UNITED STATES Nome 60° UNIMAK 50°
POINT HOPE Bering Strait ISLAND Unalaska

Chukchi Sea ČUKOTSKIJ POLUOSTROV SAINT LAWRENCE ISLAND Bering ALEUTIAN ISLANDS 170°

180° OSTROV VRANGEL'A Proliv Longa Anadyrskij Zaliv Sea

SEVERNAJA ZEML'A NORTH LAND 90° 120° NOVOSIBIRSKIJE OSTROVA NEW SIBERIAN ISLANDS OSTROV NOVAJA SIBIR' Vostočno-Sibirskoje More East Siberian Sea ANADYRSKOJE PLOSKOGORJE Anadyr MYS NAVARIN Uel'kal Velkaja Ariedj Makovo PRIBILOF ISLANDS 180°

MYS CELJUSKIN 150° OSTROV KOTEL'NYJ Arctic Circle Omolon Penžina MYS OLJUTORSKU 170°

More Laptevych Laptev Sea OSTROV BOL'ŠOJ BEGIČEV Alazeja Indigirka Kolyma JUKAGIRSKOJE PLOSKOGORJE Palana OSTROV KARAGINSKU 160°

POLUOSTROV TAJMYR Ozero Tajmyr NIZMENNOST' Nordvik Tiksi Olen'ok Kazačje Jana Zyrjanka Zaliv Šelichova POLUOSTROV KAMCATKA KAMCHATKA PENINSULA ROMANOVSKOJE

SEVERO-SIBIRSKAJA Chatanga Cheta Kolui Anabar CHREBET ČERSKOGO Jamsk SREDINNYJ Petropavlovsk-Kamčatskij ATTU

Dudinka Noril'sk Igarka GORY PUTORANA Žigansk Lena Verchojansk VERCHOJANSKIJ CHREBET Magadan Sea of Okhotsk CHREBET MYS KRONOCKAJA 170°

SREDNESIBIRSKOJE PLOSKOGORJE Jessej Jakutsk Ochotsk Ajan SANTARSKUJE OSTROVA MYS LOPATKA 160°

Jenisej Nizn'aja Tunguska Čuna Lena Lensk Amga Aldan ALDANSKOJE NAGORJE Ocha MYS JELIZAVETY OSTROV SACHALIN SAKHALIN KURIL'SKIJE OSTROVA KURIL ISLANDS 150°

IET SOCIALIST Podkamennaja Tunguska Vitim Ölokma STANOVOJ Nikolaevsk Aleksandrovsk-Sachalinskij MYS TERPENIJA 140°

Ket' Angara Čuna STANOVOJE NAGORJE Skovorodino Amur Komsomol'sk na-Amure Udа Tatarskij Proliv La Perouse Strait Asahikawa HOKKAIDO 150°

Tomsk Krasnojarsk Bratskoje Vodochranilišče Ona JABLONOVYJ CHREBET Argun Heilongjiang Chabarovsk SICHOTE-ALIN' Sapporo 40°

Kemerovo Abakan Ozero Bajkal Čita CHREBET Šilka Eergu'naihe Haerbin Ozero Chanka Hakodate Komo'i Tsugaru-kaikyo

Novokuzneck ZAPADNY SAJAN VOSTOČNY SAJAN Angara BORŠČOVOČNYJ Onon Hailaer Qiqihaer Songhuajiang Jiamusi Vladivostok Sea of Japan 40°

4506 Gora Belucha SAJAN MOUNTAINS Irkutsk Ulan-Ude Selenga Buir Nuur Hulunchi Songhuajiang Sendai HONSHŪ Niigata TOKYO

Kyzyl Chövsgöl Nuur Onon Kerulen Buir Nuur DAXINGANLINGSHANMAI Changchun Xihe HANGGUANGCALING TOKYO 140°

Uvs Nuur Chirgis Nuur Ulaanbaatar Orchon Liaohe Fushun Tongjosón-Man Nagoya Kyoto

ALTAI CHANGAJN Dzavchan NURUU MONGOLIA GOBI SHENYANG MUKDEN Andong NORTH KOREA OSAKA Hiroshima JAPAN 140°

Chol Nuur Char Us Nuur Zhangjiakou Huhehaote Liaodongwan P'yongyang SOUTH KOREA Pusan Taegu SHIKOKU

S SHAN Wulumuqi Huanghe BEIJING PEKING TIANJIN TIENTSIN Bohai Luda Dairen Korea Bay SÓUL Pusan Korea Strait Fukuoka KUSHŪ Bungo-suido 30°

Luobubo Lop Nor Ruoshui Taiyuan TAIHANGSHAN Huanghe Qingdao Tsingtao CHENGSHANJIAO Mokp'o Kagoshima AMAMI-O-SHIMA

AERJINSHANMAI QILIANSHANMAI Qinghai Yinchuan Ji'nan CHEJU DO (S. Kor.) Yellow Sea TOKONO-SHIMA

CHAIDAMUPENDI 90° 100° Lanzhou Zhengzhou Yinghe Nanjing 110° SHANGHAI 120° EAST CHINA SEA 130° 30° Yunhe Grand Canal Hongzehu CHINA

31

Southern Asia

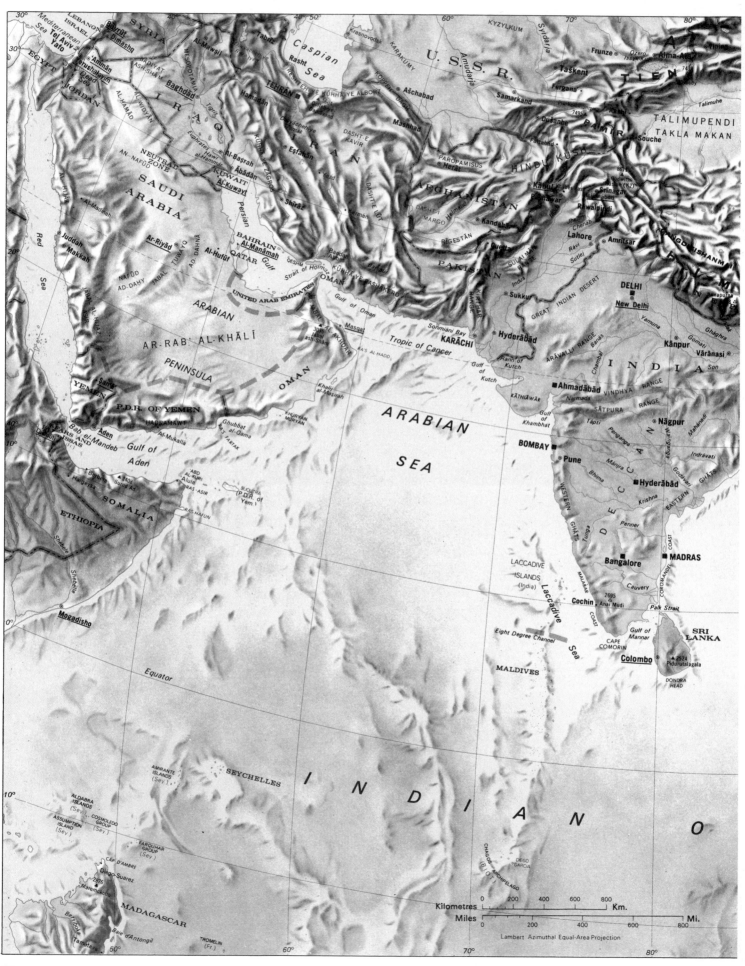

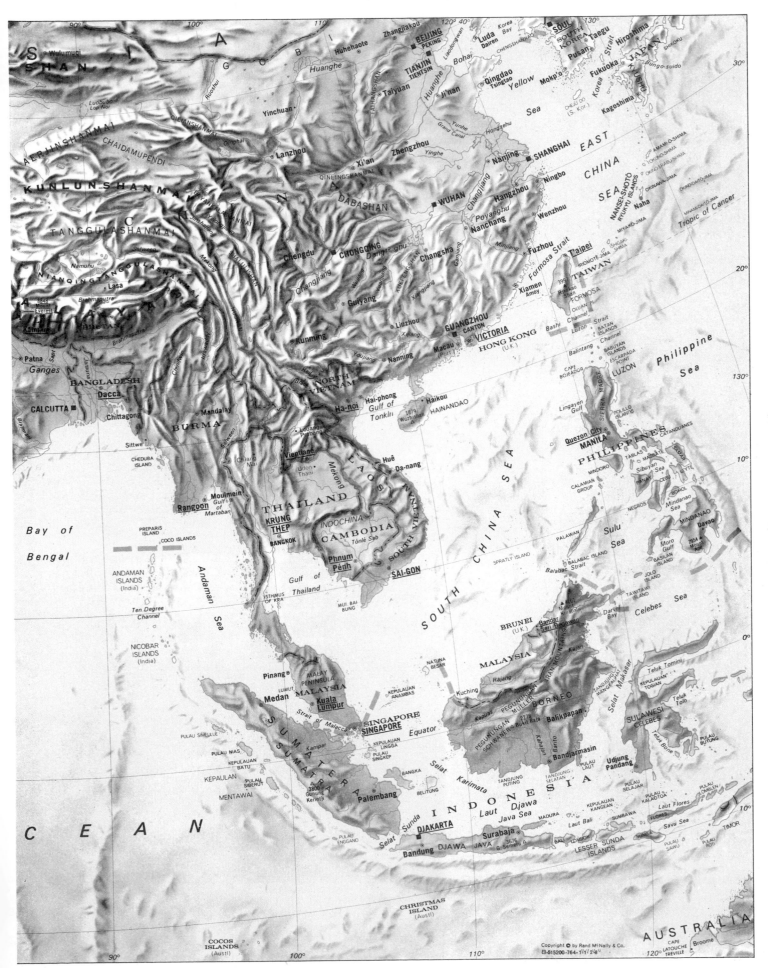

33

Earth panorama: Asia

Asia is the largest of the seven continents. The eastern and southeastern parts of the continent are fringed by a series of island arcs which have frequent earthquakes and many volcanoes: Indonesia, the Philippines, Ryukyu, Japan and the Kurils.

The Himalayas are the seam welding India and Asia proper. Similarly the Arabian peninsula is geologically part of Africa, not of Asia. The recent mountains (Caucasus, Zagros, Himalayas, Tien Shan, Altai) sometimes enclose highland plateaus such as Anatolia, the Iranian plateau and Tibet. These fringing mountains surround the geological heartland of Asia – the Siberian shield, which also extends under Mongolia and much of China.

Asia has four broad climatic domains – Mediterranean, desert, continental and monsoon. The Mediterranean zone is limited to a narrow fringe in Turkey and the Middle East. The continental zone comprises Siberia, Mongolia and Tibet and is characterized by very harsh winters. The desert climate is found from Arabia to Pakistan. Monsoon Asia extends from India to Japan.

1 The Red Sea [1] is a giant rift in the earth's surface that separates Asia from Africa. It is a cleft formed by sea-floor spreading. To the north it is split in two. The Gulf of Suez [2] follows the same line and at its inner end the Suez Canal and the Great Bitter Lake can be seen. The Gulf of Aqaba [3] is the southern end of another big rift that can be followed through the Dead Sea [4] and Lake Tiberias [5]. The Sinai is the peninsula between the gulfs of Suez and Aqaba. The dark mountains in the south are Precambrian terrains that can be traced into Egypt and Arabia.

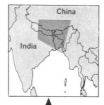

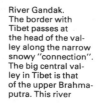

2 Lakes Neyriz [1] and Tashk [2] in the Zagros Mountains of Iran are normally dry except following rare rainfalls or the spring thaw in the mountains. The lakes are fed by the River Kur [3]. The thick salt deposits are conspicuous. The terrains to the top of the picture have been pushed over those to the bottom in a thrust line [WX], while to the left there is an ordinary fault [YZ]. An eroded anticline [4] and a dome [5] are visible. The dark patches [6] are extinct volcanoes.

3 The high mountain ranges of the Himalayas rise above the Indo-Gangetic plain [1]. Katmandu [2] is the capital of Nepal. Annapurna (8,078 m [26,503 ft]) is visible [3] above the deep valley of the River Gandak. The border with Tibet passes at the head of the valley along the narrow snowy "connection". The big central valley in Tibet is that of the upper Brahmaputra. This river runs across to the horizon on the left and then crosses the Himalayas to join the Indo-Gangetic plain. Lhasa is at [4]. Mt Everest [5] is the highest mountain in the world, reaching 8,848m (29,030ft).

4 This Gemini 9 picture of the Indian subcontinent, taken from an altitude of 740km (460 miles), has a peculiar perspective due to a wide-angle lens. The indentation at the north end of the west coast is the Gulf of Cambay. The Western Ghats are to the left and the Deccan plateau basalts are the dark areas to the upper left. The shallowness of the strait separating Sri Lanka from the mainland is apparent. The conspicuous river and delta just to the north is the Coleroon, whereas, to the north of the Bay of Bengal, the huge delta of the River Ganges can be seen. The Himalayas are hidden on the horizon by clouds.

6 Japan is an archipelago bounding the shallow epicontinental Sea of Japan on its eastern side. On Japan's Pacific coast the sea-bed plunges down to the Ryukyu and Japan trenches, part of the major Pacific trench system; thus the Japanese islands are part of the same tectonic system as other island arcs such as the West Indies and Indonesia. In this photograph of the island of Kyushu evidence of tectonic activity can be seen in the plume of smoke rising from the volcano on Sakura-Jima [1]. Aso-san [2] is the world's largest active volcanic crater.

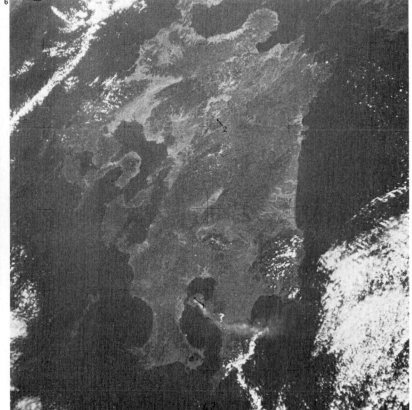

5 The complicated coastline of southeast China is due to the flooding of a worn-down peneplain by the sea, following subsidence of the land in the last few million years. The remaining knolls are predominantly made of granite and lavas. Particularly conspicuous is the island of Hainan, the land mass to the right is Taiwan. The deeper-blue current flowing north through the strait is an arm of the "black current" or Kuro Shio, which warms local climates.

Australia and Antarctica

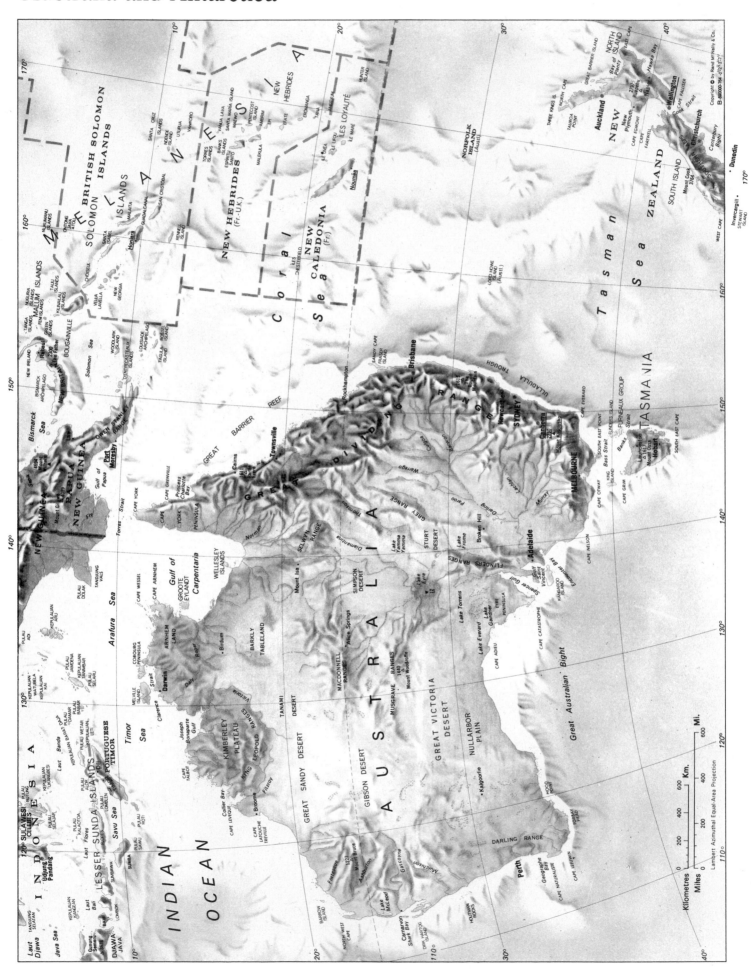

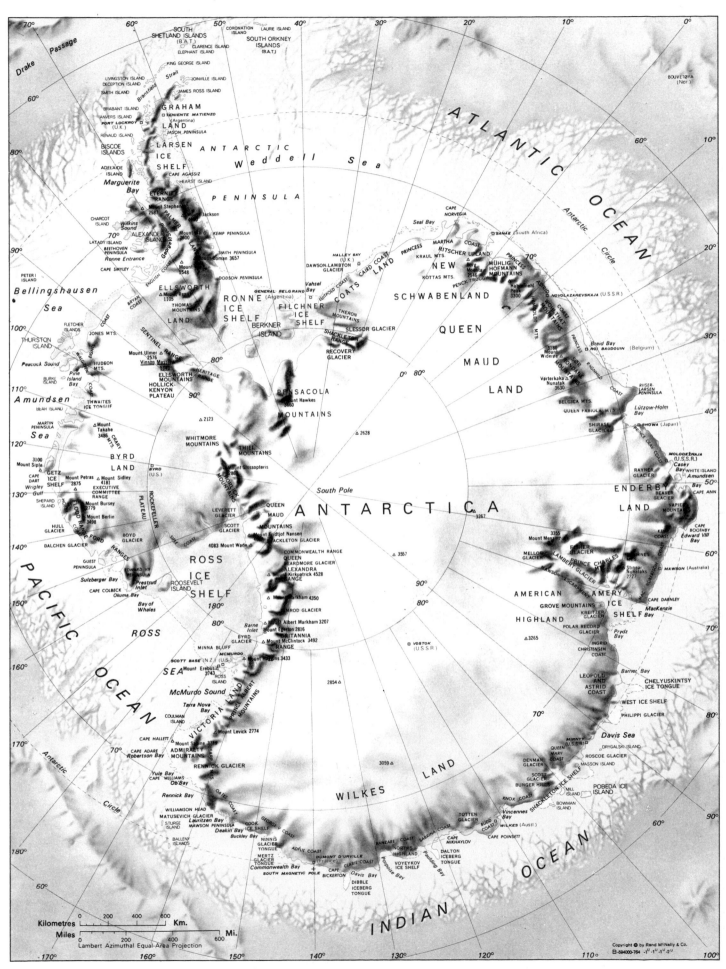

Drake Passage

70° 60° 50° CORONATION ISLAND LAURIE ISLAND 40°
SOUTH SHETLAND ISLANDS (B.A.T.) SOUTH ORKNEY ISLANDS (B.A.T.)
CLARENCE ISLAND
ELEPHANT ISLAND
KING GEORGE ISLAND
LIVINGSTON ISLAND
DECEPTION ISLAND
SMITH ISLAND
Strait JOINVILLE ISLAND
JAMES ROSS ISLAND
BRABANT ISLAND
ANVERS ISLAND
PORT LOCKROY (U.K.) **GRAHAM LAND**
Teniente Matienzo (Argentina)
RENAUD ISLAND JASON PENINSULA
BISCOE ISLANDS **LARSEN ICE SHELF**
ADELAIDE ISLAND CAPE AGASSIZ
Marguerite Bay HEARST ISLAND
CHARCOT ISLAND ETERNITY RANGE
Wilkins Sound Mount Stephenson 2987 Mount Jackson
ALEXANDER ISLAND 70° Mount Hardi 3600
LATADY ISLAND Mount Tyree KEMP PENINSULA
BEETHOVEN PENINSULA SMITH PENINSULA
Ronne Entrance Mount Coman 3657
CAPE SMILEY Mount 1548
PETER I ISLAND DODSON PENINSULA
Bellingshausen Sea **ELLSWORTH LAND**
Mount 1105
FLETCHER ISLANDS THOMAS MOUNTAINS
THURSTON ISLAND JONES MTS.
Peacock Sound SENTINEL RANGE
BURKE ISLAND Mount Ulmer 2576
Pine Island Bay HUDSON MTS. Vinson Massif
Amundsen Sea **ELLSWORTH MOUNTAINS** HERITAGE RANGE
THWAITES ICE TONGUE **HOLLICK-KENYON PLATEAU**
MARTIN PENINSULA 2123
Mount Takahe 3486 **WHITMORE MOUNTAINS**
Mount Siple 3100 **BYRD LAND** THIEL MOUNTAINS
CAPE DART GETZ ICE SHELF Mount Petras Mount Sidley 4181 2875
Wrigley Gulf EXECUTIVE COMMITTEE RANGE
SHEPARD ISLAND PLATEAU Mount Bursey 2779
HULL GLACIER Mount Berlin 3498
DALCHEN GLACIER ROCKEFELLER PLATEAU
GUEST PENINSULA **ROSS ICE SHELF**
Sulzberger Bay EDWARD VII PENINSULA *Prestrud Inlet*
CAPE COLBECK ROOSEVELT ISLAND
Okuma Bay
Bay of Whales 180°
ROSS SEA 80°
McMurdo Sound Barne Inlet
MINNA BLUFF BYRD GLACIER
SCOTT BASE (N.Z.) McMURDO (U.S.) Mount Huggins 3433
Terra Nova Bay Mount Erebus 3743 ROSS ISLAND
COULMAN ISLAND
CAPE HALLETT **VICTORIA LAND** Mount Sabine 3719 Mount Levick 2774
CAPE ADARE 70°
Robertson Bay **ADMIRALTY MOUNTAINS**
Yule Bay RENNICK GLACIER
CAPE WILLIAMS *Ob' Bay*
Rennick Bay
WILLIAMSON HEAD MATUSEVICH GLACIER
STURGE ISLAND *Lauritzen Bay* MAWSON PENINSULA COOK ICE SHELF
BALLENY ISLANDS *Deakin Bay* GEORGE V
MERTZ GLACIER TONGUE NINNIS GLACIER TONGUE
Commonwealth Bay ADÉLIE COAST DUMONT D'URVILLE (France)
SOUTH MAGNETIC POLE CAPE BICKERTON CLARIE COAST

PACIFIC OCEAN

ATLANTIC OCEAN

BOUVETØYA (Nor.)
60° 70°
CAPE NORVEGIA Seal Bay
SANAE (South Africa)
MARTHA COAST
PRINCESS RITSCHER UPLAND
HALLEY BAY (U.K.) PRINCESS MARTHA COAST
DAWSON-LAMBTON GLACIER CAIRD COAST KRAUL MTS. **NEW** 70°
Vahsel Bay COATS LAND MÜHLIG HOFMANN MOUNTAINS
GENERAL BELGRANO (Argentina) KOTTAS MTS. 2545 NOVOLAZAREVSKAJA (USSR)
GJELVIK Hansenbjell Peak PENCK TROUGH Hallvardhaugen MTS.
FILCHNER ICE SHELF THERON MOUNTAINS **SCHWABENLAND** 3300
RONNE ICE SHELF BERKNER ISLAND SLESSOR GLACIER **QUEEN MAUD LAND** 3180 Mount Widerøe
SHACKLETON RANGE RECOVERY GLACIER PRINCESS RAGNHILD COAST BREID BAY ROI BAUDOUIN (Belgium)
PENSACOLA MOUNTAINS 3650 0° 80° Vårterkaka Nunatak 3630
Mount Hawkes RIISER-LARSEN PENINSULA
BELGICA MTS. *Lützow-Holm Bay*
2628 QUEEN FABIOLA MTS. SHIRASE GLACIER
SOUTH POLE 3267 SYOWA (Japan)
ANTARCTICA MOLODEŽNAJA (U.S.S.R.)
WHITE ISLAND Casey Bay *Amundsen Bay*
ENDERBY LAND RAYNER GLACIER
BEAVER GLACIER CAPE ANN
Mount Menzies 3355 NAPIER MOUNTAINS
QUEEN MAUD MOUNTAINS 3557 MELLOR GLACIER FISHER GLACIER CAPE BOOTHBY Edward VIII Bay
Mount Fridtjof Nansen COMMONWEALTH RANGE LAMBERT GLACIER **PRINCE CHARLES** KEMP COAST
BEARDMORE GLACIER QUEEN ALEXANDRA RANGE Mount Kirkpatrick 4528 MAWSON ESCARPMENT Stinear Nunataks 2727 MAWSON (Australia)
4083 Mount Wade **AMERICAN** AMERY ICE SHELF
SHACKLETON GLACIER HIGHLAND **GROVE MOUNTAINS** KREITZER GLACIER CAPE DARNLEY
Mount Albert Markham 4350 POLAR RECORD GLACIER MacKenzie Bay
NIMROD GLACIER *Prydz Bay*
Mount Egerton 2816 INGRID CHRISTENSEN COAST
BRITANNIA RANGE Mount McClintock 3492 VOSTOK (USSR) 3265
Barrier Bay
2854 **LEOPOLD AND ASTRID COAST** CHELYUSKINTSY ICE TONGUE
WEST ICE SHELF
70° PHILIPPI GLACIER 80°
Davis Sea
MIRNYY (U.S.S.R.) DRYGALSKI ISLAND
3059 QUEEN MARY COAST ROSCOE GLACIER
WILKES LAND DENMAN GLACIER MASSON ISLAND
SCOTT GLACIER SHACKLETON ICE SHELF POBEDA ICE ISLAND
BUNGER HILLS MILL ISLAND
TOTTEN GLACIER *Vincennes Bay* KNOX COAST BOWMAN ISLAND
BANZARE COAST SABRINA COAST WILKES (Austl.)
NORTHS HIGHLAND CAPE MIKHAYLOV DALTON ICEBERG TONGUE
VOYEYKOV ICE SHELF *Davis Bay* CAPE POINSETT
DIBBLE ICEBERG TONGUE *Porpoise Bay* Paulding Bay
INDIAN OCEAN

Antarctic Circle
0°
10°
20°
30°
40°
50°
60°
70°
80°
90°
100°

Kilometres 0 200 400 600 Km.
Miles 0 200 400 600 Mi.
Lambert Azimuthal Equal-Area Projection

37

Earth panorama: the Pacific

The Pacific is the largest of all the oceans and has an area of 165 million square kilometres (64 million square miles). It is roughly circular and is bounded on three sides by Australia, Asia and America. It has wide contact south of Australia with the Indian Ocean, a limited contact with the same ocean through the Indonesian archipelago and a smaller contact with the Atlantic Ocean (through Drake Passage). To the north it has a very narrow passage through Bering Strait into the Arctic Ocean.

The hydrography of the Pacific is relatively simple. In the Northern Hemisphere there is a clockwise-current loop, driven by the northeast trade winds towards the Philippines and curving up towards Japan before carrying on towards Alaska and looping down past California back to its departure in the North Equatorial Current. The new sea-floor created by sea-floor spreading is compensated by sea-floor "sinking" into the trenches that extend from New Zealand round to Alaska and from Central America to Chile. Active volcanoes associated with these trenches circle the Pacific.

1 The oceanic hemisphere could well be another name for the expanse of the Pacific Ocean. Despite its many islands such as New Zealand, Papua and New Guinea, Borneo, Sakhalin and Japan, the proportion of dry land within the area is extremely small. The Pacific is the still-shrinking remains of the original world ocean Panthalassa that surrounded the dry land before it broke up into the continents we know today.

2 Many of the tropical Pacific Islands, for instance the Tuamotus, are coral atolls – ring-shaped islands surrounding a shallow lagoon. The atolls rise from great depths, yet the corals that built them cannot grow in depths of more than 45m (150ft). The early mariners thought that atolls were created by divine providence as convenient shelters for seafarers. Some naturalists believed that they were founded on shallow crater rims. In 1837 Charles Darwin proposed that they were once volcanic islands that sank by subsidence of the sea-floor as coral growth towards the surface kept pace.

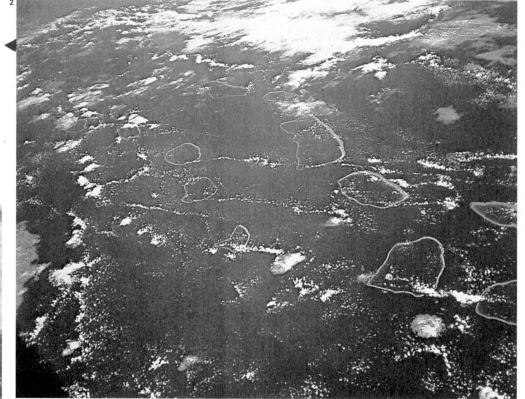

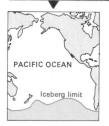

3 Icebergs shed from the huge Antarctic ice sheet drift in a northeasterly direction and are a danger to shipping. In the Pacific they can drift as far north as 41°S before they melt away. Some of them are over 600m (2,000ft) thick.

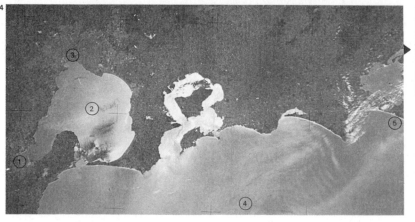

4 This section of the south coast of the state of Victoria, Australia, extends from Geelong [1] to Wilson's Promontory [5]. Bass Strait [4] separates mainland Australia from Tasmania. Melbourne [3] is at the head of Port Phillip Bay [2].

5

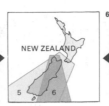

6

5 Cook Strait, named after James Cook the explorer, separates the North and South Islands of New Zealand. Wellington, the capital, can be seen [1] and also Christchurch [2]. The Tararua Range [3] and the Southern Alps [4] are covered in snow. The curvature of the earth is visible to the south.

6 The South Island of New Zealand consists of Cenozoic mountains, the Southern Alps, which were uplifted by the collision of the Pacific crustal plate to the east [left] and the Australian plate to the west. This Skylab 4 photograph was taken over Cook Strait [1] looking south, with Christchurch [2] visible.

7 The North Island of New Zealand is a volcanic area. Mount Egmont at 2,520m (8,260ft) is a symmetrical volcano although it carries several secondary cones on its flanks. Water erosion has carved several radial gullies round the craters. The limit between the volcanic scoriae and rock forming the volcano and the agricultural plain that surrounds it is distinct.

NEW ZEALAND

7

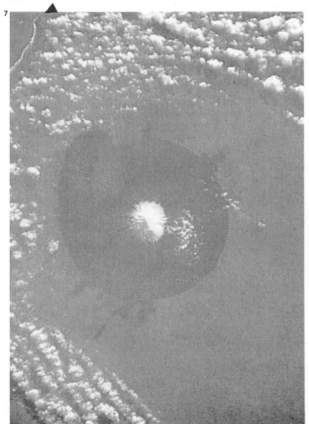

8

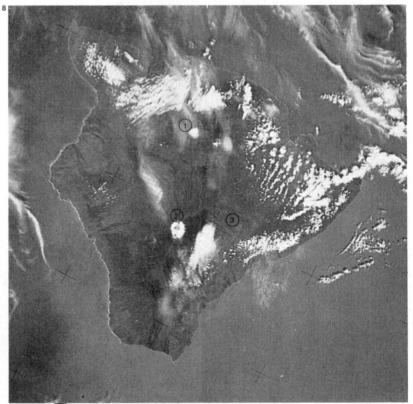

HAWAIIAN ISLANDS

8 Hawaii is the largest island in the Hawaiian archipelago. It was formed by the coalescence of two large volcanoes – Mauna Kea [1], 4,200m (13,796ft), and Mauna Loa [2], 4,160m (13,680ft). With its foot resting on the sea-floor 5,500m (18,000ft) below sea-level, Mauna Kea is the biggest mountain in the world, with a greater base-to-summit difference than even Mt Everest. It is a dormant, perhaps extinct, volcano, but Mauna Loa is one of the most active volcanoes in the world. Its most active vent, Kilauea [3], is on its southeast flank. The outer rim of the Kilauea caldera (collapse crater) is 13km (8 miles) in circumference. The caldera floor has an inner crater called Halemaumau.

North America

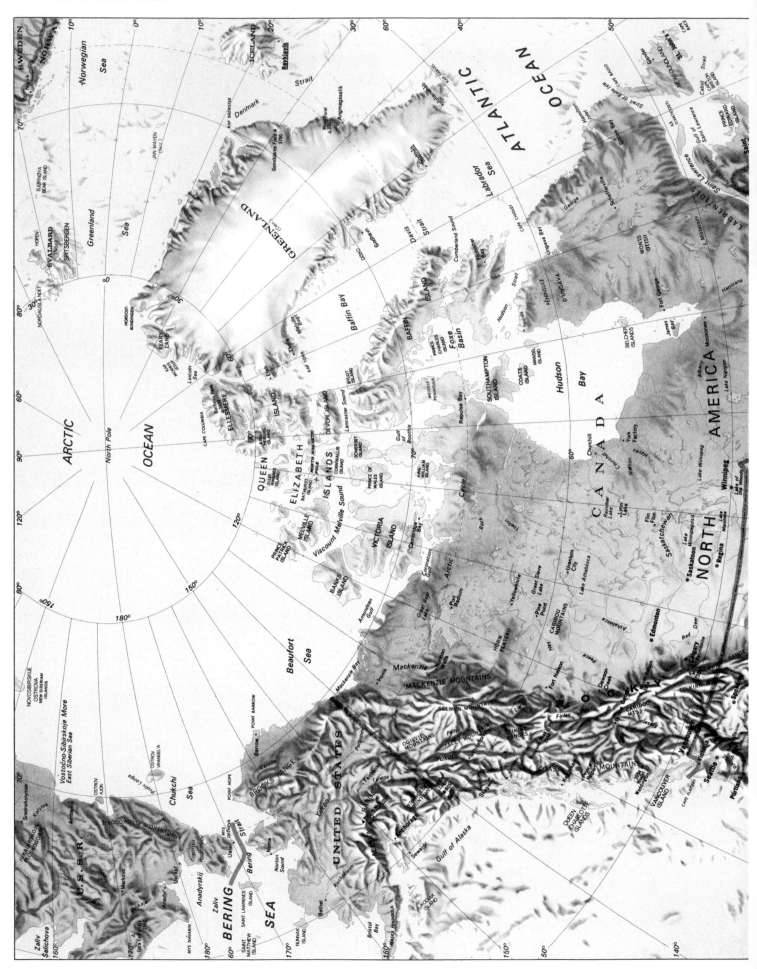

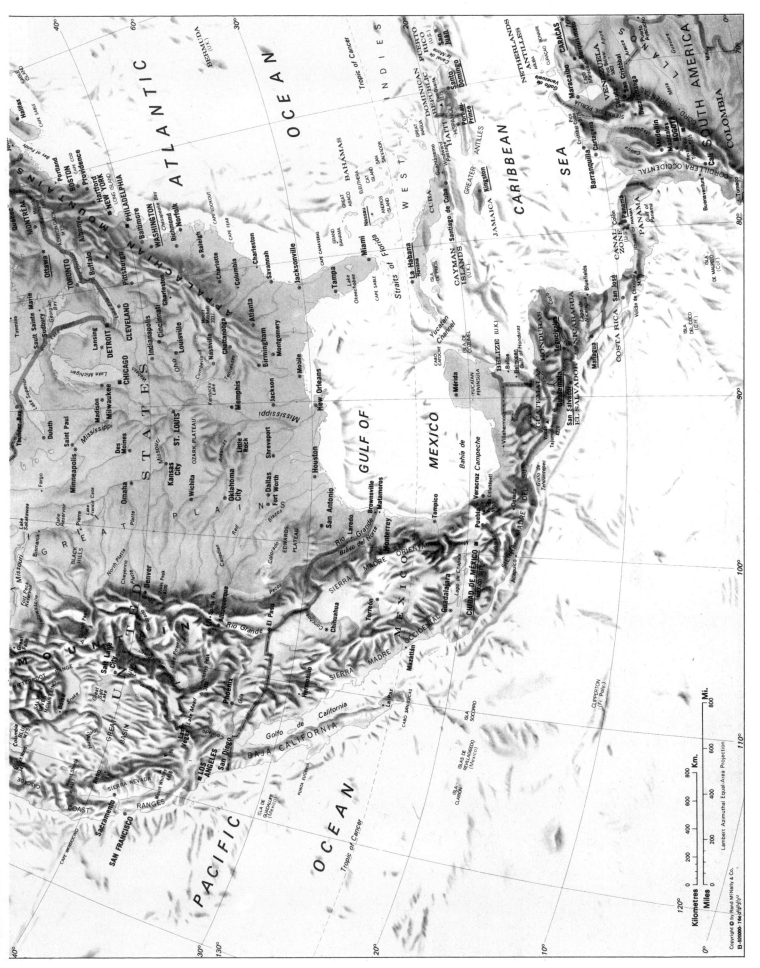

PACIFIC

OCEAN

ATLANTIC

OCEAN

GULF OF

MEXICO

CARIBBEAN

SEA

WEST   INDIES

UNITED   STATES

MEXICO

SOUTH AMERICA

COLOMBIA

VENEZUELA

CARACAS

BOGOTÁ

PANAMA

COSTA RICA

NICARAGUA

HONDURAS

GUATEMALA

EL SALVADOR

BELIZE (U.K.)

CUBA

JAMAICA

HAITI

DOMINICAN
REPUBLIC

PUERTO
RICO
(U.S.)

BAHAMAS

NETHERLANDS
ANTILLES

CAYMAN
ISLANDS
(U.K.)

GREATER   ANTILLES

Tropic of Cancer

Tropic of Cancer

SIERRA   MADRE   ORIENTAL

SIERRA   MADRE   OCCIDENTAL

SIERRA MADRE DEL SUR

BAJA   CALIFORNIA

Golfo de
California

ROCKY   MOUNTAINS

APPALACHIAN   MTS.

GREAT   PLAINS

GREAT
BASIN

SIERRA NEVADA

COAST   RANGES

BITTERROOT
MOUNTAINS

BLACK
HILLS

OZARK PLATEAU

EDWARDS
PLATEAU

BLUE   MTS.

YUCATAN
PENINSULA

Bahía de
Campeche

Straits of Florida

Yucatán
Channel

Windward Passage

Gulf of
Honduras

Gulf of
Panama

CANAL
ZONE

Golfo de
Venezuela

Mississippi

Missouri

Río Grande
(Bravo del Norte)

Río Grande

Colorado

Colorado

Lake Mead

Lake Powell

Great Salt Lake

Lake Michigan

Lake Superior

Lake Huron

San Francisco

Sacramento

LOS
ANGELES

San Diego

La Paz

Salt Lake
City

Las Vegas

Phoenix

Santa Fe

Albuquerque

Denver

Great
Falls

Boise

Hermosillo

Mazatlán

Chihuahua

El Paso

Torreón

Guadalajara

CIUDAD DE MÉXICO
MEXICO CITY

Puebla

Acapulco

Oaxaca

Veracruz

Villahermosa

Mérida

Tampico

Monterrey

Laredo

Brownsville
Matamoros

San Antonio

Houston

Dallas
Fort Worth

Oklahoma
City

Wichita

Kansas
City

ST. LOUIS

Little
Rock

Memphis

Shreveport

New Orleans

Jackson

Montgomery

Mobile

Birmingham

Nashville

Chattanooga

Atlanta

Columbia

Savannah

Charleston

Jacksonville

Tampa

Miami

Nassau

La Habana
Havana

Santiago de Cuba

Kingston

Port-au-
Prince

Santo
Domingo

San
Juan

Tegucigalpa

Managua

San Salvador

San José

Colón
Panamá

Bluefields

Maracaibo

Barranquilla

Cartagena

Medellín

Manizales

Cali

Buenaventura

Tumaco

Bucaramanga

San Cristóbal

Ciudad Bolívar

Raleigh

Charlotte

Richmond

Norfolk

WASHINGTON

Baltimore

PHILADELPHIA

NEW YORK

Hartford

Providence

BOSTON

Portland

Albany

Buffalo

Pittsburgh

Cleveland

DETROIT

CHICAGO

Milwaukee

Madison

Indianapolis

Cincinnati

Louisville

TORONTO

Ottawa

MONTRÉAL

Québec

Sudbury

Sault Sainte Marie

Thunder Bay

Duluth

Minneapolis
Saint Paul

Des
Moines

Omaha

Lincoln

Fargo

Bismarck

Pierre

Cheyenne

Lansing

Halifax

BERMUDA
(U.K.)

CUBA

Lambert Azimuthal Equal-Area Projection

Copyright © by Rand McNally & Co.

B-50000-764

Kilometres
0   200   400   600   800   Km.

Miles
0   200   400   600   800   Mi.

41

Earth panorama: North America

North America extends from 15° to 83° latitude north, from the Isthmus of Tehuantepec in Mexico to the Arctic. Nearly all types of climate are found in this great geographical region, from the polar climate in the north, through the Subarctic tundra and conifer forest climates, the temperate climates, the high-altitude climates of the Rockies and the Sierras, the tropical deserts of Arizona, New Mexico and northern Mexico to the tropical climates of Florida, the Gulf Coast and southern Mexico.

The core of the continent consists of a Precambrian basement of granite and gneiss. This is overlaid by a horizontal sedimentary cover in the Middle West Plains and reaches the surface north of the Great Lakes and the St Lawrence to form the Canadian Shield. To the west of this basement, geologically recent foldings have uplifted the Rocky Mountains which run from Alaska to eastern Mexico. To the west of these mountains lie even more recent ranges. They are still the site of faulting, folding and volcanic eruptions. To the east of the basement is an ancient and highly eroded range, the Appalachians.

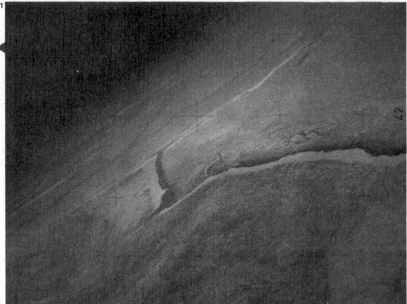

1 Hudson Bay is a large inland sea of 1,230,250km² (475,000 sq miles) which is open to navigation for only three months a year because of ice The area shown here is the Ontario and Manitoba shoreline. Hudson Bay is a shallow sea underlaid by the North American continental shield. Like the Baltic, this sea has filled a depression made by the weight of the Ice Age ice sheet and the sea-bed is now slowly rising.

2 The Great Lakes, the largest body of fresh water in the world, occupy depressions carved by the Quaternary ice sheet. The St Lawrence Waterway allows large ships to reach Duluth on Lake Superior.

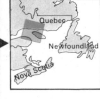

3 The Gulf of St Lawrence is icebound in winter. The elongated island is Anticosti. To the north is the mainland of Quebec and the rounded coastline to the south is the Gaspé peninsula.

4 This Skylab view of Chesapeake Bay shows the cities of Washington [below] and Baltimore [above]. The Potomac River flowing between Washington and Alexandria (on the south bank) can be seen, at the bottom. The beltways around Washington and Baltimore and the interstate 95 freeway joining the two cities are conspicuous, as is the bridge of US Route 50 across Chesapeake Bay. The US Naval Academy at Annapolis is to the south of the Washington side of the bridge. The tunnel across Baltimore's harbour can be guessed from its aerial accessways. The patterns of murkiness in the bay help in the study of sedimentation and circulation.

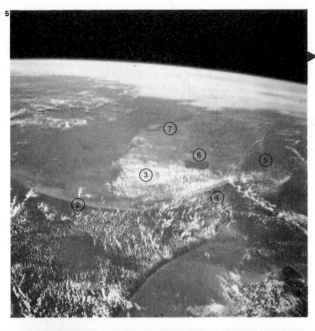

5 The Straits of Florida, through which the Gulf Stream flows, appear as a dark blue zone between the Bahama bank (bottom right) and the Florida peninsula. The Bahamas, of which only Andros [1] can be seen here, and the Florida Keys [2] are built of coral and algal reefs. The Everglades [3], Miami [4], Cape Canaveral and the John F. Kennedy Space Center [5], Lake Okeechobee [6] and Tampa Bay [7] can also be seen.

6 This swampy coast of Louisiana consists of Atchafalaya Bay [1], Atchafalaya River [2], which is a secondary effluent of the Mississippi, small muddy islands off the delta such as Isles Der- nieres and Marsh Island [3] in front of Vermilion Bay [4]. White Lake [5] is another conspicuous feature. The two smoke plumes are oil well fires. These extend 320km (200 miles) over the Gulf.

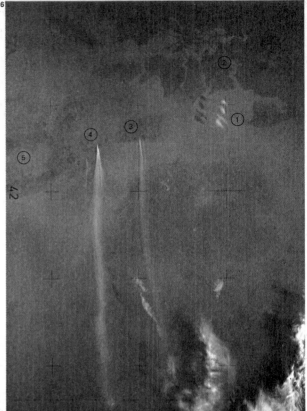

7 Baja California peninsula was part of the Mexican mainland before it drifted 480km (300 miles) in a northwesterly direction, opening up the Gulf of California. This sliding motion is also shearing California along the San Andreas Fault which starts near the mouth of the Colorado River [1]. The large amount of sediment carried by this river is shown by the discoloration of the water. The islands of Angel de la Guarda [2] and Tiburón [3] are clearly seen and so is that of Cedros [4] off Sebastian Vizcaníno Bay. At the head of this bay are two lagoons, the largest of which is Scammon's Lagoon [5] to which the California grey whale migrates each year to mate and calve.

8 The San Andreas Fault is a huge break in the earth's crust running 435km (270 miles) from the top of the Gulf of California to a point north of San Francisco. Its movement caused the 1906 San Francisco earthquake. It can be seen in this Skylab picture [X Y] running parallel and to the east of the cultivated Salinas River valley. To the west Monterey Bay can be clearly seen. The large mottled expanse to the east is the Central Valley.

South America

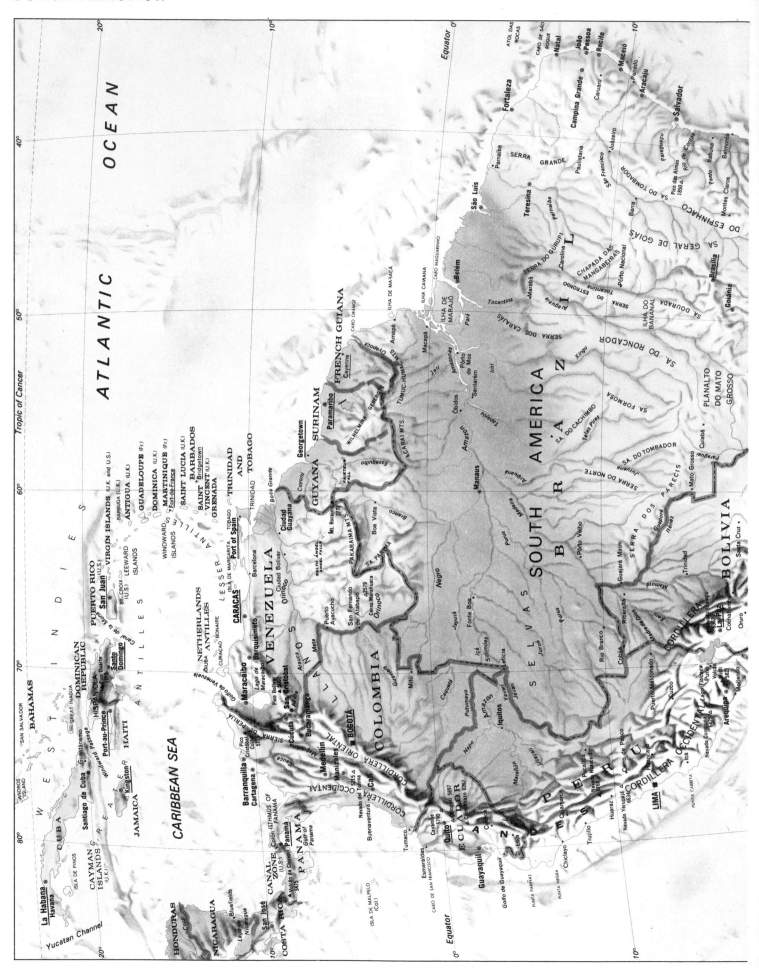

SOUTH SANDWICH ISLANDS (Falk. Is.)

ZAVODOVSKI I.
VISOKOI I.

S c o t i a   S e a

CAPE NORTH
SOUTH GEORGIA (Falk. Is.)
CAPE DISAPPOINTMENT

A T L A N T I C

O C E A N

Tropic of Capricorn

S. DOS AMORES
Bela Horizonte
Pico da Bandeira 2787
Vitória
Doce
Campos
CABO DE SÃO TOMÉ
RIO DE JANEIRO
CABO FRIO
Paraíba do Sul
MANTIQUEIRA
Pico das Agulhas Negras 2787
SÃO PAULO
Santos
S. DA CANASTRA
Paranaíba
Curitiba
SERRA
DO
Florianópolis
Porto Alegre
Rio Grande
SERRA
Lagoa dos Patos
ALTOS DO IGUAÇU (IGUAÇU FALLS)
Paraná
Santa Maria
Pelotas
Lagoa Mirim
Rocha
URUGUAY
Rivera
Montevideo
Rio de la Plata
CABO SAN ANTONIO
Mar del Plata

SERRA DE MARACAJU
PARANÁ
Paraná
SERRA
Villarrica
Posadas
Uruguay
Salto
Paysandú

Corumbá
Paraguay
Concepción
PARAGUAY
Asunción
Corrientes
Santa Fe
Rosario
BUENOS AIRES
La Plata
PAMPAS

ORIENTAL
CHACO
GRAN
Pilcomayo
Bermejo
Salado
San Miguel de Tucumán
Santiago del Estero
Córdoba
Cerro Champaquí 2884
Cerro Tres Picos 1243
Bahía Blanca
Bahía Blanca

Lago de Poopó
Potosí
Salar de Uyuní
Sucre
Nevado Sajama 6520
Salar de Atacama
Antofagasta San Pedro
Volcán Llullaillaco 6723
Cerro Galán 6600
Cerro del Toro 6380
SIERRA FAMATINA
Salado
San Juan
Mendoza
Cerro Aconcagua 6960
Paso de Bermejo 3795

Arica
Iquique
DESIERTO DE ATACAMA
CABO SAN PEDRO
PUNTA MORRO
Coquimbo
CABO BASCUÑÁN
Valparaíso
SANTIAGO
Concepción
PUNTA LAVAPIÉ
CABO CARRANZA

A N D E S

Colorado
Negro
Neuquén
Montsalvat
Viedma
GOLFO SAN MATÍAS
PENÍNSULA VALDÉS
PUNTA DELGADA
40
Rawson
Chubut
PAMPA DEL CASTILLO
Comodoro Rivadavia
GOLFO SAN JORGE
CABO DOS BAHÍAS
CABO TRES PUNTAS
PUNTA MEDANOSA
PUNTA DESENGAÑO
Río Gallegos
Punta Arenas
MESETA DE LAS VIZCACHAS
Monte San Valentín 4058
PENÍNSULA DE TAITAO
GOLFO DE PENAS
ISLA CAMPANA
ISLA WELLINGTON
ISLA MADRE DE DIOS
ARCHIPIÉLAGO REINA ADELAIDA
ISLA DESOLACIÓN
PENÍNSULA
ISLA SANTA INÉS
ISLA HOSTE
ISLA NAVARINO
CABO DE HORNOS
CABO HORN
Estrecho de le Maire
ISLA DE LOS ESTADOS
ISLA GRANDE DE TIERRA DEL FUEGO
Ushuaia
Monte Sarmiento 2300
Estrecho de Magallanes
Strait of Magellan
Bahía Grande

PATAGONIA
ARGENTINA

FALKLAND ISLANDS (U.K.)
Stanley
EAST FALKLAND
WEST FALKLAND

Puerto Montt
ISLA DE CHILOÉ
Valdivia
Osorno
Volcán Corcovado 2300
ARCHIPIÉLAGO DE LOS CHONOS
ISLA MAGDALENA

ISLAS JUAN FERNÁNDEZ (Chile)
ISLA SAN AMBROSIO (Chile)
ISLA SAN FÉLIX (Chile)
ISLA ROBINSON CRUSOE
ISLA ALEJANDRO SELKIRK

P A C I F I C

O C E A N

Tropic of Capricorn

Drake Passage

Kilomètres
Km.
Miles
Mi.
Lambert Azimuthal Equal-Area Projection

Copyright © by Rand McNally & Co.
A-540000-764   2⁰-2⁰-2⁰-2⁰,5ᴸᴵ

45

Earth panorama: South America

The structure of South America is in many ways comparable to that of North America. High recent mountains – the Andes – follow the Pacific coast and old and worn highlands are found to the east: the Guiana Highlands and the Brazilian plateau. The Andes and the eastern highlands define vast alluvial basins that are drained by large rivers such as the Orinoco, Amazon, Tocantins, São Francisco Uruguay and Paraná. More than 90 per cent of the continent's drainage is towards the Atlantic Ocean; in terms of water flow the imbalance is even higher because the Andean coast receives very little rain between 5° and 35° of latitude south.

The Andes are a young and still extremely active chain of mountains. Their geological crumpling is the result of the Andes area being squeezed between the American and the East Pacific (Antarctic) plates, which are moving towards one another.

The climate is equatorial in the north and in the Amazon basin. It is tropical south of the Amazon basin and temperate south of southern Brazil. The Andean mountains south of Ecuador have a dry, cold climate.

1 Hurricanes are prominent weather features when seen from space, as in this Apollo photograph. The Caribbean island arc experiences about a dozen hurricanes a year (the word is derived from the name of the native Mayan god of the big wind, Hunraken). Hurricanes are tropical depressions with extremely steep pressure gradients. They often originate in the Atlantic and travel westwards towards the American coast.

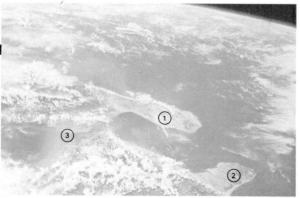

2 The Gulf of Venezuela lies between the peninsulas of Guajira [1] and Paraguaná [2]. The town of Maracaibo is on the channel leading from the gulf to Lake Maracaibo [3].

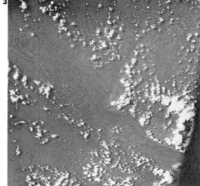

3 The Orinoco is the largest river in Venezuela. It meanders its way to the coast. Not far from its spring it links up with the Río Negro by a natural canal, the Casiquiare.

4 The large body of reddish water seen here is the Río de la Plata, between Uruguay and Argentina, which flows into the South Atlantic. The red plume is probably sediment moving seawards. Montevideo is the lighter area surrounding the deep bay where the coastline changes direction. To the west, the River Santa Lucía enters the Río de la Plata and it is the major drainage for the area. The small island at its mouth is Isla del Tigre. The white beaches and sand dunes are visible along the coast. Major thoroughfares and residential areas are seen. Green and grey rectangular patterns are fields and show local types of agriculture.

5 Taken high over the Andes, looking south, this photograph reveals their basic shape and structure. The Pacific Ocean [1] bathes the feet of the Cordillera Occidental [2], some summits of which are snow-covered. This chain is made up of Mesozoic sediments and has numerous volcanoes, some of them active, located along fault lines that run parallel to the axis. East of the Cordillera Occidental is a central zone. To the north are some high folded mountains, the Cordillera Central [3]. To the south they dip under a debris-filled highland plain, the Altiplano [4], which is a graben (depression bounded by faults). Lake Titicaca [5] drains into the salt lake Poopó (not shown), which in turn drains into the salt pans of Coipasa and Uyuni [6]. The divide between the waters draining into the Altiplano and into the Amazon basin is distinct.

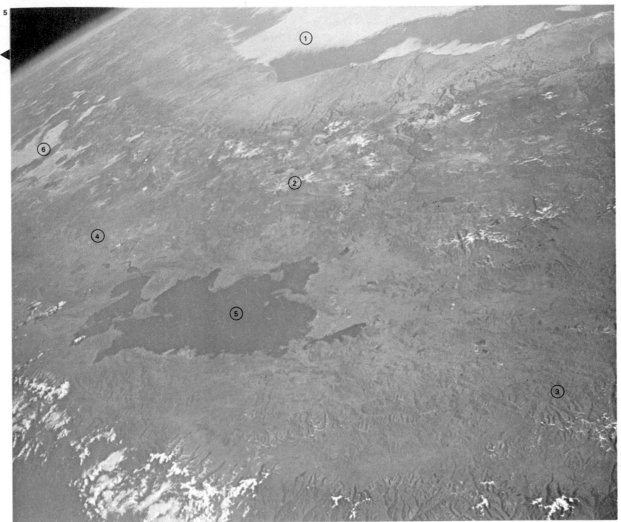

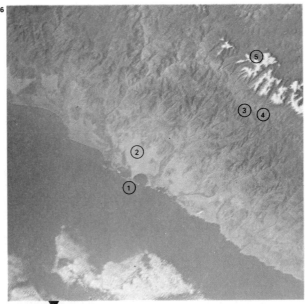

6 The direction of the sand bars [1] of this stretch of the Peruvian coast shows the northward Humboldt current's drift. The current's coldness prevents rainfall over the coast and the light areas [2] are deserts. Parallel to the coast run the Cordillera Negra [3] of volcanic origin and the snow-covered Cordillera Blanca [5]. The town of Yungay [4], in the Rio Santa valley was wiped out in 1970 by a landslide triggered by an earthquake; about 25,000 people were killed.

7 An interesting pattern of valleys is displayed in this area of the Andes between Chile and Argentina. They were carved by glaciers leaving the valley floors covered in moraine debris.

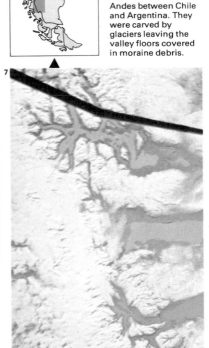

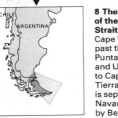

8 The eastern half of the Magellan Strait extends from Cape Virgenes [1] past the town of Punta Arenas [2] and Useless Bay [3] to Cape Froward [4]. Tierra del Fuego [5] is separated from Navarino Island [6] by Beagle Channel.

The atmosphere

The origin of the atmosphere was no doubt closely associated with the origin of the earth. When the earth was still a molten ball, it was probably surrounded by a large atmosphere of cosmic gases, including hydrogen, that were gradually lost into space. As the earth began to 'develop a solid crust over a molten core, gases such as carbon dioxide, nitrogen and water vapour were slowly released to form an atmosphere with a composition not unlike the present emanations from volcanoes. Further cooling probably led to massive precipitation of water vapour so that today it occupies less than four per cent by volume of the atmosphere. At a much later stage, the oxygen content of the atmosphere was caused by green plants releasing oxygen as a result of combining water and carbon dioxide to form carbohydrates [Key].

Heated from below

Up to a height of about 50km (31 miles) the composition of the atmosphere [1] is remarkably homogeneous, comprising a mixture of gases each with their own physical properties. Carbon dioxide, water vapour and ozone, although only small constituents of the atmosphere, play vital roles in absorption of solar and terrestrial radiation, thus allowing life on earth. Due to the action of gravity, this homogeneous mixture of gases is compressed [2] giving the highest values of density and pressure near the earth's surface; average surface density is 1.2kg/m³ and average surface pressure is 1,013 millibars (mb) (roughly 1kg/cm² or 14lb per square inch). At a height of 16km (9 miles), pressure falls to 100mb and the density is less than 11 per cent of the density at sea-level.

The constituent gases of the atmosphere largely allow the sun's radiation to pass without interception. Fortunately the small amount of ozone, concentrated most strongly at 24km (15 miles) height, but in significant amounts up to 50km (31 miles), filters out most of the ultra-violet rays harmful to life on earth. If all the ozone were brought down to sea-level, it would form a layer only 0.25cm (0.1in) thick. After scattering, reflection and some absorption in the lower, denser layers of the atmosphere, only about 46 per cent of the solar radiation reaching the upper atmos-

phere is absorbed by the solid earth's surface as heat. This input of energy raises the earth's surface to a mean temperature of 14°C (57°F). Because this is lower than the 5,700°C (10,290°F) of the sun's surface, the earth radiates energy of much longer wavelengths (infra-red or heat rays) than solar radiation and these longer waves are absorbed by the carbon dioxide, water vapour and clouds in the lower atmosphere.

This means that the atmosphere is directly heated from below, not from above as one would perhaps expect. Just as the earth radiates heat, so does the atmosphere – upwards to be lost to space and downwards to be reabsorbed by the earth. The net effect of these exchanges [3] is that together they lose as much heat to space as they gain from solar radiation, thus maintaining a balance.

Temperature distribution

In the bottom 80 per cent (in mass) of the atmosphere, temperature falls with height in accord with the heating from below [4]. This layer of the atmosphere, 8km (5 miles) deep in polar regions and 16–19km (about 11

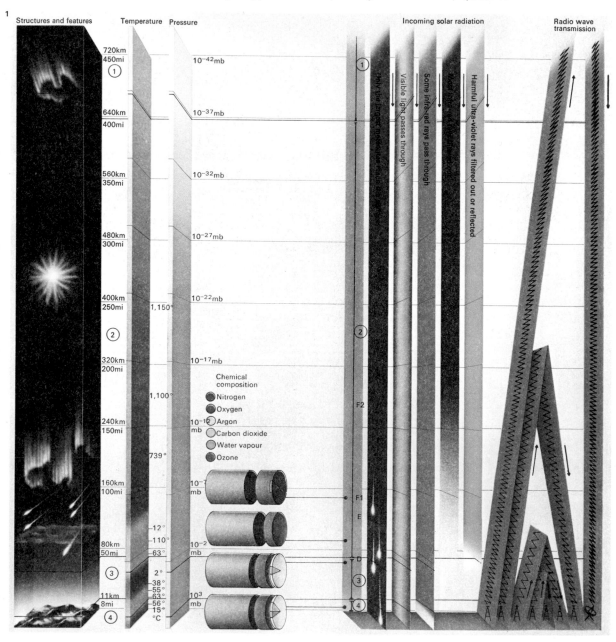

1 The atmosphere shows a surprising variety of characteristics on a vertical scale. Gravity means that air density and associated pressure increase near the surface. Pressure of about 1,000 millibars (mb) at sea-level falls to virtually nothing (10⁻⁴²mb) at a height of 720km (447 miles). Temperature also varies with height, falling and rising in several layers, ultimately increasing towards outer space. Even the mixture of gases shows variations, with water vapour being added at low levels. Four broad atmospheric layers can be identified. The exosphere [1] is a rarefied region above 400km (250 miles) with differing proportions of oxygen, helium and hydrogen. The highest aurorae are found in this region. The ionosphere [2], where charged particles (ions and electrons) occur is a deep layer comprising the mesosphere and thermosphere, subdivided into four minor layers (F2, F1, E and D). Their ion density has a marked effect on radio waves – very high frequency waves penetrate but short-wave transmissions are reflected. The stratosphere [3] contains small but vital amounts of ozone filtering out harmful solar radiation. The troposphere [4] contains the bulk of the atmosphere and all its weather. Together with the outer layers it acts as a particle and radiation shield. Temperatures decrease to its upper boundary.

miles) deep over the equatorial regions, is known as the troposphere. It is characterized by wind speeds increasing with height, lots of moisture at low levels and appreciable vertical air movement, and it is generally the source of all the "weather" we experience. The tropopause marks the boundary between the troposphere and the stratosphere.

The temperature is virtually constant throughout the lower stratosphere but this layer has strong air circulation patterns and high wind speeds in the jet streams which are used (when they blow in the right direction) by airliners. In the upper stratosphere, above about 25km (15 miles), temperature gradually increases with height to a broad maximum at the stratopause. Above the stratopause, in the mesosphere, the temperature begins to decline sharply with increasing height, to a minimum at about 85km (52 miles). Above this level, which is called the mesopause, is the thermosphere where temperature is believed to increase to the thermopause at 400km (250 miles). Beyond, in the exosphere, the pressure drops to virtually a vacuum – equivalent to that of the sun's

outer atmosphere in which the earth orbits.

Within the troposphere another type of heat balance operates. More radiant heat is received than lost in tropical latitudes and the converse is true in polar latitudes. This broad temperature gradient from equator to pole generates a pressure gradient in the same direction; warm air moves down the gradient, reducing temperature extremes by cooling the tropics and warming the polar areas [3C].

Humidity of the atmosphere
The water content of the atmosphere is primarily in vapour form. Humidity decreases with height [5] because water enters the atmosphere by evaporation from the earth's surface. The driest parts of the lower atmosphere are over the subtropical deserts, the wettest are over the equatorial and summer monsoon regions, especially ocean surfaces. Water is constantly being cycled between the earth and the atmosphere. The amount in the atmosphere at any one time is only a fraction of one per cent of the total water in the planet, but it provides enough rainfall to sustain life on earth.

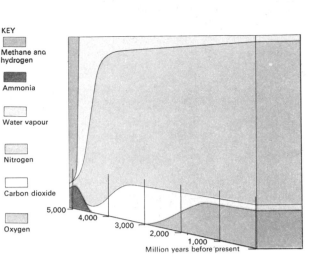

KEY

Methane and hydrogen

Ammonia

Water vapour

Nitrogen

Carbon dioxide

Oxygen

Million years before present

Important changes have occurred in the earth's atmosphere since it formed 4,600 million years ago as hydrogen, methane and ammonia. Most of the primitive hydrogen was lost to outer space and large quantities of steam and other gases were produced. This led to an atmosphere consisting mainly of nitrogen, water, sulphur dioxide and carbon dioxide. Photosynthesizing algae appeared 3,500 million years ago to produce free oxygen, and resulting ozone made up an ultra-violet shield, permitting life to spread on land.

2 Air is easily compressed, so the atmosphere becomes "squashed" by the effect of gravity. This results in the bulk (80%) of the atmosphere being in the troposphere, occupying a volume of about 6×10^9 cu km. As air density decreases with altitude, the very much smaller amounts of air present in the stratosphere (19%) and the ionosphere and above (1%) occupy a greater and greater volume.

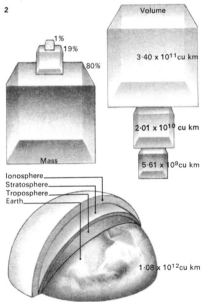

2

Volume

$3 \cdot 40 \times 10^{11}$ cu km

$2 \cdot 01 \times 10^{10}$ cu km

$5 \cdot 61 \times 10^9$ cu km

Mass

Ionosphere
Stratosphere
Troposphere
Earth

$1 \cdot 08 \times 10^{12}$ cu km

3 Temperatures in the atmosphere and on earth result mainly from a balance of radiation inputs and outputs. Average annual solar radiation reaching the earth, measured in kilolangleys (one calorie absorbed per sq cm) is highest in hot desert areas [A]. Comparison with the average annual long-wave radiation back from the earth's surface [B] shows an overall surplus radiation for nearly all latitudes but this is absorbed in the atmosphere and then lost in space, ensuring an overall balance. The extreme imbalance of incoming radiation between equatorial and polar latitudes is somewhat equalized through heat transfers by atmosphere and oceans [C]. This balancing transfer between surplus and deficit radiation is greatest in middle latitudes where most cyclones and anticyclones occur, shown at a latitude of 40° on the chart.

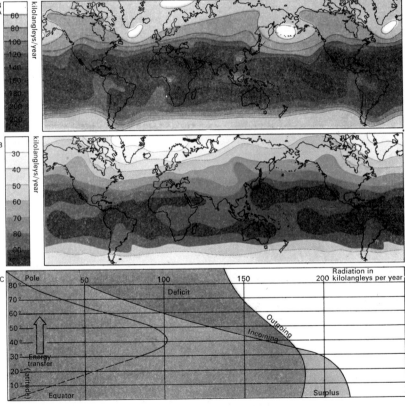

3
A

kilolangleys/year

60
80
100
120
140
160
180
200
220

B

kilolangleys/year

30
40
50
60
70
80
90

C   Pole   50   100   150   Radiation in 200 kilolangleys per year

Deficit

Outgoing

Incoming

Energy transfer (latitude)

Equator

Surplus

4 Atmospheric temperatures tend to decrease evenly with increase in height and latitude up to a level called the tropopause at a height of about 9km (5.5 miles) at the poles rising to 18km (11 miles) in tropics.

5 Humidity falls with height in the troposphere. Warm air can hold more water vapour than cold air and therefore the warmer mid-latitude atmosphere holds more water vapour than the colder air over the Antarctic region.

4

July

Summer hemisphere

Winter hemisphere

100mb

15km

-60

-60

12

-40

200

9

-20

6

0

500

3

20   0

90°N   60°   30°   0   30°   60°   90°S
1,000

5

km   mb
35

30   c15

25

20

15   100

10   Mid-latitudes

5   Antarctic   500

·0001   ·001   ·01   ·1   1   10
Water vapour mixing ratio (gm/kg) percentage

49

Winds and weather systems

Wind is the movement of air, and large-scale air movements, both horizontal and vertical, are important in shaping weather and climate. The chief forces affecting horizontal air movements are pressure gradients, the Coriolis effect and friction.

Pressure gradients are caused by the unequal heating of the atmosphere by the sun [1]. Warm equatorial air is lighter and, therefore, has a lower pressure than cold, dense, polar air. The strength of air movement from high- to low-pressure areas – known as the pressure gradient – is proportional to the difference in pressure.

The Coriolis effect, caused by the earth's rotation, deflects winds to the right in the Northern Hemisphere [3] and to the left in the Southern. As a result, winds do not flow directly from the point of highest pressure to the lowest. Instead, winds approaching a low-pressure system are deflected round it rather than flowing directly into it. This creates air systems, with high or low-pressure, in which winds circulate round the centre. Horizontal air movements are important around cyclonic (low-pressure) and anticyclonic

(high-pressure) systems. Horizontal and vertical movements combine to create a pattern of prevailing winds.

Along the Equator is a region called the doldrums, where the sun's heat warms the rising air. This air eventually spreads out and flows north and south away from the Equator. It finally sinks at about 30°N and 30°S, creating subtropical high-pressure belts, from which trade winds flow back towards the Equator and westerlies towards the mid-latitudes of the earth.

Cyclones and anticyclones

Along the polar front in the Northern Hemisphere, the warm air of the westerlies meets the polar easterlies. Waves, or bulges, develop along the polar front, some of which grow quickly in size [4]. Warm air flows into the bulge and cold air flows in behind it.

The warm, light air rises above the cold air along the warm front. Behind, the cold air forces its way under the warm air along the cold front. Gradually, the cold front catches up the warm front and the warm air is pushed above the cold in an occlusion. In cyclones in

the Northern Hemisphere, the air circulates in an anticlockwise direction (clockwise in the Southern). Along the warm front, a broad belt of cloud forms, bringing rain and sometimes thunderstorms. The cold front usually has a much narrower belt of clouds. Clouds and rain normally persist for some time along occluded fronts.

The circulation of air in anticyclones is the reverse of cyclones, being clockwise in the Northern Hemisphere and anticlockwise in the Southern. Many anticyclones are formed in warm, subtropical regions by sinking air. In winter anticyclones form over continental interiors in temperate latitudes as a result of the cooling of air.

How monsoons occur

Monsoons [2] are seasonal reversals of wind direction. The most celebrated monsoon occurs in India, where the generally northerly winds of winter are replaced by generally southerly winds in summer. The summer winds contain a lot of water vapour, which falls in heavy rain storms.

Another reversal of winds on a local scale

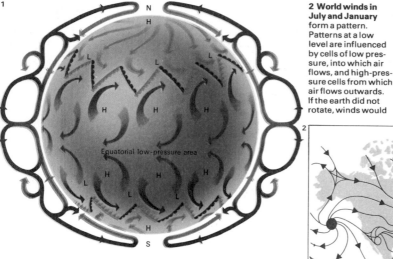

Warm air
Cool air
Cold air

Warm front
Cold front

H = High pressure
L = Low pressure

1 The earth's atmosphere acts as a giant heat engine. The temperature differences between the poles and the Equator provide the thermal energy to drive atmospheric circulation, both horizontal and verti-

cal. In general, warm air at the Equator rises and moves towards the poles at high levels and cold polar air moves towards the Equator at low levels to replace it. The pattern of prevailing winds is

complicated by the rotation of the earth, (which causes the Coriolis effect), by cells of high-pressure and low-pressure systems (depressions) and by the distribution of land and sea.

2 World winds in July and January form a pattern. Patterns at a low level are influenced by cells of low pressure, into which air flows, and high-pressure cells from which air flows outwards. If the earth did not rotate, winds would

blow directly from high-pressure cells to low-pressure cells. But the Coriolis effect causes winds to be deflected to the right in the Northern Hemisphere and to the left in the Southern Hemisphere. Wind patterns are remarkably constant between

summer and winter west of Africa. But, in the east, variations are caused by monsoons (reversals of wind flows). Monsoons arise from the unequal heating of land and sea. For example, dry winds blow outwards in winter across India from

the cold high-pressure system over southern Siberia. In summer, the land heats quickly and a low-pressure system develops over northwestern India. Moist, southeasterly trade winds are drawn into this system, bringing heavy rainfall.

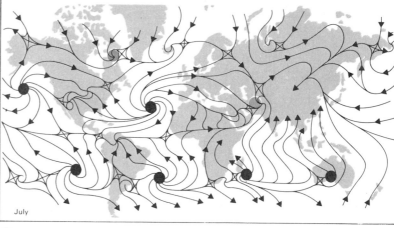

Low-pressure areas
High-pressure areas

3 A weather chart shows a "low" or depression to the south of Iceland and a "high" or anticyclone over southern Portugal and Spain. The isobars join points with equal atmospheric pressure. The values of the isobars are in millibars (1,000 millibars is the equivalent of about 750.1mm [29.53in] of mercury). Because winds are deflected, they circulate in an anticlockwise direction round a "low" and clockwise round a "high" in the Northern Hemisphere.

occurs with land and sea breezes. Sea breezes spring up on warm days along sea and lake shores when a pressure gradient is established between the rapidly heating land and the less rapidly heating water. As a result, winds blow on to land. At night, the land cools faster than the water, so a reverse gradient reverses the wind.

Thunderstorms, hurricanes and tornadoes
The most common storms are thunderstorms [6]. About 45,000 occur every day, in both temperate and tropical regions and prerequisites for their formation are strong, rising air currents. As the air rises, it is cooled and latent heat is released as condensation occurs. The release of heat provides energy that intensifies the upsurgence of air and the development of the storm. The condensation causes cumulo-nimbus clouds to rise sometimes more than 4,570m (15,000ft) from their base to their top. These clouds bring with them rain and hail and, sometimes, thunder and lightning.

Hurricanes [5], also called typhoons or tropical cyclones, form over warm oceans. They have fast spiralling winds which may reach 240–320km/h (150–200mph). The calm centre, or eye, contains warm subsiding air. The eye may be between 6.5 and 48km (4 and 30 miles) across. The hurricane itself may have a diameter of 480km (300 miles). The warmth of the air in the eye contributes to low air pressure at the surface. Warm, moist air spirals upwards around the eye. Condensation creates cumulo-nimbus clouds and releases latent heat which further increases the upward spiral of air. Hurricanes are especially destructive along coastlines where storm waves and torrential rain cause destruction through flooding.

Tornadoes [Key] are violent whirlwinds, but they cover a far smaller area than hurricanes. A tornado forms when a downward growth starts from a cumulo-nimbus cloud. When the funnel-shaped extension of the cloud reaches the ground, it may be between 50–500m (164–1,640ft) wide. It crosses land at speeds of 32–65km/h (20–40mph) and usually dies out after 32km (20 miles), although a few are known to have travelled as far as 480km (300 miles).

Hundreds of tornadoes strike the United States each year, especially in the Midwest. They may last for several hours, travelling up to 480km (300 miles) and causing great damage. At the centre winds may reach 644km/h (400mph).

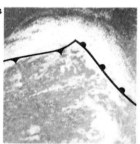
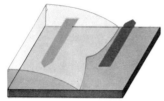
4 Fronts form in temperate latitudes where a cold air mass meets a warm air mass.

The air masses spiral round a bulge causing cold and warm fronts to develop.

The warm air rises above the cold front and the cold air slides underneath the warm.

Eventually, the cold air areas merge, and the warm air is lifted up or occluded.

4 A front is a narrow band of changing weather lying between two air masses of different temperatures and humidity. When the two air masses meet, each pushes against the other to form a cold, warm or occluded front.

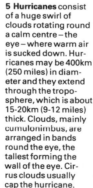

Hurricane winds

Prevailing winds

5 Hurricanes consist of a huge swirl of clouds rotating round a calm centre – the eye – where warm air is sucked down. Hurricanes may be 400km (250 miles) in diameter and they extend through the troposphere, which is about 15-20km (9-12 miles) thick. Clouds, mainly cumulonimbus, are arranged in bands round the eye, the tallest forming the wall of the eye. Cirrus clouds usually cap the hurricane.

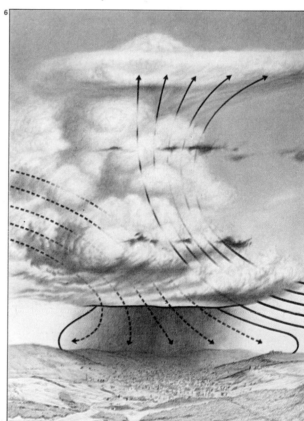

6 A storm cloud or cumulo-nimbus has developed along a cold front. These clouds occur when the air mass is unstable over a great vertical distance. Air moves upwards in a convection current and cooling causes condensation. Flat anvil-shaped cloud heads mark the level where stability is re-established. Cumulo-nimbi are formed along fronts or in overheated areas. In depressions, a line of cumulo-nimbus marks the front and thunderstorms and violent squalls occur.

Weather

"Weather" in anybody's language means rain and sunshine, heat and cold, clouds and wind. Humidity and visibility might be added to the list. In fact, if not in terminology, this layman's catalogue comprises the six elements which, for the meteorologist, make weather: in his language they are air temperature, barometric pressure, wind velocity, humidity, clouds and precipitation.

Cloud formation

Clouds are made up of millions of very small drops of liquid water or ice crystals that are too light to fall out of the atmosphere. The cloud particles form from air that contains water vapour when the temperature falls to a critical level called the dew-point. These liquid droplets may then freeze into an ice crystal. But before either water or ice particles can form, two things must happen. First, the moist air must rise, reducing its pressure and giving up its heat to the surrounding atmosphere. Second, dust particles must already be present on which the cooled vapour can condense to form droplets or ice crystals. These tiny particles are respectively

called condensation nuclei and ice nuclei.

The formation of a cloud does not necessarily mean that it will precipitate. Condensation cannot create droplets or crystals that would survive the fall to the ground. They would evaporate even if they were large enough to overcome the force of the rising air. Two other mechanisms, the Bergeron or ice-crystal process, and the coalescence process, account for precipitation-sized particles. In clouds that contain both ice crystals and droplets of supercooled water (water at a temperature less than 0°C), the droplets evaporate and the vapour condenses on to the ice crystal. Thus the crystals grow at the expense of the droplets until they are large enough to fall out of the cloud. If they melt on the way down (as frequently happens), rainfall is observed at ground level. If the cloud contains no ice crystals, precipitation particles grow by the coalescence of different-sized droplets as they fall through the cloud. The larger a drop becomes, the more efficient it is at collecting smaller ones and the greater its chance of reaching the ground.

The two basic shapes of clouds – in layers

or in heaps – are caused by the two different ways in which air can move upwards. When air rises slowly over large areas at rates of a few centimetres a second, layer or stratified clouds are formed. This frequently occurs in cyclones, particularly in warm sectors and at warm fronts. Rapidly rising air (several metres per second) occurs in convection currents which are usually only a few hundred metres across near the ground. These currents widen with altitude but the resultant heaped or cumuliform clouds are rarely more than a few kilometres across. If the atmosphere is unstable they may grow into very large cumulo-nimbus clouds.

The easiest way to identify a cloud [1] is by its shape and height above ground. This was recognized by Luke Howard, a London chemist, in 1833 when he presented his first cloud classification. This still forms the basis of the World Meteorological Organization's International Classification of ten cloud types, which fall into three families according to their height. The highest clouds – about 8–10km (5–6 miles) – made of ice, are called cirrus, cirro-stratus and cirro-cumulus; the

1 The different cloud types are best illustrated within the context of the familiar mid-latitude frontal depression. Most of the major types occur within such cyclones. Here a schematic, generalized Northern Hemisphere depression is viewed from the south as it moves from west [left] to east [right]. It is in a mature state, prior to the occlusion stage, and both warm [1] and cold [2] fronts are clearly visible. Over the warm front, which may have a slope ranging from 1/100 to 1/350, the air rises massively and slowly over the great depth of the atmosphere. This results in a fairly complete suite of layer-type clouds ranging from cirrus [3] and alto-cumulus [4] to nimbo-stratus [5]. The precipitation area often associated with such cloud types, and especially with nimbo-stratus, usually lies ahead of the surface warm front and roughly parallel to it [6]. Turbulence may cause some clouds to rise and produce heavy convective rainfall, as well as the generally lighter and more widespread classical warm front rainfall. Stratus often occupies the warm sector, but a marked change occurs at the cold front. Here the wind veers (blowing in a more clockwise direction) and cumulus clouds [7] are often found in the cold air behind the front. At the front itself the atmosphere is often quite unstable and cumulus clouds grow into cumulo-nimbus formations [8]. The canopy of cirrus clouds – of all types – may extend over the whole depression and is often juxtaposed with the anvil shape of the nimbus. These cloud changes are accompanied by pressure, wind temperature and humidity changes as the fronts pass the individual observer on the ground.

middle clouds – 3–8km (2–5 miles) – of water and ice, are called alto-cumulus and alto-stratus; and the low clouds – below 3km (2 miles) – usually made of water, are called stratus, strato-cumulus and nimbo-stratus. The two remaining types are cumulus and cumulo-nimbus. There are, however, many variations on these ten types. Rarely is a cloud seen in isolation or conforming exactly to its textbook form; clouds of different types occur together and, as a result many hybrid forms are to be found.

Sun, wind and humidity
Long periods of sunshine are, of course, marked by clear skies, which usually result from sinking air in anticyclones. The longest periods of sunshine occur in the polar summer when the sun never sets, but the highest intensities and temperatures occur in the main deserts of the world which lie roughly at the latitudes 30°N and S. The daily maximum temperature in these areas may be more than 35°C (95°F), falling to below freezing at night.

Wind speed and direction at low levels are affected by friction between the air and the ground and by local topography. Friction means the wind speeds near the ground are generally less than at high levels and it also accounts for the generally higher speeds over water as compared with the rougher land surface. Air flow is often channelled in both valleys and urban areas.

There are several ways of expressing the humidity of the air but relative humidity is the most widely used. This is the percentage of water vapour actually held in a given volume of air relative to the amount that the air could hold if saturated at the same temperature. In middle latitudes the daily values usually lie between 60 and 80 per cent, but they can range from 8 to 100 per cent.

Fog, a modern menace
Visibility has assumed a great importance in our communications-conscious world. Fog [3], which is cloudy air at ground level, presents dangers to aircraft, ships and motor vehicles alike. It can also affect the man in the street; if fog becomes contaminated with pollutants it may become lethal smog.

The structure of a hurricane may be difficult to discern at ground level but from a satellite in orbit the pattern of air movements involved can be clearly seen.

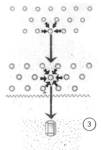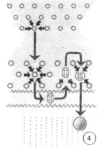

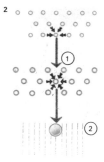

3 Advection fog is caused by warm, damp air blowing over cold land or water. In warmer latitudes, heat rises to warm the air above (upward blue arrows). When the air passes into cooler areas, it loses heat (blue arrows and upward red arrows) and as the temperature of the air reaches dew point, fog gradually forms.

4 Radiation fog occurs when air is cooled to its dew-point by contact with land that has itself been cooled by long-wave radiation loss [long brown arrows]. As the ground cools, surrounding air transfers heat by conduction [short brown arrows]. The cooling of the air is shown by the grey arrows.

2 Repeated coalescence of droplets [1] forms drops [2] too large to float on air currents. Ice crystals collect in hexagonal patterns [3] then agglomerate into snowflakes. Water can freeze round an ice embryo [4] to form hail.

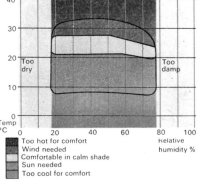

Temp °C

☐ Too hot for comfort
☐ Wind needed
☐ Comfortable in calm shade
☐ Sun needed
☐ Too cool for comfort

Relative humidity %

Too dry Too damp

5 A Campbell-Stokes recorder registers the duration of sunshine. A glass ball focuses the sun's rays on to a specially prepared piece of card on which a trace is burnt as long as the sun shines brightly. The instrument must be orientated to the noonday sun at an angle determined from the declination of the sun. Three sets of grooves in the bowl behind the glass sphere will accommodate the different cards which are used for summer, winter and the equinoxes.

6 Human beings can tolerate only certain ranges of temperature and humidity. Even within these ranges, other elements such as sun and wind are needed to produce comfortable conditions in which people can live and work.

7 The power of the wind to erode and transport is well seen in this photograph of an approaching dust storm in the Midwest of the United States of America. These storms occur only in arid areas where the soil is loose.

Forecasting

Day-to-day weather depends on the movements of huge air masses, which take their characteristics of temperature and humidity from the land or water surface beneath them and shift slowly over the surface of the earth. Some are virtually static, providing steady weather conditions for days or weeks on end in their area of origin. These produce, for example, the constant, predictable weather of tropical deserts and oceans and the heartlands of the great continents. Other air masses are affected by the earth's rotation and, as a result, they move and swirl rapidly, interacting in different ways with neighbouring masses. These provide the changeable weather of temperate latitudes, which is much more difficult to predict accurately.

Factors that influence the weather

To predict the weather over a particular area, the forecaster must first know the pattern of air masses that overlies it at any given time. Then he must try to predict how the pattern will change during the period of forecast – usually the next few hours or days – drawing on his experience of the ways in which similar patterns have changed in the past.

Weather forecasting originated in the observations of farmers and sailors, whose especial interest caused them to watch the weather closely and discover the patterns underlying it. Even in temperate regions this is not as difficult as it may seem at first. For example, much of western Europe's weather depends on a west-to-east procession of cyclones or depressions, and the passage of "fronts" – planes of contact between neighbouring air masses of differing temperature and humidity. Fronts that bring the worst weather lie generally in the southern half of the depressions. An observer who sees the barometer falling and notices a change of wind (often veering to the southwest accompanied by a thickening and lowering of cloud from high cirrus to cirro-stratus, alto-stratus and nimbo-stratus), is keeping track of the movement of a depression and warm front. He can predict fairly accurately the sequence of weather that will arise from it, and even the speed with which the changes will take place. Similarly, a rising or high and steady barometer, with clear skies and light breezes, usually means that an anticyclone has formed. This often brings clear, steady weather for several days until the next depression moves in to replace it.

The forecaster at work

The professional forecaster begins his work by preparing a synoptic chart [3], that is, an accurate map of the weather prevailing at the time over a large area surrounding his position. In this he is helped by observations from many surface stations, which come to him through teleprinter and radio networks.

There are more than 8,000 surface stations providing this service round the world; they include mountain outposts, ships at sea, polar bases and automatic (unmanned) units which record the weather and send information out at regular intervals.

In his synoptic chart the forecaster plots pressure, wind, temperature, cloud types, humidities and pressure tendency, and makes a note of past and present weather. This enables him to draw in isobars (lines connecting points of equal atmospheric pressure) and the position of fronts. Knowing the weather

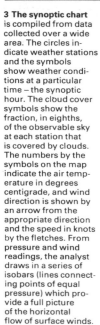

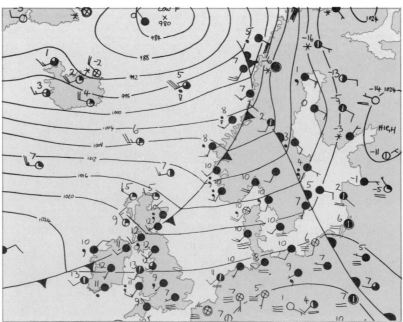

1 Red skies at night, as shepherds have long known, usually indicate good weather for the next day, while red skies at dawn may mean foul weather before the day is out. These observations are not infallible but often make meteorological sense. Red skies in the evening are caused by the scattering of light by dust particles in the atmosphere and are found in anticyclonic conditions of calm, stable weather. Dust tends to settle during the night and so a red sky in the morning is more likely to be due to scattering of light from water droplets in a damp atmosphere at low levels. Moist conditions such as these indicate that a depression is forming.

2 Analysis and forecasting require simultaneous, standard and regular observations at many stations. The international, standardised weather station includes a variety of equipment. The Stevenson screen [1] is a box that shelters thermometers and other instruments from sunlight; it contains wet- and dry-bulb thermometers and recording instruments. Open land [2] allows the state of the ground to be assessed. A grass minimum thermometer [3] records the lowest ground temperature during the past 24 hours. The anemometer and arrow [4] show wind speed and direction. The Campbell-Stokes sunshine recorder or radiometer [5] records hours of sunshine. Radiosonde balloon [6] and theodolite [7] show wind speed and direction, and other data from high altitude. A rain-gauge [8] records the amount of precipitation. The weather office also has a barometer and barograph, to record atmospheric pressure.

3 The synoptic chart is compiled from data collected over a wide area. The circles indicate weather stations and the symbols show weather conditions at a particular time – the synoptic hour. The cloud cover symbols show the fraction, in eighths, of the observable sky at each station that is covered by clouds. The numbers by the symbols on the map indicate the air temperature in degrees centigrade, and wind direction is shown by an arrow from the appropriate direction and the speed in knots by the fletches. From pressure and wind readings, the analyst draws in a series of isobars (lines connecting points of equal pressure) which provide a full picture of the horizontal flow of surface winds.

CLOUD	
○	0
◑	1 or less
◓	2
◕	3
◔	4
◑	5
●	6
◗	7 or more
●	8
⊗	Sky obscured
⊠	Doubtful data

WEATHER	
≡	Mist
≡	Fog
'	Drizzle
' •	Rain and drizzle
•	Rain
*	Rain and snow
✳	Snow
▽	Rain shower
▽	Rain and snow shower
▽	Snow shower
▽	Hail shower
ℝ	Thunderstorm

WIND	
○	Calm
	1-2
	3-7
	8-12
	13-17
▲▲▲▲	Cold front
▲▲▲	Warm front

picture, and the rate at which it is changing, he is then able to predict what the weather will be like at any point on his map in the near future. His work is nowadays made easier by upper-air observations (taken by weather balloons with radiosonde attachment) and photographs from weather satellites [6] that give him an astronaut's eye-view of patterns. Much of the forecaster's work of plotting and analysis has been automated and mathematical analysis plays an increasing role in forecasting as more accurate data from all levels of the atmosphere become available.

Short-term and long-term forecasting
Short-term forecasting is still of great importance to farmers and sailors, and the safety of many millions of airline passengers depends on it each year. There is also an increasing demand for long-term forecasting, covering periods of from five days to six months ahead. Different techniques of analysis are required for this kind of forecasting. In areas of the world where the climate varies little from one year to another, comparatively simple statistical methods are used to relate the

character of one season to the next as a basis for prediction. More variable climates demand more sophisticated methods and detailed research into the nature, origins and movements of air masses. Recently, analysis of relationships between the atmosphere and the ocean have been of great value to long-range forecasters. Britain's predominantly maritime climate depends on air masses that have passed over the ocean, and anomalously cold or warm patches of ocean can have marked effects on weather to come.

The first attempt to co-ordinate meteorological observations on an international basis was not made until 1853, when the major maritime nations formulated a system of weather observations over the oceans to help navigation. In 1878 the International Meteorological Organization (IMO) was set up to keep a constant watch on the weather. International co-operation continued to improve during the years that followed, and in 1951 the IMO was reorganized to become the World Meteorological Organization (WMO), which was recognized by the United Nations.

KEY

Television brings the daily weather forecast into viewers' homes. From internationally collected data, the presenter prepares a simplified synoptic chart. On this he explains the pressure situation, discusses the position and movement of fronts and predicts the kind of weather to be expected during the next few hours.

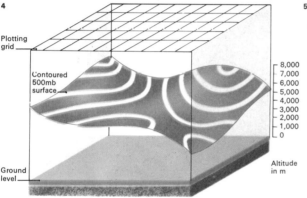

4 Basic mathematical models are designed to forecast the altitude of a pressure surface, usually about 500 or 600 millibars (mb). From them, air flow at that level can be defined and the future position of cyclones and anticyclones plotted. Pressure surfaces are contoured in the same way as ground maps: surface heights are plotted by calculation over a grid. This method is suitable for large-scale forecasting, usually on a 250km (155 mile) grid. A two-level model may be used, on which two pressure surfaces – eg the 500mb and 1,000mb surfaces – are plotted at the intersections of the same grid.

5 Accurate weather forecasting involves the processing of large quantities of data that flow into the weather centres several times each day. The introduction of computers and plotting machines allows forecasters to handle the data more rapidly. Recent developments in plotting machinery display processed data in map form using a line printer or plotting table. Here both types of output are shown; isobars can be interpolated from the pattern of figures [left], or the isobars can be computed and drawn in automatically [right]. These techniques can produce maps like this one in seconds rather than hours.

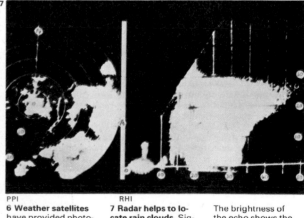

PPI   RHI

6 Weather satellites have provided photographs of clouds since 1960, with steady improvement in photographic quality and coverage. A sequence of photographs showing developing cloud patterns greatly helps the work of the forecaster.

7 Radar helps to locate rain clouds. Signals are reflected by raindrops and ice particles, registering on the Plan Position Indicator (PPI) showing the pattern over an area, or on the Range Height Indicator (RHI) showing the vertical distribution. The brightness of the echo shows the intensity of precipitation. Rangemarkers (radiating from the centre of the PPI and bottom left of the RHI) are in miles while heights (on the right of the RHI) are shown in thousands of feet.

Climates

The climate of an area is its characteristic weather considered over a long period. Climate depends first on latitude, which determines whether an area is hot or cold and how strongly marked are its seasons. It depends also on the moving air masses that prevail in the area; these may be purely local in origin or they may have moved into the area from several hundred kilometres away, bringing cooler or warmer, wetter or drier conditions with them. Climate is also influenced by the relative distribution of land and sea, high ground and low, and the presence nearby of forests, lakes, valleys, glaciers and many other physical factors.

On a world scale, macroclimate is defined primarily in terms of temperature and rainfall and the world can be divided into large climatic zones on this basis. On a smaller scale, humidity, wind strength, aspect in relation to the sun and other local features determine local climate. On an even smaller scale, microclimate refers to the conditions in a particular woodland or under a particular stone.

The range of climates can be broadly grouped under three headings, according to latitude. Tropical climates are hot and dominated by equatorial air masses throughout the year. Temperate climates of the mid-latitude zone are variable, dominated alternately by subtropical and sub-polar air masses, and usually seasonal. Polar climates of high latitudes are uniformly cold, under the continuous control of sub-polar and polar air masses and strongly seasonal.

Characteristics of tropical climates
Because of constant daily sunshine, equatorial and tropical regions are warm throughout the year and the moving air masses that affect them are also warm [6, 7]. The wettest regions lie in a belt of shallow depressions and convection formed where the trade winds meet. This belt shifts north and south seasonally on either side of the Equator, but temperatures vary only slightly and rainfall is fairly steady throughout the year. Monsoon climates of India, South-East Asia and China occur where seasonal winds blow from almost opposite directions; warm, moist winds alternate with warm, dry ones, giving cloudy, wet "summers" and drier "winters".

Dry, tropical climates occur in broad zones on either side of the Equator between latitudes 15° and 30°. These are anticyclonic areas of warm, dry air, where cloudless skies bring strong sunshine and little rain except in rare torrential thunderstorms.

Temperate climates and their features
The middle latitudes of both hemispheres are battlegrounds where warm subtropical and cool sub-polar air masses jostle for position. The day-to-day battle-lines are the warm and cold fronts of the weather charts, which tend to occur along broad frontal zones. On the equatorial side of these zones warm air is present for most of the time. The zones shift north and south with the seasons so that an area such as the south of France may bask reliably in subtropical air throughout the summer but suffer occasional draughts of cold sub-polar air in winter. On western flanks of the continents in the warmer zone the air tends to be dry, bringing hot, dry summers and mild, damper winters – the "Mediterranean" climate of California, southwestern Australia and the eastern

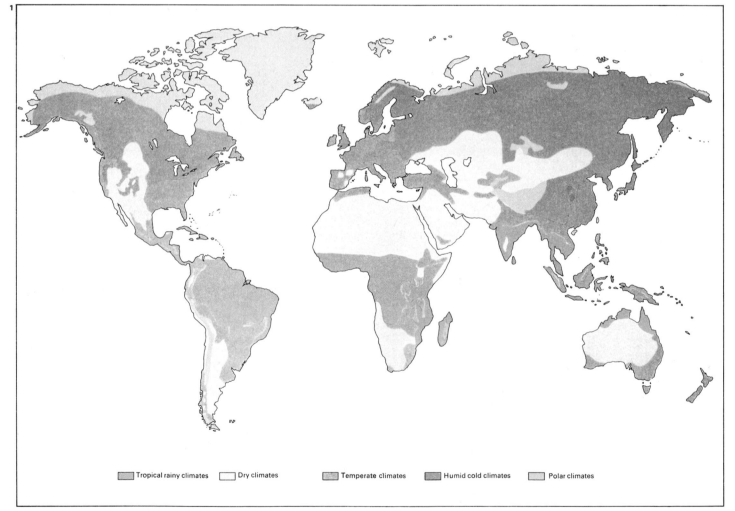

Tropical rainy climates · Dry climates · Temperate climates · Humid cold climates · Polar climates

1 Climate on a global scale presents a bewildering variety and has provided would-be classifiers with a challenge for more than a century. The most generally accepted classifications reflect the close links that exist between vegetation and climate.

A system in wide use today is that of W. Köppen (1846–1940), a German biologist who devoted most of his life to climatic problems and modified his own system many times before he was satisfied with it. The Köppen system of classification

recognizes five major climatic categories, each quite distinct. These are equatorial and tropical rain climates, dry climates, temperate climates of the (mainly) broadleaf forest zone, humid cold climates and polar

climates. Each category is defined in terms of temperature and some in terms of rainfall too. Köppen also devised additional symbols for times of year in which most rain falls and other climatic qualities that affect the growth of vegetation.

The map locates the hot, wet tropical rain forests of South America, Africa and the Far East. Farther away from the Equator the world's great deserts, dominated by the Sahara, straddle subtropical latitudes and the edges of the tropics, as a

result of the stable high pressures there. The deserts are more evident in the Northern than in the Southern Hemisphere, mainly because of the extensive southern oceans. Nearer the poles, a mosaic pattern of mid-latitude cli-

mates occurs. This is less complex over the huge continental areas of Siberia and North America, particularly in tundra and boreal regions. The extreme polar and highland climates (dissimilar but with common features) occupy smaller areas.

Mediterranean itself. Eastern flanks of the continents draw moist, unstable air from over the sea; they tend to be warm all year, with frequent thunderstorms in summer.

In higher latitudes, farther from tropical influences, cool sub-polar air masses prevail. A procession of cyclones or depressions, swinging eastwards round the earth, brings moist maritime air to the western flanks of North America and Europe. Britain and western Canada stand in prevailing southwesterlies, giving mild, cloudy and damp conditions in winter and summer alike. Alternating air masses from the eastern continents bring cold, clear winter and hot, dry summer weather, and air from the north is usually cold and crisp. Central and eastern regions of the continents tend to be drier, with colder winters and hotter summers.

The cold, dry polar climates

Nearer the poles are climatic regions controlled by polar air masses [2]. Despite brief, sunny summers they tend to be cold and dry throughout the year. The broad boreal zone is forested, the tundra zone supports shrubs,

rough grassland and mosses. The true polar climate, which covers the northern fringes of Canada, Europe and Asia and the whole of the Antarctic continent, is generally too cold and dry to support any but the most meagre and hardy vegetation. The coldest regions of the Northern Hemisphere lie in the heartlands of northern Canada and northeastern Siberia, where winter temperatures fall well below −30°C (−22°F). On the high polar plateau of Antarctica summer temperatures are about −30°C (−22°F), while winter temperatures average −70°C (−94°F) or lower.

Geological evidence suggests that the modern situation in which different parts of the globe have certain well-defined climatic patterns is unusual. In past ages climates tended to be fairly even over most of the earth's surface. For example, the Permian period 280 million years ago was characterized by extensive desert areas over most of the continents and Jurassic sediments 195 million years old show evidence of warm, wet conditions in most places. The present pattern may be due, in part, to the fact that the earth is still recovering from the last Ice Age.

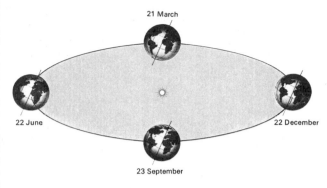

21 March

22 June

23 September

22 December

The seasons are primarily controlled by the rotation of the earth round the sun and the inclination of the earth's axis to the plane of rotation. Inclination of 23.5° means that the sun is directly over the Tropic of Cancer (23.5°N) on 22 June and over the Tropic of Capricorn (23.5°S) on 22 December. At the equinoxes, 21 March and 23 September, the sun is over the Equator. The sun's apparent movement is accompanied by a similar shift in belts of pressure and wind.

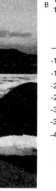

Arctic Bay 11 metres above sea level (asl)

2 Polar climates, as in Arctic Bay [A], are very cold and dry. Only three months of summer are frost-free [B]. There is little precipitation but much surface water due to poor drainage and low evaporation.

3 A continental climate is found in Calgary, Canada. Temperatures there are high in summer and low in winter; annual precipitation is low. This type of climate supports grasslands and cereal crops.

10 Calgary 1079 metres asl

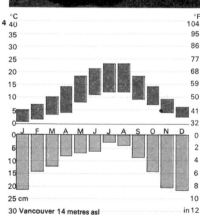

4 The Canadian city of Vancouver has a mid-latitude maritime climate, with warm summers and mild winters. Monthly temperature ranges are greater in summer, precipitation is highest in winter.

5 A Mediterranean climate is typified by Rome [A] and its environs [B], with hot, dry summers and warm, moist winters. Similar latitudes, of western USA, South America and Australia, enjoy similar climates.

30 Vancouver 14 metres asl

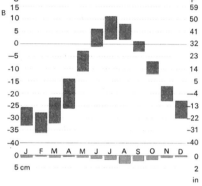

Rome 115 metres asl

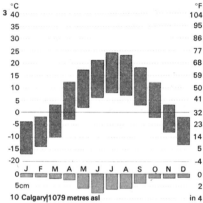

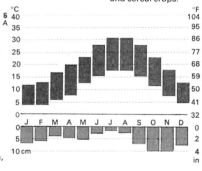

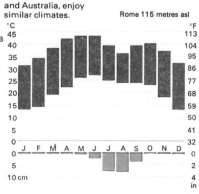

6 Hot deserts, near Timbuktu [A] for example, show little annual variation of temperature but extreme monthly variation [B]. The scarce rainfall occurs as a result of convectional summer storms.

7 An equatorial climate, that of Manaus in central Amazonia for example, is typified by high, constant temperature throughout the year and very heavy rainfall. There is no dry season, although the level of rainfall may vary from time to time.

Timbuktu 301 metres asl

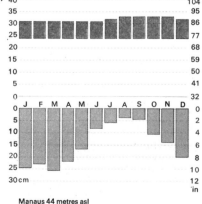

Manaus 44 metres asl

The sea and seawater

Photographs of the earth from space suggest that "Ocean" would be a more suitable name for our planet, because the oceans cover 70.8 per cent of the earth's surface [Key]. There are three major oceans, the Pacific, the Atlantic and the Indian, but the waters of the Arctic and Antarctic are also described as oceans. These five oceans are not separate areas of water but form one continuous oceanic mass. The boundaries between them are arbitrary lines drawn for convenience.

The study of oceanography

The vast areas of interconnected oceans contain 97.2 per cent of the world's total water supply. The study of oceans, including their biology, chemistry, geology and physics, has become a matter of urgency, because man's future on earth may depend on his knowledge of the ocean's potential resources of food, minerals and power.

The most obvious resource of the oceans is the water itself. But seawater is salty, containing sodium chloride (common salt), which makes it unsuitable for drinking or farming. One kilogramme (2.2lb) of sea-water contains about 35g (1.2oz) of dissolved material, of which chlorine and sodium together make up nearly 30g (1oz) or about 85 per cent of the total.

Seawater is a highly complex substance in which 73 of the 93 natural chemical elements are present in measurable or detectable amounts [1]. Apart from chlorine and sodium seawater contains appreciable amounts of sulphate, magnesium, potassium and calcium, which together add up to over 13 per cent of the total. The remainder, less than one per cent, is made up of bicarbonate, bromide, boric acid, strontium, fluoride, silicon and trace elements. Because the volume of the oceans is so great there are substantial amounts of some trace elements. Seawater contains more gold, for example, than there is on land, although in a very low concentration of four-millionths of one part per million [3].

Also present in seawater are dissolved gases from the atmosphere, including nitrogen, oxygen and carbon dioxide. Of these, oxygen is vital to marine organisms. The amount of oxygen in seawater varies according to temperature. Cold water can contain more oxygen than warm water. But cold water in the ocean deeps, which has been out of contact with the atmosphere for a long period, usually contains a much smaller amount of oxygen than surface water.

Other chemicals in seawater that are important to marine life include calcium, silicon and phosphates, all of which are used by marine creatures to form shells and skeletons. For cell and tissue building, marine organisms extract such chemicals as phosphates, certain nitrogen compounds, iron and silicon. The chief constituents of seawater – chlorine, sodium, magnesium and sulphur – are hardly used by marine organisms.

The salinity of the oceans

The volume of dissolved salts in seawater is called the salinity of the sample. The average salinity of seawater ranges between 33 and 37 parts of dissolved material per 1,000 parts of water. Oceanographers usually express these figures as 33 parts per thousand (33°/₀₀) to 37°/₀₀. The salinity of ocean water varies with local conditions [6]. Large rivers or

Trace elements 0·01%
Fluoride F⁻ 0·003%
Strontium Sr⁺⁺ 0·04%
Boric acid H_3BO_3 0·07%
Bromide Br⁻ 0·19%
Bicarbonate HCO^-_3 0·41%
Potassium K⁺ 1·10%
Calcium Ca⁺⁺ 1·16%

Magnesium Mg⁺⁺ 3·69%

Sulphate SO 7·68%

Sodium Na⁺ 30·61%

Chloride Cl⁻ 55·04%

1 Nearly all elements are found in seawater. Sodium and chloride make up common salt and form more than 85 per cent of the total substances in seawater. Trace elements include aluminium, manganese, copper and gold. If the salt in the oceans were precipitated, it would cover the earth's land areas with a layer 153m (520ft) thick.

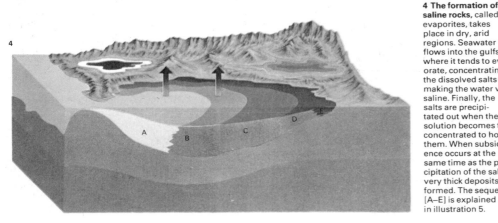

2 The salt in the world's salt mines was formed either from ocean water or from saline water in inland seas. The salt layers accumulated over extremely long periods in basins where evaporation caused the salt to precipitate from the water. The salt mines of Wieliczka, Poland, contain a layer of salt 366m (1,200ft) thick, while those of Texas are up to 3,658m (12,000ft) thick. A column of seawater about 305m (1,000ft) high would precipitate only about 4.6m (15ft), so very thick salt deposits are difficult to explain. Illustration 4 depicts the creation of salt and other saline rock deposits.

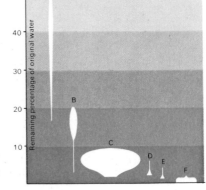

3 One of the elements in seawater is gold. Although gold forms only 0.000004 part per million, the total amount of gold in ocean water, represented by the large cube, is about 6ₓ 10⁹ kg, about 100 times more than all the gold in man's possession, which amounts to 6ₓ10⁷kg, represented by the small cube. The Germans once tried to extract oceanic gold to pay war debts, but it was too expensive.

4 The formation of saline rocks, called evaporites, takes place in dry, arid regions. Seawater flows into the gulfs where it tends to evaporate, concentrating the dissolved salts and making the water very saline. Finally, the salts are precipitated out when the solution becomes too concentrated to hold them. When subsidence occurs at the same time as the precipitation of the salts very thick deposits are formed. The sequence [A–E] is explained in illustration 5.

5 When half a sea-water sample has evaporated, calcium and magnesium carbonates [A] precipitate out. They are completely removed from the brine when it is 15% of its original volume. At about 20% calcium sulphate [B] starts precipitating followed by sodium chloride or common salt [C], other sulphates [D], rare salts of magnesium, potassium, sodium and borates and fluorides [E]. Finally magnesium and potassium chloride precipitate [F]. White areas show amounts of salts.

Remaining percentage of original water

melting ice reduce salinity, for example, whereas it is increased in areas with little rainfall and high evaporation. The Baltic Sea, which receives large quantities of fresh water from rivers and melting snow, has a low salinity of 7.2⁰/₀₀. The highest salinity of any ocean is in the Red Sea where it reaches as much as 41⁰/₀₀.

To produce fresh water from seawater the dissolved salts must be separated out. This desalination can be carried out by electrical, chemical and change of phase processes. Change of phase processes involve changing the water into steam and distilling it, or changing it into ice, a process that also expels the salt. Eskimos have used sea ice as a source of fresh water for hundreds of years [8] and primitive coastal tribes still take salt from the sea by damming water in pools and letting it gradually evaporate in the sun.

Density, light and sound
The density of seawater is an important factor in causing ocean currents and is related to the interaction of salinity and temperature [7]. The temperature of surface water varies between −2°C and 29°C (28°F and 85°F). Ice will begin to form if the temperature drops below −2°C (28°F).

The properties of light passing through seawater determine the colour of the oceans. Radiation at the red or longwave end of the visible spectrum is absorbed near the surface of the water [9] while the shorter wavelengths (blue) are scattered, giving the sea its blue colour. The depth to which light can penetrate is important to marine life. In clear water light may penetrate to 110m (360ft) whereas in muddy coastal waters it may penetrate to only 15m (50ft).

Water is a good conductor of sound, which travels at about 1,507m (4,954ft) per second through seawater, compared with 331m (1,087ft) per second through air. Echo-sounding is based on the measurement of the time taken for sound to travel from a ship to the sea floor and back again. However, temperature and pressure both affect the speed of sound, causing the speed to vary by about 100m (328ft) per second and creating phenomena such as sound "shadow" zones and slow velocity zones [10].

KEY

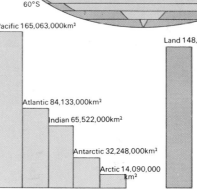

Pacific 165,063,000km²
Atlantic 84,133,000km²
Indian 65,522,000km²
Antarctic 32,248,000km²
Arctic 14,090,000 km²
Land 148,900,000km²

The oceans cover about 70 per cent of the earth's surface. No other planet in the Solar System has as much water. The five oceans are connected together and can be thought of as one large oceanic mass. Oceanography is the study of this great area of water.

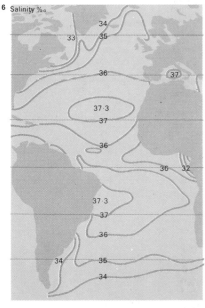

6 Salinity ‰

6 In an isohaline map of the Atlantic Ocean the lines join the places of equal salinity. The range of salinity in most of the ocean is between 33 and 37 parts per thousand. The map shows that salinity in the tropics, where evaporation is considerable, is relatively high. In the almost enclosed Mediterranean Sea it is higher still. In the Arctic, however, the salinity is lowered by melting ice and rainfall. In Hudson Bay the salinity falls considerably below the normal ocean values because of the inflow of fresh water from rivers. In the tropics, large rivers, such as the Amazon, reduce the salinity locally.

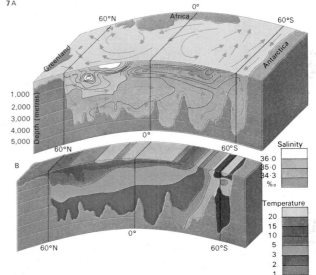

7A
7B

7 The physical properties of seawater, including the salinity [A] and temperature [B], are relatively constant at depth compared with the variations produced by local conditions at the surface. The surface salinity varies greatly with inflows of fresh water and variations in the rate of evaporation but it remains quite constant at depth as mixing of water by deep currents is very slow. The same is true of the temperature, which remains fairly constant at depth despite the climatic variation at the surface. In the Atlantic Ocean, as illustrated, a larger body of cold water exists at the south than the north and this has some effect on the temperature range.

Salinity
36·0
35·0
34·3 ‰

Temperature
20
15
10
5
3
2
1
0 °C

8 One of the ways of removing salt from seawater is the direct freezing method. This happens naturally when the temperature of seawater with a salinity of 35 parts per 1,000 falls below −2°C (29°F). This freezing results in the formation of surface ice that contains little if any salt. Eskimos and other peoples living in polar climates have long used sea ice as a source of fresh water. Such freezing leads to an increase in the salinity of the water beneath the ice.

9 Seawater reduces the intensity of sunlight (attenuates it) selectively according to its wavelength. Attenuation is minimum for blue and maximum for red and infra-red and is caused by absorption and the scattering of light in all directions. The blue wavelengths, being less absorbed, are more scattered. As a result clear seawater looks blue. Impurities in seawater, such as organic life and silt, especially around coastlines, greatly increase the attenuation. The diagram shows the attenuation in pure seawater and depicts the attenuation for different light wavelengths, the bottom of each band being the point at which only one per cent of the light intensity at the surface remains.

10 The velocity of sound in seawater is more than 4.5 times as great as it is in air but it can vary with pressure, salinity and temperature. Sound waves passing through water in which these vary are refracted, or bent like light passing through a lens. Such refraction can take place at a thermocline – the boundary between warm surface water and cold water at depth. Submarines and other naval vessels can make use of this effect to hide the sound of their passage from an enemy.

9 Sea-level
50m
100m
150m
200m
White light
UV

10
Thermocline
Sound of submarine cannot be detected on surface
Thermocline

Ocean currents

No part of the ocean is completely still, although, in the ocean depths, the movement of water is often extremely slow. Exploration of the deeper parts of the oceans has revealed the existence of marine life. If the water were not in motion, the oxygen – upon which life depends – would soon be used up and not replaced. Life would therefore be impossible. The discovery that all ocean water moves is of great significance. It was once thought that dangerous radioactive wastes could be dumped in sealed containers in the ocean depths. If the containers were to corrode, the radioactive substances would be released into the water and gradually circulate around the globe, poisoning marine life.

Causes of ocean currents

Surface currents in the oceans have been recorded since ancient times and were used by early navigators. In 1947, Thor Heyerdahl sailed on his raft, the *Kon-Tiki*, from Peru to the Tuamotu Islands east of Tahiti in 101 days. The journey, of nearly 7,000km (4,300 miles), was powered partly by the wind, but the raft was mainly carried by the Peru Cur-

rent and the South Equatorial Current.

Prevailing winds sweep surface water along to form drift currents. These surface currents do not conform precisely with the direction of the prevailing wind because of the Coriolis effect [Key] caused by the rotation of the earth. This effect, which increases away from the Equator, makes currents in the Northern Hemisphere veer to the right of the wind direction and currents in the Southern Hemisphere veer to the left. The result is a general clockwise circulation of water in the Northern Hemisphere and an anticlockwise circulation in the Southern Hemisphere [5].

Other factors affecting currents are the configuration of the ocean bed and the shapes of land masses. For example, in the Atlantic Ocean, the North Equatorial Current flows towards the West Indies. Most of this current is channelled into the Gulf of Mexico where it veers northeastwards, bursting into the Atlantic between Florida and Cuba as the Gulf Stream. (The term "stream" is used for currents with fairly clear boundaries.) This current, properly known as

the North Atlantic Drift once it leaves the American coast, then flows at four to five knots in a northeasterly direction. However, even this marked current is confined to waters near the surface. At a depth of about 350m (1,150ft), its effect is hardly noticeable. In the late 1950s, another large current was discovered flowing under the Gulf Stream in the opposite direction.

Variations in density

The causes of currents that are not powered by winds are related to the density of ocean water, which varies according to temperature and salinity. Heating at the Equator causes the water to become less dense. Cooling round the poles has the opposite effect. Salinity is affected by the inflow of fresh water from rivers, melting ice and rainfall, and by evaporation. For example, a high rate of evaporation in the Mediterranean Sea increases the salinity and therefore the density of the water [2]. As a result, currents of less dense (less salt) water flow into the Mediterranean from the Atlantic and the Black Sea. Smaller counter-currents of a

1 A

18°C
16°C
14°C
12°C

1 **Upwelling** [A] occurs when a longshore wind [1] pushes surface water away from a coast at an angle [2], allowing subsurface water to rise [3]. This slow motion can best be seen as temperature gradients [4] as the deeper water is colder. Subsurface water often contains many nutrients and so areas where upwelling occurs are often exceptionally rich fishing grounds, such as off the west coast of South America [B].

B

2

Fresh water

Increasing salinity

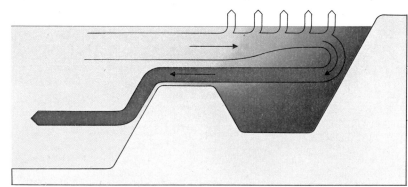

2 **The water of the Mediterranean** is constantly evaporating from its surface causing its salinity to increase. A current of normal salinity flows in and the excess salt is carried out by a deep-water current.

3 **In the Baltic,** a surface current of low salinity flows outwards. The overall salinity of the Baltic is maintained by a small undercurrent bringing in as much salt as the amount that is carried away by the outflow.

3
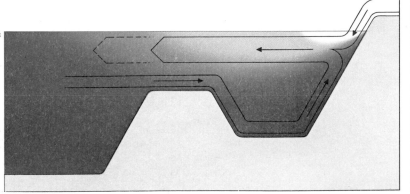

4

4 **Current meters** are the most accurate instruments used to measure and record the direction and rate of flow of ocean currents. The meters are sometimes attached to buoys or they may be anchored to the sea-bed and left to measure the current over a period of time. They usually contain some kind of propeller that is turned by the moving water and a vane connected to a compass, which orients the meter so that it always faces the current.

higher density or salinity flow outwards beneath these currents so that the salt content of the basin remains constant.

One of the simplest ways of measuring the speed and direction of surface currents is to record the movement of floating objects such as icebergs or wreckage. Ships record the flow of currents, sometimes by trailing a drift buoy and noting its movements. Current meters [4] of many kinds are also used.

Effects of ocean currents

One of the most important effects of ocean currents is that they mix ocean water and so affect directly the fertility of the sea. Mixing is especially important when sub-surface water is mixed with surface water. The upwelling [1] of sub-surface water may be caused by strong coastal winds that push the surface water outwards, allowing sub-surface water to rise up. Such upwelling occurs off the coasts of Peru, California and Mauritania. Sub-surface water rich in nutrients (notably phosphorus and silicon) rises to the surface, stimulating the growth of plankton which provides food for great

shoals of fish, such as Peruvian anchovies. The anchovies are adversely affected by another current: when the winds fail, about the end of December, disaster occurs in the form of a warm current called El Niño which flows into the area, killing the cold-water plants and animals.

Water has a high heat capacity and can retain heat two and a half times as readily as land. The heat of the sun absorbed by water around the Equator is transported north and south by currents. Part of the North Atlantic Drift flows past Norway warming offshore winds and giving northwest Europe a winter temperature that is 11C° (20F°) above the average for those latitudes [6]. The northward-flowing Peru and Benguela currents have a reverse effect, bringing cooler weather to the western coasts of South America and southern Africa. In such ways, currents have a profound effect on climate. Currents from polar regions can also create hazards for shipping. The Labrador and East Greenland currents carry icebergs and pack ice into shipping lanes and fog often occurs where cold and warm currents meet.

Surface currents are caused largely by prevailing winds. The Coriolis effect results in the deflection of currents to the right of the wind direction in the Northern Hemisphere.

In the same manner, the surface motion drives the sub-surface layer at an angle to it, and so on. Each layer moves at a slower speed than the one above it and at a greater

angle from the wind. The spiral created has the overall effect of moving the water mass above the depth of frictional resistance at an angle of about 90° from the wind direction.

Warm currents ➝

1 North Pacific
2 Alaska
3 Kuro Shio
4 Gulf Stream
5 North Equatorial
6 South Equatorial
7 Counter Equatorial
8 Brazil
9 Indian Counter Equatorial
10 Equatorial
11 East Australian

Cold currents ➝

12 California
13 Oya Shio
14 Canaries
15 Peru
16 Benguela
17 West Wind Drift
18 West Australian

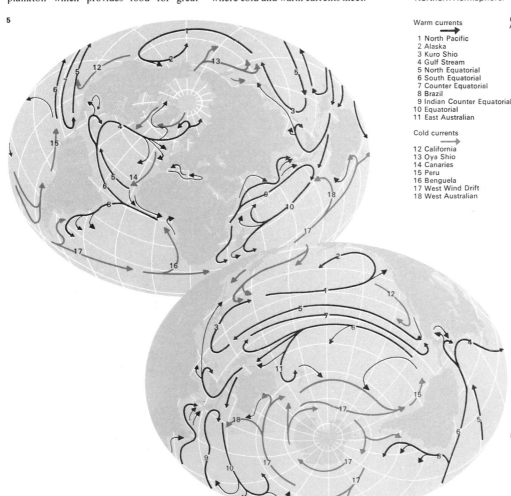

6 Climate is profoundly affected by ocean currents. Where winds blow off the warm sea rather than the cold land the North Atlantic Drift can bring mild weather to some European coasts. New

York City [A] lies at a latitude only 160km (100 miles) north of Lisbon [B]. While New York has average January temperatures of −1°C (31°F), Lisbon has a sunny average of 10°C (50°F) at the same time.

5 The surface currents of the world circulate in a clockwise direction in the Northern Hemisphere and in an anticlockwise direction in the Southern Hemisphere. These circulatory systems are called gyres. There are two

large clockwise gyres in the Northern Hemisphere (in the North Atlantic and in the North Pacific) and three anticlockwise gyres in the Southern Hemisphere (in the South Atlantic, the South Pacific and the Indian Ocean). Beneath the surface

are undercurrents whose direction may be opposite to those at the surface. Beneath the northeastward flowing Gulf Stream off the eastern USA lies a large, cold current flowing south from the Arctic. The Gulf Stream finally splits in the

North Atlantic, branching past eastern Greenland, northern Europe and southern Europe, while part of the current returns southwards to complete the gyre. Surface cold currents in the Northern Hemisphere generally flow southwards. In

the Southern Hemisphere, cold water circulates around Antarctica, while offshoots flow northwards. The warm currents are very strong in tropical and sub-tropical regions. They include the Equatorial and Indian currents.

Waves and tides

Waves and tides are the most familiar features of oceans and seas. Sometimes, the energies of waves, tides and high winds combine with devastating effect. In January 1953, a high spring tide, storm waves and winds of 185km/h (115mph) combined to raise the level of the North Sea by 3m (10ft) higher than usual. This "surge" in the sea caused extensive flooding in eastern England, but in The Netherlands, 4.3 per cent of the entire country was inundated, about 30,000 houses were destroyed or damaged by the waters and 1,800 people died.

Waves and wave movements

Some wave motion occurs at great depth along the boundary of two opposing currents. But most waves are caused by the wind blowing over an open stretch of water. This area where the wind blows is known as the "fetch". Waves there are confused and irregular and are referred to as a "sea". As they propagate beyond the fetch they combine into more orderly waves forming a swell which travels for large distances beyond the fetch. Waves are movements of oscillation –

that is, the shape of the wave moves across the water, but the water particles rotate in a circular orbit with hardly any lateral movement [Key]. As a result, if there is no wind or current, a corked bottle bobs up and down in the waves, but is more or less stationary.

Waves have two basic dimensions [1]. Wave height is the vertical distance between the crest and the trough. Wave length is the distance between two crests. At sea, waves seldom exceed 12m (39ft) in height, although one 34m (112ft) high was observed in the Pacific [3] in 1933. Such a wave requires a long fetch measuring thousands of miles and high-speed winds. Wave motion continues for some way beneath the surface, but the rotating orbits diminish and become negligible at a depth of about half the the wave length; this is known as the wave base.

Waves that break along a seashore may have been generated by storms in mid-ocean or by local winds. As waves approach shallow water [1], which is defined as a depth of half a wave length, their character changes. As a wave "feels" the bottom, it gradually slows down and the crests tend to crowd together.

When the water in front of a wave is insufficient to fill the wave form, the rotating orbit, and hence the wave, breaks. There are two main kinds of breakers. Spilling breakers occur on gently sloping beaches, when the crests spill over to form a mass of surf. Plunging breakers occur on steeper slopes.

Tsunamis – tidal waves

Tsunamis [4] are sometimes called tidal waves but they have no connection with tides. Tsunamis are caused mainly by earthquakes, but also by submarine landslides and volcanic eruptions. At sea, the height of the wave is seldom more than 60–90cm (2–3ft). But the wave length may be hundreds of miles long and tsunamis travel at hundreds of kilometres per hour because of their long wave length. For example, an earthquake in the Aleutian Trench in the far north of the Pacific in 1946 triggered off a tsunami which devastated Honolulu. The tsunami took 4 hours 34 minutes to reach Honolulu, a distance of more than 3,220km (2,000 miles) – a speed of about 700 km/h (438mph). Waves more than 15m (50ft) high struck Honolulu,

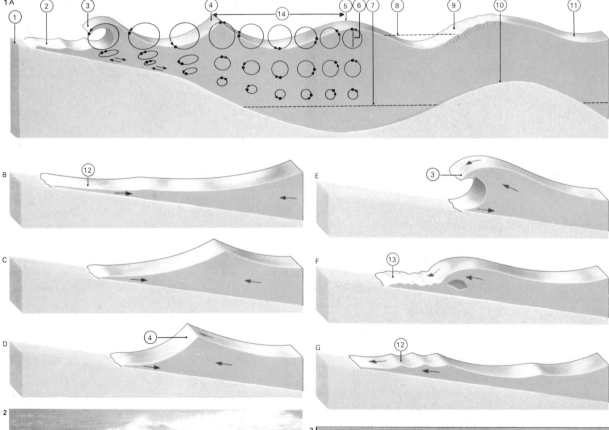

1 Waves have length and height [A]. The wave length [14] is the distance between one crest [5] and another, in this case, a peaking wave [4]. Between crests is a trough [11]. The wave height [6] is the distance between the crest and the trough. If wave action ceased, the water would settle at the "still water level" [8]. Wave action extends to the wave base [7]. Wave distortion is caused by frictional drag on the bottom. If waves pass over a sand bar [10], a spilling breaker [9] may form. Sometimes, waves in shallow water move the whole body of the water forward in translation waves [2] towards the shore [1]. In the development of a breaking wave, B shows backwash [12]. C shows the advance of the next wave which peaks [4] in D and then becomes a plunging breaker [3] in E. F and G shows swash [13] rushing up the beach after the wave has broken. Backwash then begins the cycle again.

2 Surfing is a popular sport in many countries, such as Australia. Surf forms as the crest of a wave breaks over.

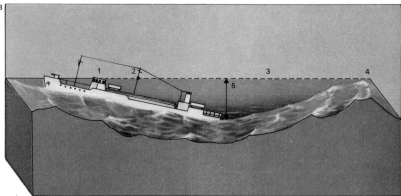

3 The tallest recorded wave in open sea was 34m (112ft) high. An officer on the USS *Ramapo*'s bridge [1] in the Pacific in 1933 saw the crest of a wave [4] in line with the horizon [3] and the crow's nest [2], enabling him to work out the wave height [5].

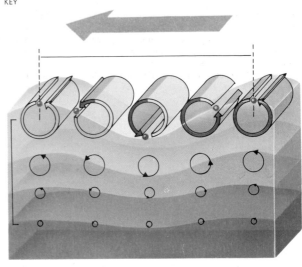

Most waves are generated by the wind.
As a wave travels in deep water, however, the water particles

do not move up and down but rotate in circular orbits. As depth increases, the rotations of the

water particles diminish rapidly. This is why submarines escape the effects of severe storms.

causing $25 million damage and killing 173 people. Although the height of the crest is low at sea, tsunamis have immense energy, which, as they lose speed in shallower water, is converted into an increase in height. The waves, on reaching the shore, may be 38m (125ft) or more high.

Most destructive tsunamis occur in the Pacific [5], but they have been recorded in the Atlantic. A tsunami battered Lisbon shortly after the earthquake of 1755. It was later felt in the West Indies in the form of a destructive wave 4–6m (13–20ft) high. Other tidal waves can be due to the surge of water when the barometric pressure is exceptionally low, such as in a hurricane.

Tides and their causes

Tides are alternate rises and falls of the sea's surface, caused chiefly by the gravitational pull of the moon and the sun [6]. The tidal effect of the sun is only 46.6 per cent that of the moon. Tides are also affected by the shapes of ocean basins and land masses. The moon's gravitational pull makes the waters of the earth bulge outwards when the moon is

overhead at any meridian. Another bulge occurs on the opposite side of the earth at the same time. Because the moon orbits the earth once every 24 hours 50 minutes, it causes two high tides and two low tides in that period.

Spring tides [7] occur when the earth, moon and sun are in a straight line. The combined gravitational attraction makes high tides higher and low tides lower, giving a high tidal range. Neap tides, which have the lowest tidal range, occur when the sun, earth and moon form a right-angle.

In the open sea, the tidal range is no more than a few feet and in enclosed basins, such as the Mediterranean, it is little more than 30cm (12in). However, in shallow seas, it may be more than 6m (20ft) and in tidal estuaries 12–15m (40–50ft). The highest tidal range recorded is about 16m (53ft) in the Bay of Fundy in eastern Canada. In some estuaries, including those of Hangchow Bay in China and the Severn in England, tidal bores occur. Bores are bodies of water with a wall-like front that surge up rivers. They form because estuaries act as funnels, leading to a rise in the height of the water as it flows upstream.

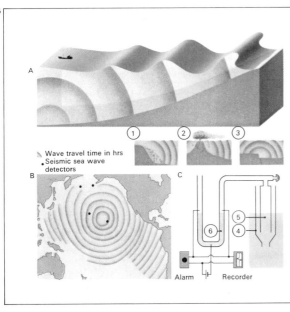

Wave travel time in hrs
Seismic sea wave detectors

Alarm   Recorder

4 Tsunamis [A], caused by landslides [1], volcanoes [2] or earthquakes [3], reach great heights near land. Pacific warning stations [B] use detectors [C]. A container [4], half in seawater, has air in a tube [5]. When a wave increases the pressure, mercury is forced around [6], closing an electrical circuit and setting off an alarm.

5 Tremendous damage is caused by tsunamis. They occur mainly in the Pacific Ocean.

→ Average gravitational pull
→ Actual gravitational pull
→ Tide generating force

6 Water on the earth [A] is attracted to the moon [B] on the near side but pushed away on the far side. This causes tidal bulges at the nearest [1] and farthest [2] points, tidal flows at [3] and [4] and low tides at median points [5]. The force at work [red arrows] is the difference between the moon's actual gravitational pull and its average pull at the earth's centre [6] where it is exactly balanced by centrifugal force.

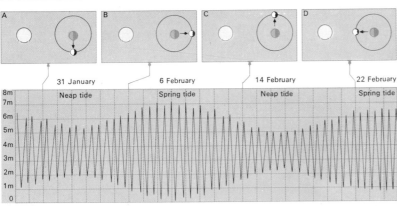

31 January   6 February   14 February   22 February

| | Neap tide | Spring tide | Neap tide | Spring tide |

8m
7m
6m
5m
4m
3m
2m
1m
0

7 The height of tides varies according to the positions of the sun and moon in relation to the Earth. When the moon is in its first quarter [A], and again when it is in its last quarter [C], the moon, earth and sun form a right-angle. The gravita-

tional forces are therefore opposed, causing only a small difference between high and low tide. Such tides are called neap tides. However, the moon, earth and sun form a straight line at full moon [B] and at new moon [D]. The high tides then

become higher and the low tides lower. These are called spring tides. Because of friction and inertia, both spring and neap tides come about two days after the moon's phases. The graph shows the tidal range over the period of a month.

8 At low tide [A] the sea recedes from Mont St Michel, off the northern coast of Britanny, making it part of the mainland. At high tide [B], the sea surrounds it and it becomes an island. A similar feature in Cornwall, England, is St Michael's Mt.

The sea-bed

The floor of the deep ocean has always fascinated man. Pluto's legendary lost continent of Atlantis, "beyond the Pillars of Hercules", has never lost its hold on the imagination although there is no geological evidence to support the belief that it lay south of the Azores, on the mid-Atlantic Ridge.

Early knowledge of the sea-bed was restricted to depth soundings, taken by lead and line, of the areas around the known islands. Magellan tried – and, of course, failed – to reach the bottom of the Pacific with 370 m (1,200 ft) of rope. The first true oceanic sounding was made by James Clark Ross in 1840, when he measured a depth of nearly 3,700m (12,140ft) with a line.

Probing the sea-floor

The epic voyage of HMS *Challenger* which led to the first true oceanic depth survey was made between 1872 and 1876. The *Challenger* expedition used soundings weights with tube-like cups to obtain a sample of the material forming the sea-floor. Thus, when Jules Verne (1828–1905) wrote *Twenty Thousand Leagues under the Sea* (1870),

man first developed a systematic knowledge of the deep sediments. Their classification, which was developed by the *Challenger* expedition's geologist John Murray (1841–1914), and others who studied the samples after the ship's return, has been improved but never completely discounted.

Even so, the widely prevalent idea that the ocean floor consisted of a sandy waste extending for thousands of miles, dotted with a few islands and occupied by exotic fish, was gradually discarded. The early samples of sediment obtained by *Challenger*, and the soundings obtained on the mid-Atlantic which actually mapped the mid-Atlantic Ridge, did not lead to a full understanding of the variation in the extent and thickness of the sediments. They did not supply any scientific reasons for this variation nor was it appreciated that mid-ocean ridges ran through all the world's major oceans.

During this century, improved coring devices greatly enlarged the collective knowledge of oceanic sediments.

The actual topography of the deep ocean has been revealed by echo-sounding using

sonic or ultra-sonic signals. Scientists can calculate the depth of the water by noting how much time passed between sending the signals and receiving the echo. Since the 1940s seismic methods have also been used; they have shown that the ocean floor is made up of hills, volcanic mountains, island complexes – of which the islands are only the visible tips – and of huge and complex submarine mountain chains, with median rift valleys, faults and numerous flanking ridges.

The continental shelf

If one walks down a pebbly beach, the pebbles usually give way to sand, which continues out to sea. This is the continental shelf [1, 2] which may be covered by relatively coarse sediments or muds and silts. It is inhabited by seaweeds of many kinds, as well as numerous animals: corals, sea anemones and other coelenterates, many species of burrowing worms and minute colonial rock-encrusting animals (Bryozoa), and clams, mussels, oysters, scallops and other molluscs. There are sea-urchins, starfish, brittle stars, sea-cucumbers and sponges. Bottom-

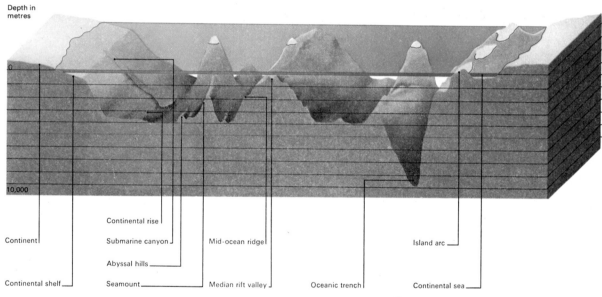

1 The sea-bed consists of different zones, the shallowest of which is the continental shelf that lies between the coast and the 200m (656ft) depth contour. The shelf area occupies 7.5% of the sea-floor and corresponds to the submerged portion of the continental crust. Beyond, the downward slope increases abruptly to form the continental slope, which occupies some 8.5% of the sea-floor. This area may be dissected by submarine canyons. The continental slope meets the abyssal basins at a more gentle slope called the continental rise. The basins lie at depths of 4,000m (13,200ft) and show many mountain ranges and hills.

Depth in metres

Continent | Continental rise | Mid-ocean ridge | Island arc
Continental shelf | Submarine canyon | Abyssal hills | Seamount | Median rift valley | Oceanic trench | Continental sea

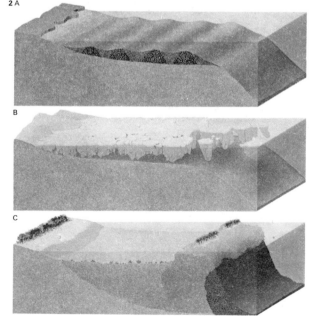

2 Continental shelves are the regions immediately off the land masses. There are several different sorts. Off Europe and North America the shelf [A] has a gentle relief, often with sandy ridges and barriers. In high latitudes, floating ice wears the shelf smooth [B] and in clear tropical seas a smooth shelf may be rimmed with a coral barrier like the Great Barrier Reef off eastern Australia [C], leaving an inner lagoonal area "dammed" by the reef.

3 Submarine canyons like the 1.5km (5,000ft) deep gorge off Monterey, California [B], are found on the continental slopes [A]. They can be caused by river erosion before the

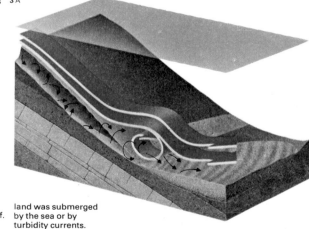

land was submerged by the sea or by turbidity currents. Mud and sediment-laden water often pour out of major estuaries scouring gorges out of slope rock and sediment. These canyons compare with the Grand Canyon [C].

dwelling fish such as plaice and flounder also live on the continental shelf.

This is the region of sand banks and sand waves (underwater dunes). In the North Sea, sand waves are formed as masses of loose sand move around like sand dunes in the desert, propelled by currents. Here, too, vast oil and gas reservoirs, sometimes associated, as in the Gulf of Mexico, with salt domes, are found in the continental rocks deep beneath the surface sand.

At the edge of the continental shelf, at about 200m (656ft) depth, the sea-floor begins to dip markedly down: this is the upper boundary of the continental slope. It is dissected in places by submarine canyons [1, 3], in which underwater avalanches, known as turbidity currents, carry mud, pebbles and sand far out to sea and deposit them at the foot of the slope, on the continental rise [1], at depths of about 2,000m (6,560ft). Life is much more scarce on the continental slope and rise: large free-swimming molluscs – octopuses, cuttle fish and large squid – brittle stars, worms and strange fish are among the most common species.

The continental rise leads to the abyssal plains – vast empty basins occupied by few, even stranger fish, worms, brittle stars, and deep-sea free-swimming molluscs, with no plant life to speak of. From these plains rise huge mountain ranges [1], the mid-ocean ridges, from 4,000m (13,200ft) deep to some 1,000m (3,300ft) below the surface with occasional peaks reaching the surface as islands. Seamounts [5] also rise from the abyssal plains, sometimes part of island chains like the Hawaii-Emperor chain in the Pacific, but often isolated. They are nearly all volcanic and may be crowned with coral, formed when they were near the surface.

Sea-bed maps

On the six pages following, the floors of the five oceans are mapped. The projections used were chosen to maximize coverage of sea areas relative to land and the colours reflect those thought to exist on the sea-bed. Continental shelves are shown in the greyish-green of the terrigenous oozes, while the calcareous oozes of the deeper areas are shown in pale greys and buff.

KEY

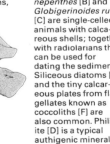

The existence of manganese nodules on the deep ocean floor was discovered by the *Challenger* expedition. These potato-sized and -shaped nodules form on the ocean bed by processes that are not fully understood, although a great deal of research is going on to find out how they grow. They consist of a rock nucleus surrounded by concentric layers of metal oxide and are of potential economic importance because they contain enough copper, cobalt and nickel, as well as manganese, to last the world for many thousands of years.

4 **Basalt** is the rock most commonly found on the sea-floor. It is a lava that forms the bulk of the seamounts and ocean ridges and it underlays the marine sediments in the abyssal plains. Submarine eruptions produce lumps of basalt "frozen" into pillow shapes (pillow lavas). The submarine basalt shown here is seen through a microscope. It shows small crystals, glassy patches and gas bubbles now filled with green mica.

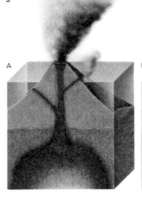
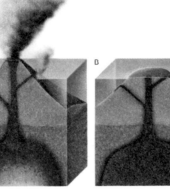

5 **Seamounts** are submarine mountains rising at least 1,000m (3,300ft) above their surroundings; they are nearly always volcanoes. Some seamounts called tablemounts or guyots have flat tops at depths down to 2,500m (1.5 miles). These tops are often too large to be explained as ancient craters filled to the rim by sediments. Thus it was proposed that guyots were volcanoes above sea-level [A] which after extinction were worn flat by waves [B] and which then sunk as the sea-level rose or as the sea-bed subsided [c]. This has been confirmed by the presence of beach pebbles.

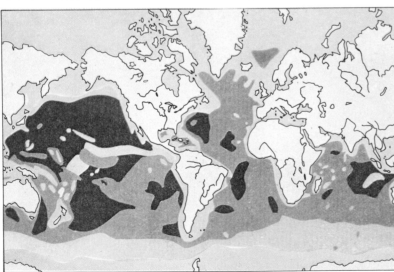

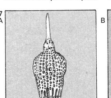
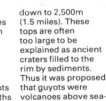
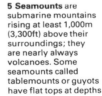

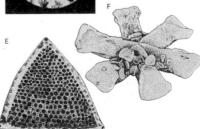

Terrigenous deposits

Red clay

Globigerina ooze

Pteropod ooze

Diatom ooze

Radiolarian ooze

6 **Deep-sea sediments** are related to surface water temperature, depth and distance from land. Terrigenous deposits consist of mineral particles derived from the weathering of land rocks. They are carried out to sea by rivers and winds and are found near the coasts. The deep sea floor is often blanketed by ooze which is formed by the endless "snowfall" of the shells or skeletons of countless tiny planktonic animals and algae. Globigerina and radiolarian ooze are made from the remains of single-celled animals with calcareous and siliceous skeletons respectively. Occasionally the shells of pteropods, small swimming molluscs, form deposits of pteropod ooze. In cold seas, silica-shelled microscopic algae, the diatoms, thrive and form diatom ooze. In areas away from land and where planktonic life is scarce, atmospheric dust settles very slowly as abyssal red clays.

7 **Constituents of marine sediments** include micro-organisms and new (authigenic) minerals formed on the sea-bed, as well clays. Radiolarians, such as *Calocycletta virginis* [A] are single-celled animals with siliceous skeletons. Foraminifera such as *Globigerina nepenthes* [B] and *Globigerinoides ruber* [C] are single-celled animals with calcareous shells; together with radiolarians they can be used for dating the sediments. Siliceous diatoms [E] and the tiny calcareous plates from flagellates known as coccoliths [F] are also common. Philipsite [D] is a typical authigenic mineral of the deep sea.

65

The Atlantic Ocean

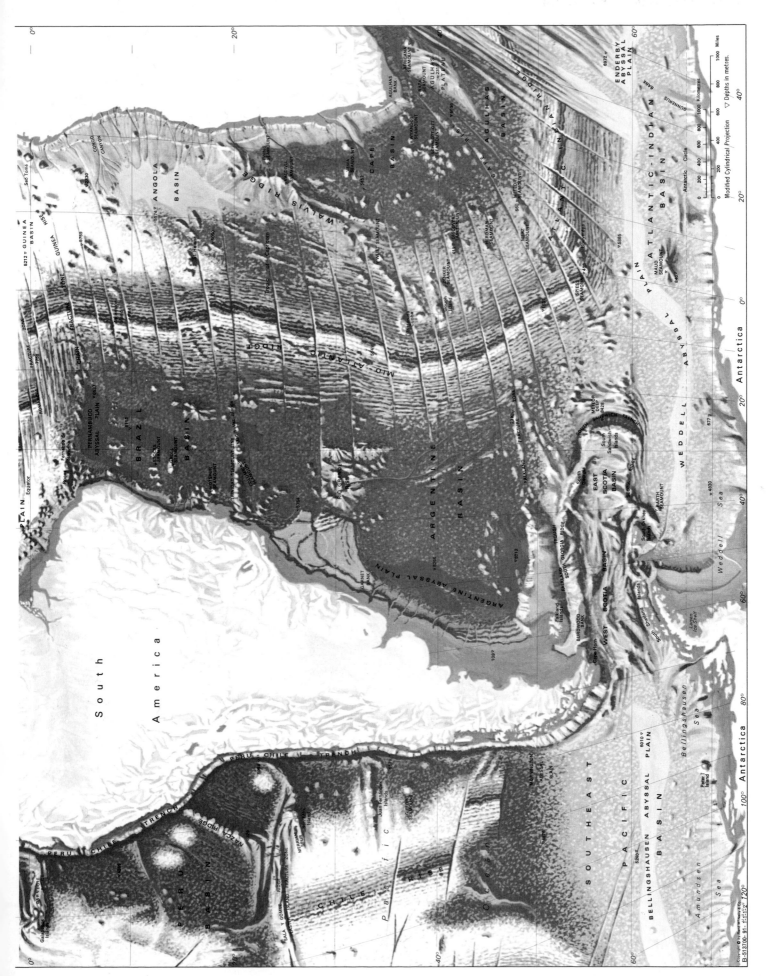

The Pacific Ocean

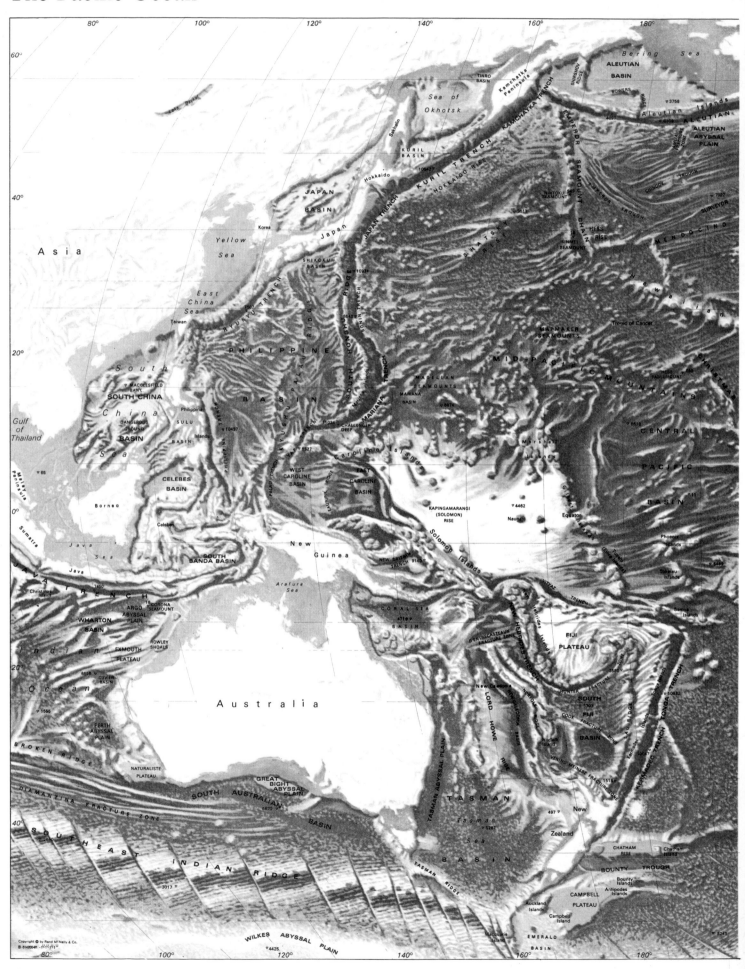

160°   140°   120°   100°   80°   60°   40°

Hudson Bay

LABRADOR BASIN

KODIAK GUYOT (SEAMOUNT)

ALASKA ABYSSAL PLAIN

TRENCH

∇3626

TUFTS ABYSSAL PLAIN

∇6257

North America

NORTH AMERICAN BASIN

∇331

Great Lakes

FRACTURE ZONE

JUAN DE FUCA RIDGE
BLANCO FRACTURE
CASCADIA

FRACTURE ZONE

PIONEER FRACTURE ZONE

DELGADA FAN

MONTEREY FAN

∇236

MUSICIANS SEAMOUNTS

∇6288

MURRAY

FRACTURE ZONE

∇5120

∇1795

∇9009

Guadalupe Island

Cortes Trench

Gulf of Mexico

MEXICO BASIN

SIGSBEE KNOLLS ∇4023

WEST FLORIDA SHELF

BLAKE PLATEAU

MOLOKAI FRACTURE ZONE

HAWAIIAN FRACTURE ZONE

∇1657

BAJA CALIFORNIA SEAMOUNT PROVINCE

Mexico

CAMPECHE BANK

MOLOKAI

PENSACOLA SEAMOUNT

SUITCASE SEAMOUNTS

CLARION FRACTURE ZONE

RIVERA FRACTURE ZONE

OROZCO FRACTURE ZONE

MIDDLE AMERICA TRENCH

CAYMAN TRENCH

Caribbean Sea

∇11

BEATA RIDGE

EAST

∇4200

CLARION FRACTURE ZONE

∇4085

Clipperton Island

SIQUEIROS FRACTURE ZONE

∇6868

PACIFIC

∇720

GUATEMALA BASIN

PANAMA BASIN

∇4220

Malpelo Island

BASIN

20 GERMAINE BANK

COCOS RIDGE

∇5349

CLIPPERTON FRACTURE ZONE

GALAPAGOS RISE

Christmas Island

∇5029

GALAPAGOS FRACTURE ZONE

Galapagos Islands

CARNEGIE RIDGE

0°

Marquesas Islands

∇5405

∇5851

PERU BASIN

∇4389

PERU-CHILE TRENCH

MARQUESAS FRACTURE ZONE

BAUER FRACTURE ZONE

Society Islands

Tuamotu Archipelago

Tahiti

∇4525

NAZCA RIDGE

20°

∇9214

Cook Islands

Tubai Islands

320

∇806

Tropic of Capricorn

Pitcairn Island

Sala y Gómez SALA Y GOMEZ RIDGE

San Felix Island

∇1080

Chapa

Easter Island

EASTER ISLAND FRACTURE ZONE

CHILE BASIN

SOUTHWEST PACIFIC BASIN

∇3841

CHILE RISE

Juan Fernandez Islands

∇4795

CHALLENGER FRACTURE ZONE

FERNANDEZ

GIFFORD SEAMOUNT

EAST PACIFIC RISE

CORDILLERA

FRACTURE ZONE

∇3977

ALBATROSS

1447

Atlantic Ocean

SOUTHEAST

109

ELTANIN FRACTURE ZONE

PACIFIC

∇4876

BASIN

Falkland Islands

SOUTH GEORGIA RIDGE

South America

Cape Horn

WEST SCOTIA BASIN

0   400   800   1200   Kilometres
0   400   800   1200   Miles
Modified Cylindrical Projection   ∇ Depths in metres.

160°   140°   120°   100°   80°   60°

69

The Indian Ocean and the polar seas

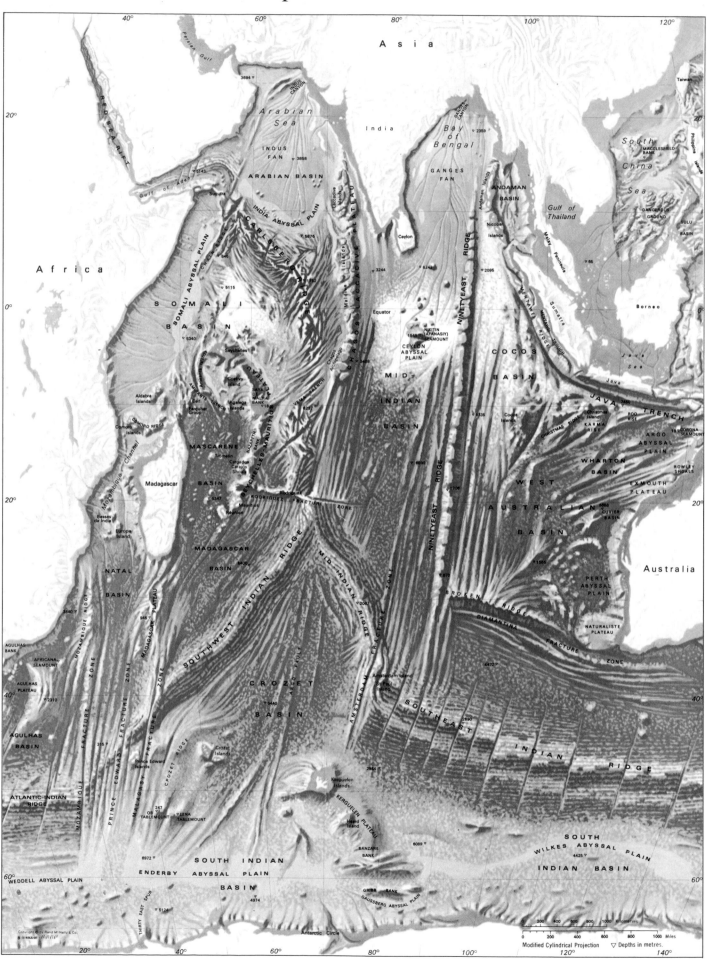

Modified Cylindrical Projection   ▽ Depths in metres.

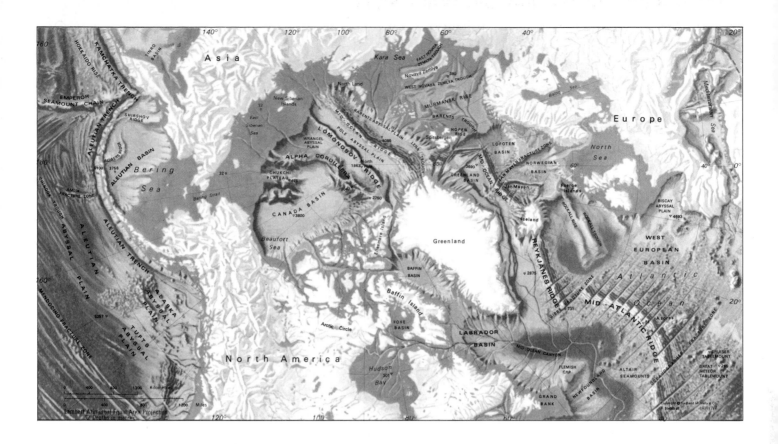

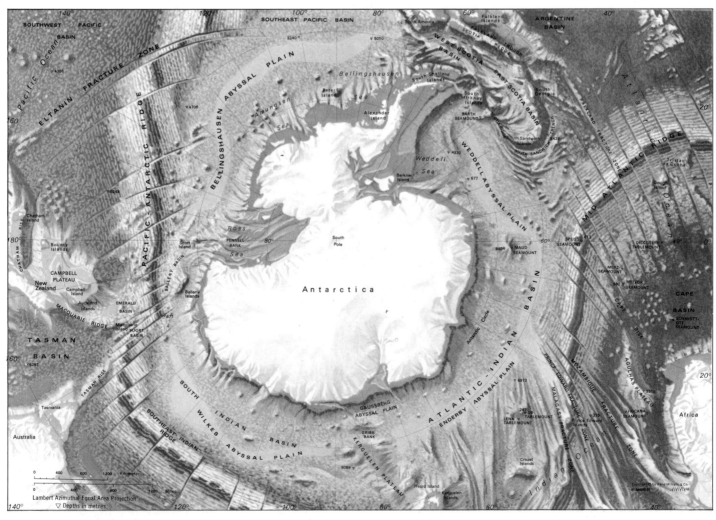

Oceanographic exploration

The topography of the ocean floor is hardly more familiar to man than that of the hidden side of the moon. Much remains to be discovered about the oceanic two-thirds of our planet and oceanographic research is not just a matter of scientific curiosity – man is only just beginning to appreciate and to exploit the vast untapped food, mineral and energy resources of the sea.

Early observations

The earliest scientific observations of the sea were recorded by Aristotle (384–322 BC) who described 180 marine animal species. Little further progress was made until the age of discovery during the fifteenth and sixteenth centuries which advanced the geographical knowledge of the seas and their currents. In 1670 the Irishman Robert Boyle (1627–91) published his *Observations and Experiments on the Saltiness of the Sea* in which he correctly deduced that the salt is derived from the weathering of the land. He introduced the silver nitrate test to measure the chloride content of seawater, a method which is still used today.

The Italian count Luigi Marsigli (1658–1730), a contemporary of Boyle, deserves to be called the first oceanographer because he studied the whole realm of the sea, from its flora and fauna to its currents. He invented the propeller current meter and discovered the deep counter-current in the Bosporus, correctly attributing it to differences in salinity between the Black Sea and the Mediterranean. (The Black Sea receives more water from rivers than it loses through evaporation, hence the main surface current flows towards the Mediterranean.)

In the eighteenth century the American Benjamin Franklin (1706–90) published a chart of the Gulf Stream which successfully shortened the passage time of the mail packets between North America and England. James Cook (1728–79), during his famous Pacific voyages from 1768 to 1779, finally exploded the geographical myth of a great southern continent in the South Pacific where he took soundings down to 1,243m (4,078ft) which hinted at even greater depths.

At the very beginning of the nineteenth century the German Alexander von Humboldt (1769–1859) described the cold current that flows up the Andean coast to the Galapagos Islands. In 1835 the English naturalist Charles Darwin (1809–82) visited these islands during his round-the-world voyage in HMS *Beagle*. Darwin made many sea-related observations, including some on plankton (the microscopic life forms of the sea). He also proposed a theory on the origins of coral reefs which after more than a century of heated debate was finally proved correct by the well-drilling on Eniwetok atoll in 1952. In the middle of the nineteenth century, Lieutenant Matthew Fontaine Maury of the US Navy (1806–73) published *Wind and Current Charts*, the first pilot charts, compiled from the data in ships' log books.

The *Challenger* expedition

The findings of the early scientists and the many unanswered questions they posed induced the British Government in 1872 to finance a scientific expedition to circumnavigate the world, for which the Royal Navy provided a ship – HMS *Challenger*.

Challenger, under the scientific direction

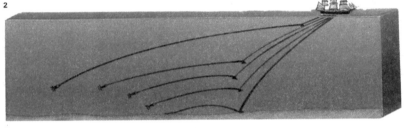

1 **The natural history laboratory** aboard HMS *Challenger* was fitted for the study of marine, bird and island life. The first true oceanographic ship, *Challenger* was a converted man-of-war and this laboratory was installed on her gun deck and lit by a gunport.

2 **Dredging** on the *Challenger* expedition was a slow, tedious operation and was nicknamed drudging by the crew who failed to share the enthusiasm of the scientists. The dredge was streamed out at the end of a warp and was made to sink by the attachment of a sliding weight.

3 **Instruments used on the *Challenger*** included a current drag [A], which was lowered to a predetermined depth, the drift being shown at the surface by a buoy. The Baillie sounding machine [B] measured depth and collected samples of sediment. The slip water bottle [C] was used for sampling the bottom water for in-board analysis.

4 **This dredge** was used on the *Challenger* for collecting biological specimens from the sea-floor.

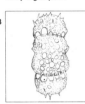

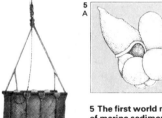

5 **The first world map of marine sediments** was provided by the *Challenger* expedition. Vast areas of the sea-floor were found to consist of dead shells of single-celled animals (mainly Foraminifera and radiolarians) and algae (diatoms).

Foraminifera, such as *Globigerina digitata* [A], have calcareous shells whereas radiolarians, such as *Panartus tetrathalamus* [B], have siliceous shells. The *Challenger* discovered 3,508 new species of radiolarians.

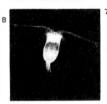

6 **The *Challenger* expedition** also studied the species and individuals forming plankton, such as the comb jelly [A], a ctenophore and the copepod [B], a crustacean.

7 **The plankton net** is a cone of fine muslin kept open by a hoop and weighted by a sinker on its bridle. The small end is tied to the neck of a jar in which the plankton is collected.

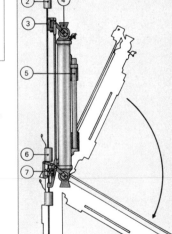

8 **The Nansen bottle** is used for taking deep-water samples. Bottles are attached at suitable intervals on the hydrographic wire [1]. When the desired depth is reached a messenger weight [2] is slid down until it hits the latch [3] of the uppermost bottle which then swings around its lower grip, closing the valves [4] and tripping the thermometers [5]. The messenger then slides farther down the wire [6] and trips the lever [7], releasing a new messenger to operate the next bottle down.

of Charles Wyville Thomson (1830–82), sailed 69,000 nautical miles between 1872 and 1876. Among other observations, ocean depths and surface currents were measured, water samples taken for analysis [3] and sea life was dredged or trawled [2, 4]. The ship was also fitted with laboratories [1]. The *Challenger* expedition outlined the broad features of the sea-floor and the nature of its sediments, and discovered some 4,417 new species of animals and plants. It also showed that life existed in the most extreme depths. Thus modern oceanography began.

Modern oceanography
Many expeditions were to follow using improved techniques and instruments. The Norwegian polar explorer Fridtjof Nansen (1861–1930) invented the deep-water sampling bottle [8] that bears his name. It can carry thermometers for determining the temperature at depth [9]. Plankton nets [7] were perfected and many ingenious instruments, such as the bathythermograph [10], were invented. A breakthrough came with the discovery of echo-sounding [13] just

before World War I, but it was only perfected for use at great depths after World War II.

A new era in marine geosciences was introduced in 1961 by the Mohole project on the US drilling ship *CUSS I* (from the initials of the participating oil companies). The aim to drill down to the earth's mantle was not achieved, but the accumulated experience was put to use in the American Deep Sea Drilling Project that started in 1968. This project confirmed the sea-floor spreading theory, which states that new sea-floor is generated along the mid-oceanic ridges.

The emphasis in oceanography has changed since the early days when the main object was to collect samples of sediment, water and marine life. While this is still part of the research, the aims are increasingly to find new food and physical resources (minerals and energy), to control pollution and to conserve the biological resources of the sea. Oceanography has become an advanced science involving satellite navigation, expensive ships [Key] with on-board computers and laboratories and backed up by sophisticated shore-based facilities.

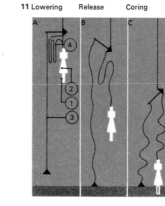

Modern research vessels such as the AGOR–class R/V *David Starr Jordan* of the Scripps Institution of Oceanography, USA, are designed for versatility. This ship is 80m (254 ft) long and carries four laboratories. She has two winches and two cranes for lowering scientific gear. A central well through the hull allows further use as a drilling platform. Propulsion is provided by two cycloid-al propellers, which give total manoeuvrability in all directions. The ship has an automatic satellite navigation system which provides a digital display of both the latitude and longitude.

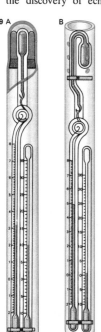

9 Deep-sea reversing thermometers (DSRT) are fixed on Nansen bottles. The protected thermometer [A] is insulated from pressure and records the temperature when the bottle is tripped. The unprotected thermometer [B] is similar but the hydrostatic pressure squeezes the reservoir so that the reading is a function of both temperature and depth. The small auxiliary thermometers indicate the temperature at the time of the reading and this must be introduced as a correction.

10 The bathythermograph simultaneously records temperature and depth down to 300m (1,000ft) but it lacks the precision and the depth range of the DSRT.

11 The gravity corer, which takes samples of the sea-floor sediments, consists of a metal tube [1] with a lead weight [2] and a tripping device [3]. The instrument is lowered in the sea [A] with the lower part of the wire coiled [4]. When the tripping device touches the bottom [B] the coil is released and the core barrel falls and punches into the sediments [C]. It is then brought back to the surface [D].

13 Echo-sounding is a method of measuring depth from the speed of sound in seawater – The lapse is timed between sending a sound signal and receiving its echo which has bounced off the bottom. In A both the sound receiver [1] and the transmitter [2] are on the ship, and the water depth is measured. In B a transmitter [3], weighted by a sinker [4] sends signals direct to a single receiver and bounces others off the bottom to calculate the depth.

12 The piston corer is an improvement on the gravity corer. Its penetration is increased by an internal piston [1] which sucks the corer deeper into the sediment. Piston cores can exceed 20m (60ft) in length whereas gravity cores seldom exceed 2m (6ft).

14 The American deep-sea drilling vessel *Glomar Challenger* maintains its station by dynamic positioning; the drift of the ship is computed relative to a sonar beacon [1] and is automatically corrected [A, B, C] by side thrusters [2] and the main propeller. After a worn drill bit at the end of the drill string [3] is renewed, the string is guided back to the hole by fitting the core barrel with a sonar device [4], which determines its position relative to three sonar reflectors [5] placed around the re-entry funnel [6]. The drill is then guided into the funnel by a sideways jet [7].

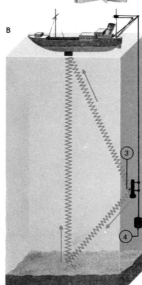

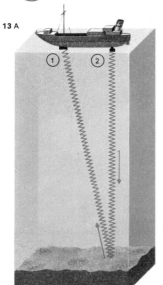

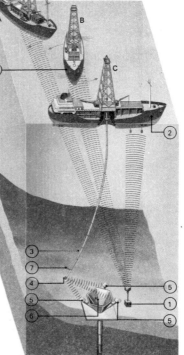

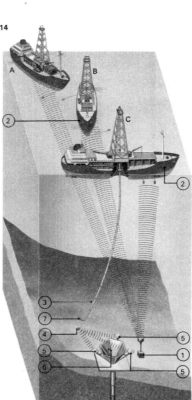

Man under the sea

For centuries man has striven to conquer the world beneath the sea. Even in the fourth century BC Alexander the Great (356–323 BC) was lowered into the sea in a large glass barrel and he used divers in military operations such as the siege of Tyre (334 BC).

Early diving apparatus

The earliest reliable diving bells, which were open at the base and supplied with air by a hose from the surface, date from the sixteenth century. In 1663–4 one such bell was used to recover 53 cannons from the Swedish galleon *Vasa*. The first practical bell holding more than one diver was built by Edmond Halley (1656–1742) [1] in 1690, and bells are still used for harbour construction and salvage. The familiar "hard hat" diving suit introduced by Augustus Siebe in 1837 is still used extensively in underwater engineering down to 60m (200ft) but it is the aqualung [3], developed by Jacques Yves Cousteau and Emile Gagnan in 1943, that gives the diver greatest mobility.

The air supplied to divers, whether from a pump or from aqualung tanks, must be at the same pressure as the surrounding water so that the diver's body is not crushed. At a depth of less than 10m (33ft) water pressure equals that of the atmosphere (1.03kg/sq cm [14.7lb/sq in]); each 10m from the surface increases pressure by one atmosphere. The result of breathing air at higher than normal pressure is that nitrogen (which forms 80 per cent of air) becomes highly concentrated in the blood and tissue fluids. This dissolved nitrogen can turn back into a gas in the organs and blood-stream if pressure is lowered too suddenly, leading to decompression sickness, usually called "the bends". If a diver rises from below 14m (45ft) too quickly, the nitrogen in his blood is not expelled in the normal way through his lungs; and the bubbles formed in his system prevent the proper circulation of his blood. To avoid the bends, divers are raised in stages, stopping for a set period at predetermined depths as they ascend. If for any reason this has not been possible the diver can be put into a decompression chamber [5]. This subjects him to the same pressure at which he was working under water and then slowly returns him to normal atmospheric pressure.

At depths greater than 40m (130ft) dissolved nitrogen can produce narcosis, a state in which a diver becomes so confused or euphoric that he may even remove his air supply. Narcosis can be avoided by using a mixture of oxygen and helium, but the mixture alters the diver's voice, making his speech almost unintelligible, and causes him to lose body heat rapidly – a hazard in cold waters unless he wears a heated suit.

The deepest dive made at sea to date using self-contained underwater breathing apparatus (SCUBA) gear was 133m (437ft), accomplished in 1968. Much deeper dives have been simulated in compression chambers, in 1970 two Royal Navy divers went to an equivalent of 457m (1,500ft) for ten hours. The "dive" and subsequent decompression took 15 days to complete.

Saturation diving

The disadvantages of the need for decompression after each dive are being overcome by saturation diving techniques. Twenty-four hours' exposure to nitrogen-

1 Edmond Halley's diving bell was 2.4m (8ft) high and 1.5m (5ft) wide at the base. It was wooden with glass portholes and was weighted with lead. Air was supplied from one of two lead-lined barrels. When the first barrel was exhausted it was pulled back to the surface to be refilled.

2 The standard diving suit consists of a heavy metal helmet with breastplate, tough watertight diving dress, heavily weighted boots and a flexible tube carrying air pumped from the surface.

3 The aqualung (or SCUBA) diver wears a rubber suit. Compressed air carried in tanks is delivered at ambient water pressure (equal to that of the surrounding water) via a demand valve.

4 This atmospheric diving suit, dubbed "Jim" by its inventors, has a working depth to 300m (1,000 ft). The articulated arms and legs permit only limited movement; tools are gripped by manipulators. The diver works at surface rather than ambient pressure, which avoids decompression. Soda lime scrubbers remove exhaled CO_2, and oxygen is replenished from two cylinders in the back pack.

5 A submerged decompression chamber can be used to treat an injured diver or one who is suffering from the bends. He can be admitted to the main chamber through an air lock from a portable pressure vessel [left], which has its own bottled air supply. The rate of decompression to ordinary pressure can then be carefully controlled.

free artificial air (such as a mixture of oxygen and helium) under pressure causes a diver to become "saturated" at that pressure. He can remain under pressure for several weeks, greatly increasing his working capacity, after which only one decompression is necessary. Divers working under saturation conditions live in a large deck decompression chamber; they then transfer under pressure into a smaller chamber from which they work. On their return the transfer is reversed.

Underwater habitats such as Conshelf, Tektite [6] and Sealab, are variations on the saturation diving system. The living chamber lies on the sea-bed and divers enter and leave through an entry trunk. These habitats are used mainly for scientific research in depths down to 100m (328ft).

Submersibles for industry and research

Cornelius van Drebble built one of the earliest submersibles in 1620. Powered by 12 oarsmen, it travelled 5m (16ft) below the surface of the Thames. Subsequent development of small submarines was largely directed towards military objectives. Only in the 1960s was much attention paid to the development of submersibles for scientific research or underwater engineering [Key]. Since 1960 more than 50 submersibles have been built with depth ranges from 100m to 2,000m (329–6,560ft) and displacements of between five and 100 tonnes.

The present generation of working submersibles, used in biological and geological research, are mostly in the 10–20 tonne range and carry a pilot and one or two observers who enter the submersible on the mother ship. The interior is at atmospheric pressure throughout the dive.

Since 1973 submersibles have been used increasingly by the offshore oil and natural gas industry for pipeline inspection, repairs and platform site surveys. The serious quest to probe great depths began in 1930 when Otis Barton and William Beebe descended to 425m (1,400ft) off Bermuda in a steel pressure sphere, or bathysphere, lowered on a cable from a ship. On 23 January 1960 Jacques Piccard and Donald Walsh descended 10,917m (35,820ft) to the bottom of the Challenger Deep in the Mariana Trench.

Submersibles are used in both research and engineering. They carry hydraulic arms for handling equipment, TV and photographic cameras. The maximum operational depths of some research submersibles are shown in this diagram.

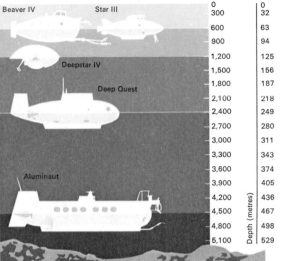

Depth (metres)	Pressure (kg/cm²)
0	0
300	32
600	63
900	94
1,200	125
1,500	156
1,800	187
2,100	218
2,400	249
2,700	280
3,000	311
3,300	343
3,600	374
3,900	405
4,200	436
4,500	467
4,800	498
5,100	529

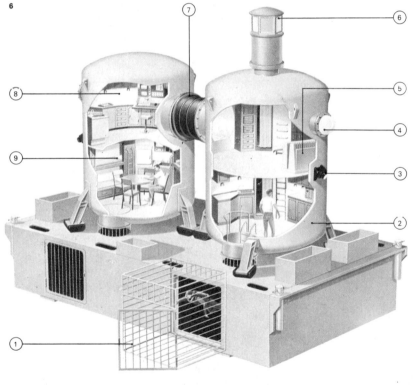

1 Shark cage protecting the entrance
2 Wet room
3 External light
4 Observation port
5 Air conditioning and purification equipment
6 Beacon light
7 Connecting passage
8 Control and communication room
9 Living quarters

6 Tektite was designed to study the reactions of scientists working underwater for long periods under saturated diving conditions. It has four chambers and accommodates four or five people.

7 The submersible Pisces III is 5.8m (19ft) long, weighs 10.8 tonnes and has a maximum operating depth of 1,100m (3,600ft). It is launched from an A-frame at the stern of the mother ship.

8 The bathyscaphe FRNS 3 consists of a pressure sphere fitted with an entrance hatch and a conical Plexiglas window. Entry is through an air lock. The buoyancy tanks are in compartments built of light sheet metal and filled with petrol for buoyancy. To descend, the remaining tanks and air lock are flooded. Electric motors provide lateral movement at depth and lead shot ballast is jettisoned for ascent.

9 The submersible VOL L-1 operates down to 365m (1,200ft). The pilot, diving supervisor and observer travel in the forward compartment at atmospheric pressure while the two divers in the lockout are pressurized to the working depth.

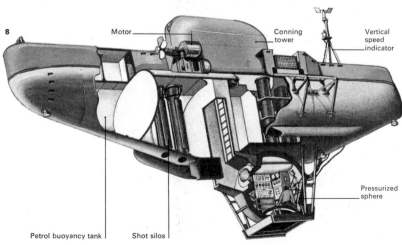

Motor
Conning tower
Vertical speed indicator
Pressurized sphere
Petrol buoyancy tank
Shot silos

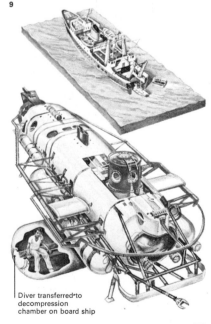

Diver transferred to decompression chamber on board ship

Shapes and structures of crystals

Most solid matter is composed of crystals. Table salt and sugar are perhaps the most obviously crystalline substances in common use, but even substances such as clay and steel are made up of crystals. It is often difficult to recognize that a substance is crystalline; the basic regularity of its true form is frequently masked because a number of minute crystals aggregate to produce no particular shape.

Many minerals however, crystallize in nature in set shapes, and well-formed crystals can be grown artificially. The science of crystallography began when the Danish scientist Nicolaus Steno (1638–86) discovered in 1699 that the angles between the faces in different quartz crystals are constant. In 1783, the Frenchman Jean-Baptiste Louis Romé de l'Isle (1736-90) established that the angles between the faces of a crystal are characteristic of the substance of which it is formed. Another Frenchman, the abbot René Just Haüy (1743–1822), explained that the angles between the faces are constant because a crystal is composed of tiny identical blocks of substance (known today as unit cells) packed together in a regular array. He also described the seven basic crystal systems [2–8] and the principles of their symmetry. In 1912, crystallography became an important branch of science with the discovery by the German physicist Max von Laue (1879–1960) that the internal structure of crystals could be revealed by X-ray diffraction [9]. The principles of this method were largely developed by William Henry Bragg (1862–1942), a Briton, and his Australian son, William Lawrence (1890–1971). X-ray analysis of metals has since given us an understanding of the properties of alloys, and the determination of the structure of nucleic acids and proteins an insight into the workings of the body.

Crystal lattices and crystal systems

Within a crystal, particles (atoms, ions or molecules) are arrayed in similarly oriented identical unit cells [1] to make up a lattice or network of particles. For example, the unit cell of a crystal of halite (common salt or sodium chloride) can be considered as a cube [9D] with eight chloride ions [red] at the corners plus another six at the centres of the faces. Twelve sodium ions [black] lie at the centres of the edges of the cube and one more in the centre of the cube itself. All the particles except the central ion are shared by the adjacent unit cells.

The external shape of a well-formed crystal reflects precisely the symmetry, although not necessarily the shape, of the unit cell. The unit cell of sodium chloride is a cube, but the crystal shape of halite may be either a cube or some other form with the same kind of symmetry, such as an octahedron.

The elements of symmetry that can be found in crystals are axes, planes and centres. A unit cell or crystal has an axis of symmetry if it can be rotated by an angle of less than 360° and produce an identical configuration. A plane of symmetry is like a mirror; on either side of the plane, the shapes of the unit cell or crystal are mirror images of each other. A centre of symmetry is such that every feature of a crystal or unit cell is repeated upside down on the other side of the centre at an equal distance from it. Combinations of these elements give rise to 32 crystal classes, which

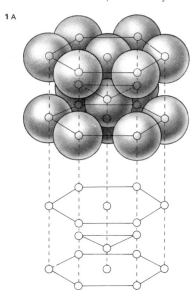

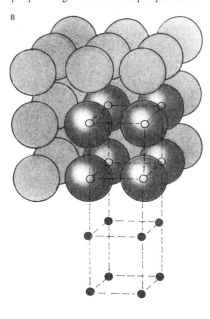

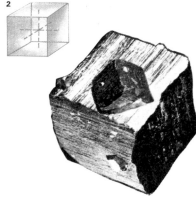

1A   B

1 Crystals are formed by the regular repetition of identical building blocks. The regularity of the three-dimensional array is described by the lattice, here hexagonal [A] and simple cubic [B]. The pictures show how the smallest possible building block, the unit cell, can be stacked to reproduce the crystal. Within the unit cell there may be one or more atoms, or ions, or molecules. The simplest crystals, such as copper, silver and gold, have a single atom in the unit cell. Inorganic crystals may have up to, perhaps, 100 atoms or molecules, and organic compounds such as proteins may have up to 100,000 atoms within each unit cell.

2 Pyrite (iron sulphide) crystallizes in the cubic system. The unit cell is such that all the axes are of equal length and the angles between them are 90°. Of the seven crystalline systems, only the cubic one does not polarize light passing through it. Cubic crystals sometimes exhibit the related octahedron and dodecahedron shapes. Garnet, halite and fluorite are also cubic.

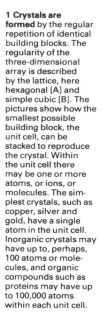

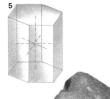

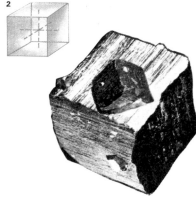

3   4   5   6

3 Chalcopyrite (copper iron sulphide) belongs to the tetragonal system. The unit cell is a straight prism on a square base.

4 Calcite (calcium carbonate) crystallizes in the trigonal system. The unit cell is like a cube stretched along a solid diagonal.

5 Beryl (beryllium silicate) belongs to the hexagonal system. The unit cell is a hexagonal prism.

6 Topaz (aluminium silicate and fluoride) belongs to the orthorhombic system. The unit cell is a straight prism on a rectangular base.

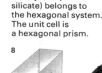

7   8

7 Augite, a calcium, magnesium, iron, alumino-silicate of the pyroxene family, crystallizes in the monoclinic system. The unit cell is a straight prism on a parallelogram base.

8 Chalconthite, a form of blue hydrated copper sulphate, belongs to the triclinic system. The unit cell has three axes of different lengths, none of which is at right-angles.

can be grouped into one of the seven different crystal systems.

X-ray diffraction

X-rays are used to determine the shape and size of unit cells and the positions of the particles within them because X-rays have wavelengths of the same size as the distances between adjacent parallel lattice planes in crystals. A rotating single crystal is irradiated in a homogeneous X-ray beam [9A]. The beam is diffracted (bent) as it passes between the particles in adjacent planes [9B], acting as if it were reflected from the planes, and interference produces a pattern of varying intensities that is recorded on a cylindrical photographic film [9A] or a flat plate [9C] or by detecting instruments. At maximum intensity, the distance d between the planes, the wavelength λ of the X-rays and the angle of the incidence θ of the beam on the planes are related by Bragg's law: $\lambda = 2d \sin \theta$. By using X-rays of known wavelengths and measuring the angles of incidence at which diffraction occurs, it is possible to calculate the distances between the planes and the sizes and positions of the particles. Fourier synthesis (a mathematical computation) of the many diffracted X-ray intensities yields a contour picture of the atoms or ions in a molecule or unit cell of a crystal [13].

The properties of crystals

The size and configuration of crystals in a metal affect its mechanical properties: stress behaviour, fatigue and resistance depend on the crystals. Impurities in the lattice, in concentrations of only a few parts per thousand million, account for the electrical properties of semiconductors. The magnetic properties of many materials are influenced by the internal disposition and shapes of crystals. Some crystals respond to vibrations by generating electricity (piezo-electricity) and this is the principle behind some record-player pickups; the converse is used in ultrasonic transducers and radio-tuning and clock-regulating crystals. Transparent crystals of all systems except the cubic rotate the plane of polarized light. Polaroid polarizing sheets or glasses (as used in sunglasses) contain very small oriented crystals.

Crystal shapes, when apparent, are related to the underlying lattice forming them, but the same lattice can produce different shapes. The dogtooth calcite shown here has the same lattice as the Iceland-spar calcite shown in illustration 4. Both types of crystals have the same internal symmetry.

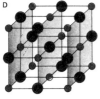
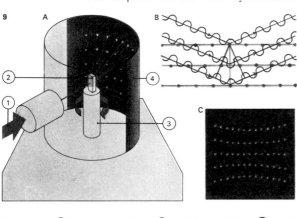

9 X-rays are scattered in various directions by crystal lattices, depending on the distance between the lattice planes. In diffraction apparatus [A], the source [1] generates single-wavelength X-rays to hit an oriented crystal [2] on a revolving support [3]. Diffraction occurs as the beam passes between the lattice planes [B] in accordance with Bragg's law. The diffracted rays are in phase at certain angles, producing rows of spots on a cylindrical photographic film [4] or curved lines of spots on a flat plate [C]. Different planes [D] with different orientations may exist within the same crystal.

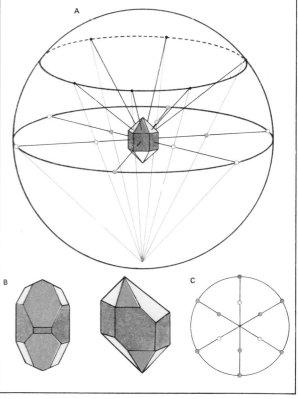

10 Stereographic projection represents a three-dimensional crystal as a two-dimensional figure. The mathematics are quite complex but in theory the crystal is placed at the centre of a sphere and lines drawn from its centre, perpendicular to each face, are extended to the surface of the sphere [A]. The points so produced at the equator of the sphere and over the northern hemisphere are then connected to the south pole. The points at which these connecting lines cut the equatorial plane form a pattern. This pattern is the stereographic projection of the crystal [C]. In any crystal the angles between the corresponding faces are always equal no matter how distorted the crystal may be, and so the stereographic projection will always be the same. Hence the two distorted crystals of quartz [B], despite the differences in size of their corresponding faces, will produce the same projection.

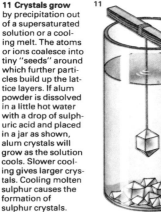

11 Crystals grow by precipitation out of a supersaturated solution or a cooling melt. The atoms or ions coalesce into tiny "seeds" around which further particles build up the lattice layers. If alum powder is dissolved in a little hot water with a drop of sulphuric acid and placed in a jar as shown, alum crystals will grow as the solution cools. Slower cooling gives larger crystals. Cooling molten sulphur causes the formation of sulphur crystals.

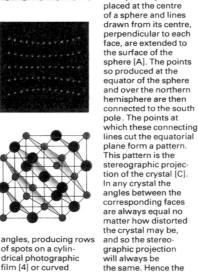

12 The colours of mineral crystals in a thin section of rock viewed through a polarizing microscope can help to identify the minerals in that rock section. Polarized light (light vibrating in one plane) passing through the microscope and through the thin section is distorted by the internal structure of the crystals and these distortions give rise to the colours observed. In this example the large yellow crystals are of pyroxine while the small grey ones are of felspar.

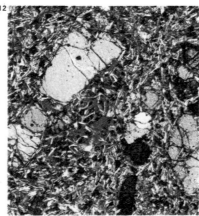
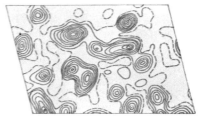

13 An electron density map is like a contour map, showing not the height of mountains but the distribution of electron density within the atoms, ions or molecules that make up the crystal. The map is derived mathematically, using the intensities and positions of the X-ray diffraction spots. A large number of rings implies a lot of electrons – either an atom or ion – or several seen end-on.

Earth's minerals

A rock is not a homogeneous mass of material with a constant chemical composition throughout its bulk. If a rock is examined closely it is seen to be made of many components, each quite different from the others and usually forming discrete crystals. These individual components are the minerals.

The economic minerals such as precious stones and the ores of useful metals are those that usually come to mind when minerals are mentioned, but these actually represent a small part of the mineral kingdom. The largest components are the rock-forming minerals, the building blocks from which the earth's crust and all its rocks are constructed. These can be so attractive, with their great variety of crystal shapes and range of colours, that finding and collecting minerals has been a popular hobby for thousands of years.

The constituents of the rocks

Minerals are defined as naturally occurring inorganic substances made up of one or more elements. Most have a constant chemical composition and are usually crystalline [1]. There are exceptions to this, however. Some minerals, such as opal [1B], are non-crystalline and in others the chemical composition varies: in olivines and pyroxenes, for example, the proportions of magnesium and iron atoms are not constant.

The quantities of the earth's elements are reflected in their relative abundance in minerals. The element oxygen is most abundant, thus a large number of minerals contain oxygen. Haematite [7] is an oxide of iron. Silicon is the next most abundant, so silica, the oxide of silicon, plays a large part in the composition of minerals. Quartz [2, 3] can be pure silica and is an extremely common mineral but the silica is more often found in combination with other elements to produce the numerous rock-forming minerals known as silicates. Olivine, for instance, is a common silicate mineral in igneous rocks where no pure quartz is present and consists of silica combined with varying amounts of iron and magnesium. Other groups of minerals found are compounds of sulphur such as anhydrite, gypsum [13] and galena [9] and carbonates such as calcite and malachite [1C, 12]. Occasionally, as with native copper and gold [8], a mineral has only one element.

Many minerals crystallize from the molten state. The overall composition of magma, the molten material from which igneous rocks are formed, is fairly constant but when it starts to solidify the minerals that crystallize out vary greatly from place to place. The resulting rock has a composition very different from that of another rock formed elsewhere from the same magma.

The formation of minerals

Olivines have a high melting-point so they tend to crystallize first from a cooling magma. Once crystallized they may sink to the bottom of the magma chamber and leave the rest of the liquid deficient in iron and magnesium. Other minerals such as felspar [3, 14B], in which sodium, calcium, potassium and aluminium combine with what silica is left, then crystallize out, leaving a cooling magma with yet another composition that solidifies into even more minerals.

Some minerals are formed in sedimentary environments. For example, when seawater evaporates in restricted basins the salts dis-

1 A crystal is a solid in which the molecules, atoms or ions are arranged along regular and repetitive lattices, its external shape reflecting its internal symmetry. Not all crystals

are minerals – sugar [A] is a crystalline organic substance. Opal [B] is an "amorphous" mineral without a crystalline internal structure. Calcite [C], as most minerals, is crystalline.

2 Where a mineral such as quartz grows unimpeded it shows its typical "automorphic" shape, with plane faces that reflect the internal lattice structure of its atoms.

3 The last minerals to crystallize in a rock are crowded by the others and are xenomorphic – unable to assume their normal external crystalline form. They have irregular shapes

although the internal crystalline lattice is retained. This section of granite contains xenomorphic quartz crystals [shown grey] surrounded by automorphic felspar crystals.

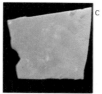

4 Pseudomorphism is the replacement of one mineral with an external crystal shape by another that is in every way identical in shape and volume, but not in internal crystalline lattice.

The quartz shown is forming a pseudomorph of a fluorite crystal that was dissolved. The quartz would normally form a six-sided prism but has filled the octahedral shape of the fluorite.

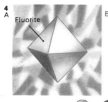
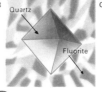

- Ca A
- O
- C

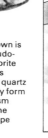
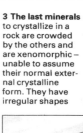

- Na B
- O
- N

5 Minerals of different chemical composition may possess identical lattice structures and will have similarly shaped crystal faces under normal circumstances. This is called isomorphism and is shown for calcite

[A] and soda-nitre [B] crystals. Because of a near similarity in size the ions of isomorphic minerals can readily substitute for each other in the structure of a crystal if they are also chemically similar.

6 Compounds that can assume more than one crystalline structure are said to be polymorphous and they form three different kinds of minerals. The type of crystal lattice in which the compound will crystallize is determined

by the pressure and temperature at the time of formation. Kyanite, sillimanite and andalusite are three different crystal types and minerals of the same silicate compound that is common in metamorphic rocks.

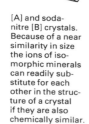

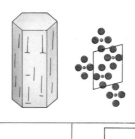
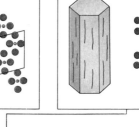

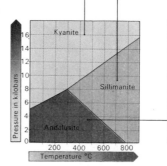
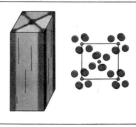

Kyanite
Sillimanite
Andalusite

Pressure in kilobars
16
14
12
10
8
6
4
2
0
200   400   600   800
Temperature °C

- Oxygen
- Aluminium

solved in it are crystallized out and form sedimentary rocks consisting of minerals such as halite (sodium chloride) and gypsum (hydrated calcium sulphate).

Other minerals form under metamorphic conditions where the minerals of rocks already formed are altered by heat or pressure to produce new minerals. Kyanite (an aluminium silicate) is found in schists formed under great pressure while andalusite (which has the same chemical composition) is formed when rocks are altered under conditions of moderate heat and low pressure [6].

Related to the metamorphic minerals are those formed by metasomatism – the movement of hot fluids from igneous bodies through rocks already present. Quartz is often formed by these movements as well as by the more usual process of direct crystallization from a molten magma [3].

Mineral identification

There are many different ways in which minerals can be recognized and identified even by an amateur. The crystal shape is the best clue, but it is rarely well defined because

the minerals usually suffer from the effects of weather before they are studied, or lack definite shapes due to being formed too close to other growing crystals. Akin to this is the way a mineral breaks, the fractures formed being related to the crystal lattice.

The hardness of a mineral is significant in identification and can be determined by the mineralogist; he finds out whether the mineral can be scratched by a number of different substances whose hardnesses are known. The colour is not usually definitive because impurities almost invariably creep in to the mineral as it is formed and discolour it. But when a mineral is scratched against a white surface it leaves a streak of colour that is usually distinctive. The lustre – the way in which the light is reflected from the surface – is different in different minerals. Quartz has a glassy lustre while mica [14C] can be pearly or metallic in appearance.

These diagnostic features are used by the geologist and amateur collector in the field to make tentative identifications. It is only when the specimen is back in the laboratory that its chemical composition can be investigated.

An open-pit copper mine in Montana, USA, produces ore in the form of the sulphide minerals of copper. Where an exploitable mineral occurs near the surface it can be extracted in this way; once the overburden of soil and rock is removed the exposed ore is blasted loose or – if soft enough – scooped up by machinery. Minerals such as bauxite, iron and gypsum are mined in open-cast pits.

7 Mineral identification seldom needs the complexities of a laboratory and is in fact an easy and fascinating hobby. Haematite, an iron ore, is identified by its colour, hardness and density. Rubbed against a piece of unglazed china, it leaves a dark red streak. It scratches glass but is not scratched by a knife. It is heavy. In further tests, powdered and heated in a blue (reducing) flame it becomes magnetite and will be picked up by a magnet after cooling. Heated in concentrated hydrochloric acid it will dissolve and colour the acid rust. Cut into thin sections in laboratory tests it will be shown to be black or red in transmitted light, but bright and metallic when exposed to reflected light.

8 Gold – like silver, copper and sulphur – is a naturally occurring native element found in igneous formations but at such low concentrations that it can hardly be said to be an ore.

9 Galena is lead sulphide; sulphides are formed by the combination of one or more metals with sulphur and provide many commercially valuable ores. Galena is widely used in electronics.

12 Malachite is a copper carbonate. Carbonates, which are second only to silicates in abundance, are formed by carbon, oxygen and one or more metals and sometimes water.

13 Sulphates are made of a sulphur oxide combined with a metal; gypsum, which also contains water, is the most common. Barite can assume shapes like the "desert rose" shown here.

10 Oxygen combined with one or more metals forms the oxide minerals. Cassiterite (SnO_2), a reddish-brown mineral with a distinctive, pyramid-ended structure, is tin oxide.

11 Rock salt or halite is sodium chloride, a mineral found in thick deposits precipitated during the evaporation of shallow seas and lakes, such as those in Utah, USA.

14 Silicates are by far the most common and important rock-forming minerals. Their basic framework is the tetrahedron formed by silicon surrounded by four oxygen atoms. These tetrahedrons can form chains as in asbestos [A], sheets as in mica [C] and three-dimensional structures as in orthoclase felspar [B] and quartz. Felspars are the most abundant of rock-forming minerals in the earth's crust.

Gems and semi-precious stones

Gems are valued by man for their beauty, rarity and durability. The most precious gems are naturally occurring minerals such as diamonds, emeralds, sapphires and rubies. Some organic substances are also considered to be gems: amber is a fossil resin, coral is made by tiny sea creatures and pearls are formed from nacre, the iridescent substance forming the inner layer of many sea shells, especially the oyster. Fashion often determines the popularity of gems. Jet, a hard, shiny black fossilized wood, was widely used in jewellery in the years after 1861, when Queen Victoria was in mourning.

Formation of gems
Gems that are of inorganic origin and occur as natural minerals are formed in several different ways. Many gems are found in igneous rock, that is, rock formed directly from magma that has welled up from the earth's interior and solidified beneath the surface. As magma cools, the elements tend to separate into regions where they form different minerals. Pockets of gases and superheated water often dissolve many ele-

ments; these finally cool and combine to form precious and semi-precious minerals. Pegmatites – light-coloured, coarse-grained igneous rocks – are formed by superheated gas and water and they often contain stocks of gems including beryl, quartz, tourmaline and felspar. Gases in the cooling pegmatites help form minerals such as the fluorine-bearing topaz and tourmaline [6].

Other gems are formed when heat, pressure or chemical action alter the structure of existing rocks causing them to recrystallize or re-form in different ways as metamorphic rocks. Olivine [14] (also common in lavas), emerald and garnet [7] are found in metamorphic rocks. Great heat and pressure were probably responsible for diamond formation from carbon in kimberlite [3]. Many gem materials, including diamond, are found as crystals or rolled pebbles in alluvial gravels of river beds.

Properties of gems
Gem minerals can be identified by a number of qualities such as the shape of the uncut crystals, their colour, hardness, refractive

index and specific gravity (density). A gem's value is established by rarity, brilliance, purity, colour and hardness. Demand also determines the value of a gem; diamonds are in constant demand for industrial use as cutting instruments as well as for jewellery.

One of the main factors that determines the beauty of a gem is its properties with regard to light – namely, how light is reflected, refracted (bent) and dispersed (split up) into the spectrum by the gem. Each stone has its own refractive index. This index is measured by dividing the sine of the angle of incidence (the angle between the ray of light and the normal, which is a line drawn perpendicular to the surface) by the sine of the angle of refraction. Of all natural gems diamond has the highest index of refraction. Its ability to disperse white light gives the diamond its special fire, or flashes of spectral colour and characteristic brilliance.

The colours of diamonds are generally due to a lattice defect in the crystal and rarely to trace elements. Most other gemstones are coloured by metal oxides that are either impurities or components. Colour, however,

1
- ◆ Diamond
- ● Ruby
- ▲ Sapphire
- ■ Emerald
- ● Turquoise
- ▲ Pegmatite gems
- ■ Malachite
- ◆ Zircon
- ▲ Lapis lazuli
- ● Amber

- ◆ Rhodochrosite
- ■ Garnet
- ○ Cordièrite
- □ Quartz
- ◇ Opal
- △ Chalcedony
- ○ Jade
- △ Amethyst
- □ Peridot

1 The gem-producing regions of the world are shown on the map. The diamond, ruby, sapphire and emerald are classed as precious stones; all the other gems are classed as semi-precious stones.

2 The Kimberley Great Hole is a disused diamond mine 300m (1,000ft) deep. Diamonds were found at Kimberley in 1871 and some three tonnes of gems were removed before work ended in 1909.

3 Diamonds are made by intense heat and pressures in volcanic plugs or kimberlite pipes, deep below the earth's crust [A]. As pressure increases gas collects in fissures and explodes, forming a hollow in

the earth's surface [B]. Diamond-bearing kimberlite wells up the fissures [C] to fill the cavity [D]. The kimberlite may rise above the surface [E]. Shafts are sunk for easier access to it [F].

4 A rough diamond is cut to shape along the cleavage planes [A]. These are first grooved [B] and then cleaved with a blade [C] until a workable shape [D] is obtained. Cutting is done first with a coarse [E] and

then a fine [F] saw to give the final shape [G, H, I, J]. Polishing is done on a lap [K], covered in diamond powder, producing the facets [L, M] that reflect light from the interior giving the stone its fire [N].

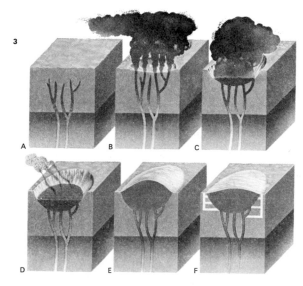

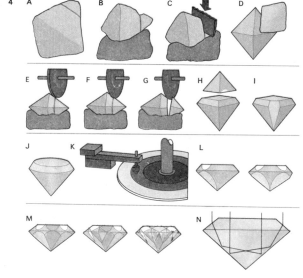

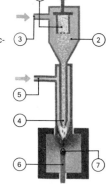

5 Synthetic gems are produced by a flame-fusion process, known as Verneuil's method, after the inventor. Alumina powder in the container [1] falls into the chamber [2]. Oxygen [3] mixes with the alumina and carries it to the tip of the torch [4] where it burns with hydrogen entering through the tube [5]. In the intense heat produced, the fine alumina particles fuse into gem droplets and fall onto a support [6] on which the body of the gem is being formed [7].

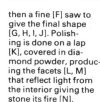

is the feature that gives many gems their special quality. The transparent red ruby [13] and the blue sapphire [15] (both of which are forms of a normally dull, grey or colourless mineral called corundum), the green emerald, a form of the mineral beryl and the yellow topaz are all admired because of their pure tints. Opaque or cloudy gems such as opals depend entirely upon their colour to make them attractive.

Specific gravity is the weight of the mineral compared with the weight of an equal amount of pure water. Diamond, for example, has a specific gravity of 3.52 which means that it weighs 3.52 times an equal amount of pure water, whereas amber has a specific gravity of 1.07. The weight of a diamond is usually expressed in carats – one carat is equivalent to 200 milligrammes.

Hardness ensures durability and accordingly the most valuable gems are stones that will wear for a long time. Hardness is measured on the Moh's scale, which consists of numbers from one to ten, indicating the relative hardness of substances. The diamond has a hardness of ten on this scale and is by far the hardest of all natural substances. It is about 90 times harder than corundum, which rates as nine on the scale. Some gems are quite soft and are valued for other properties.

Polishing and cutting of gems

The beauty of gems is greatly enhanced by skilful cutting and polishing [4], for this removes the surface flaws and heightens the colour or brilliance of a stone. The oldest form in which gems were cut was a rounded shape called *cabochon*, a French word for head. The *cabochon* is used for stones showing the effects of chatoyancy (cat's-eyes) and asterism (star-stones), which are caused by reflections from inclusions.

Faceting – first started by Indian cutters polishing small facets on diamonds – soon became applied to other stones. Thus evolved the brilliant, step and mixed cuts, which depend on various facets being ground and polished in symmetrical arrangements on the stones. The facets on a diamond are cut and polished in one operation but other precious stones have their facets first ground and then subsequently highly polished.

The largest cut diamond in the world is the Star of Africa, weighing a little over 530 carats. It came from the biggest diamond ever found, the Cullinan. This stone, found in 1905 in the Premier mine, South Africa, was named after Thomas Cullinan, chairman of the mining company. It weighed 3,106 metric carats (0.60kg [1.3lb]) but was cut into two large stones, seven medium, and 96 smaller stones. The largest of these, the Star of Africa, is now among the British Crown Jewels in the Tower of London. Another diamond in this collection is the Indian diamond Koh-i-noor (Mountain of Light), which was given to Queen Victoria in 1850 by the East India Company.

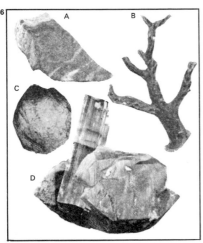

6 Most gems are minerals. Lapis lazuli [A] is the name given to a rock rich in lazurite. Tourmaline [D] is a complex boro-silicate. Organic gems include coral [B] (the skeletons of coral polyps) and amber [C] which is a fossil resin.

7 Garnet [A], the birthstone for January, symbolizes faithfulness. Garnets are formed from silica and two metals [B]. Those with aluminium and magnesium are the prized ruby-red pyrope.

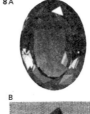

8 Amethyst [A], the birthstone for February, symbolizes sincerity. Amethysts are a form of transparent quartz [B], with a violet or purple colour. They are mined in USSR and South America.

9 Aquamarine [A], one of the March birthstones, symbolizes courage. Aquamarines are a blue or blue-green variety of the mineral beryl [B]. The best are mined in Brazil and the Urals.

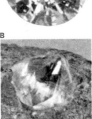

10 Diamond [A], the April birthstone, symbolizes innocence. Diamonds are pure crystalized carbon [B], the hardest natural substance. South Africa is the main source. The most prized are colourless.

11 Emerald [A], the birthstone for May, represents love. Emerald is a gem-quality, rare green variety of the mineral beryl [B]. The best emeralds occur in Colombia in South America.

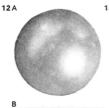
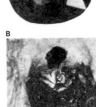

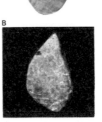
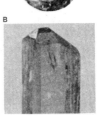

12 Pearl [A], one of the June birthstones, symbolizes health. Pearls are organic gems produced mainly by oysters [B] from nacre, the iridescent substance forming the inner layer of the shell. Pearls are prized for their lustre.

13 Ruby [A], the July birthstone, represents contentment. Ruby is a red variety of the hard grey or colourless aluminium oxide mineral, corundum [B]. The finest rubies, from Burma, are coloured a deep bluish-red by a chromium impurity.

14 Peridot [A] is one of the birthstones for August. It symbolizes married happiness. Peridots are a transparent green variety of the mineral olivine [B], which is a magnesium-iron silicate, finest come from Burma and Thailand.

15 Sapphire [A], the September birthstone, represents clear thinking. Sapphire, like ruby, is a variety of the mineral corundum [B]. It occurs in many colours but the most valued are blue. The best kinds come from Burma and Thailand.

16 Opal [A] is the October birthstone. It symbolizes hope. Opals are a form of hydrated silica [B]. The most prized specimens are the so-called black opals found in Australia, which show flashes of several iridescent colours.

17 Topaz [A], the birthstone for November, symbolizes fidelity. The most prized varieties are yellow. Topaz is a mineral compound of aluminium, silica and fluorine [B]. It is found mainly in Brazil, USSR and the United States.

18 Turquoise [A], the birthstone for December, represents prosperity. Turquoise is a hydrous copper-aluminium phosphate [B] sometimes containing iron. The most prized colour is sky blue and comes from Iran. Its name means Turkish stone.

The rock cycle and igneous rocks

The rocks on the earth's surface can be divided into three kinds: igneous, metamorphic and sedimentary. Igneous rocks have formed by the cooling of molten magma [3]. Metamorphic rocks have formed by the baking or the compression of older rocks. New crystals have grown in the rock and because these were under pressure they grew in only one direction and are thus aligned. Sedimentary rocks are composed of the weathered or eroded fragments of older rocks or of the remains of living organisms.

Each of these three classes formed under very different conditions from the others. Sedimentary rocks formed on the surface of the earth under extremely low pressures, metamorphic rocks formed below the surface where both the temperature and pressure are high, and intrusive igneous rocks formed, again beneath the earth's surface, but where the temperatures are even higher.

Rock cycle

The rock cycle [2] is the relationship between these three types of rocks. The first part of the rock cycle takes place on the earth's sur-face. This is the erosion and weathering of older rocks to soil and sand and the transportation of the resulting sediment by rivers down to the sea. Nearly all the sediment produced, whether on the land or along the coast, is eventually transported to deep basins under the sea. In these areas great thicknesses of sediment accumulate. For instance, the Mississippi has been pouring sediment into the Gulf of Mexico at the rate of approximately 500 million tonnes a year for the last 150 million years. The pile of sediment is now 12km (7 miles) thick.

Formation of rocks from sediments

The water circulating through the sand deposits iron oxide, silica or lime between the grains and this "cements" the loose sand into sandstone. Mud is squeezed by the weight of the sediment above until all the water is pressed out and it becomes shale. This process of changing sediment into rock is called lithification.

Most great thicknesses of sedimentary rocks accumulate in long, narrow depressions on the sea-floor called geosynclines. These depressions are caused by descending convection currents which, over a period of millions of years, carry the crust of the earth down into the earth's interior where both the pressure and temperature are high. The sedimentary rock in the depression is carried down with the crust. It is folded and squeezed and heated up to between 200°C (392°F) and 500°C (932°F). This changes the sedimentary rock to a metamorphic rock.

The movement of the earth's crust may carry the rock as much as 700km (454 miles) below the surface. Here the temperature and pressure will be even higher and the rock will begin to melt. Molten rock is lighter than solid rock and it will begin to rise up through the overlying rock towards the surface. If it reaches the surface as a lava flow it will immediately be ready for weathering and erosion and the start of a new cycle. More often the molten rock solidifies underground and then all the rock above it must be eroded away before it can begin the cycle again.

Although the complete cycle is from sedimentary to metamorphic to igneous, many rocks short-cut the cycle, usually by

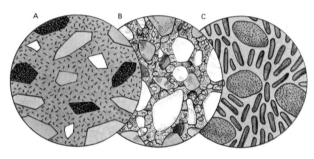

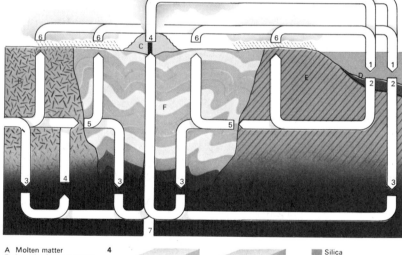

1 Textures can be used to identify rock types. Igneous rocks [A] show well-developed crystals, sedimentary [B] contain older pieces and metamorphic [C] show the stresses under which they formed.

2 The rock cycle is the slow change from one rock type to another. Erosion produces sediments which harden to form sedimentary rocks. If these are deeply buried the temperature and pressure turn them into metamorphic rocks. Intense heat at great depths melts metamorphic rocks. This rock may be pushed up to the surface where it cools to form igneous rocks. There erosion begins the cycle again.

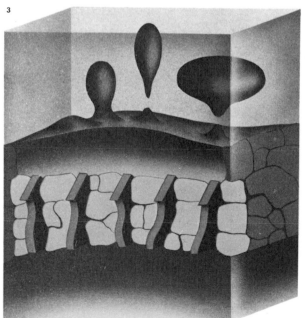

A Molten matter
B Intrusive igneous rocks
C Extrusive igneous rocks
D Sediments
E Sedimentary rocks
F Metamorphic rocks

1 Deposition
2 Lithification
3 Fusion
4 Solidification
5 Metamorphism
6 Erosion
7 Emplacement of new material from earth's interior

3 Granite is the most abundant igneous rock. It is formed by the partial melting of older deeply buried rocks. Initially, the molten liquid stays between the remaining grains but later it migrates to form small pods which in turn collect together into layers. Because the liquid is lighter than the surrounding rock it rises upwards and intrudes the rock above, forming large masses called batholiths.

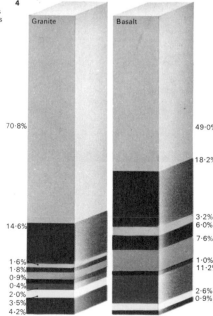

Silica
Alumina
Ferric oxide
Ferrous oxide
Magnesia
Titanium oxide
Calcium oxide
Sodium oxide
Potassium oxide

Granite 70·8%
14·6%
1·6%
1·8%
0·9%
0·4%
2·0%
3·5%
4·2%

Basalt 49·0%
18·2%
3·2%
6·0%
7·6%
1·0%
11·2%
2·6%
0·9%

4 Basalt and granite are the two commonest rocks found on the earth's surface. Both rocks are composed mostly of the elements silicon and oxygen. These are combined with minor amounts of other elements into natural chemical compounds called minerals. Basalts occur either as lava flows or dikes, while granites occur as batholiths.

missing out the igneous or metamorphic stages. For instance, a sediment may be lithified to a sandstone but then may be uplifted out of the sea and eroded.

Igneous rocks

Igneous rocks [5] are divided into extrusive and intrusive rocks. Extrusive rocks are those that were ejected by volcanoes and cooled as lavas on the surface of the earth. Intrusive rocks are those that solidified beneath the earth's surface. The grain or crystal size of a rock depends on how fast it cooled; coarse-grained rocks are the result of slow cooling which has given crystals time to grow to sizes greater than two millimetres in length. Rocks cool slowly when deep in the earth's crust and coarseness is characteristic of intrusive rocks. Fine-grained rocks have cooled rapidly either on or near the earth's surface; most extrusive rocks are fine grained although some are cooled so rapidly that no crystals have time to grow and obsidian is formed.

Igneous rocks are classified by the amount of silica they contain [6], and the size of the grains. The chemical composition [4]

and the silica content in particular depends on the origin of the magma from which the rock was made. The magma may have resulted from the partial melting of the rocks beneath the earth's crust or from the melting of the crust itself as part of the rock cycle. Magma from the crust contains more silica than that from below it and produces light coloured rocks, whereas the magma from below the crust gives dark-coloured rocks.

The partial melting of the rocks beneath the earth's crust produces basalts (fine-grained extrusive lavas), dolerite (medium-grained intrusive rock) and gabbro (coarse-grained intrusive rock) [7]. Basalts form the floors to the oceans and occur extensively in Iceland and in some continental areas. Dolerites are found in thin extensive sheets called dikes and sills [5] injected in or between the sedimentary rock layers. Gabbro occurs in large layered intrusions which were the source of the dolerite and basalt.

The melting of rocks which were once sediments on the crust produces granites [3] and andesites. Granites occur in very large intrusions called batholiths [5].

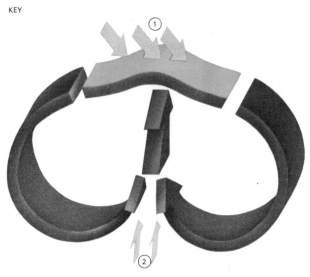

The energy to power the rock cycle is derived from the heat of the sun [1], which indirectly breaks down existing rocks to sediments, and the heat from the earth's interior [2], due to radioactivity which melts existing material to give igneous rock and also causes the movements of the earth's crust.

6 Igneous rocks comprise varying amounts of minerals in which the quantity of silica (SiO_2) determines the acidity of the rock and thus its classification. This proportion of silica determines the type

Intermediate (Diorite)

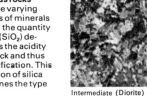

Acidic (Granite)

6

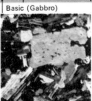

and proportion of the minerals present. Thin rock sections examined by polarized light reveal the individual minerals in distinctive colours, helping to identify them and to classify the rock.

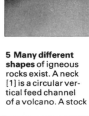

5 Many different shapes of igneous rocks exist. A neck [1] is a circular vertical feed channel of a volcano. A stock [2] is a large mass of rock which solidified at great depth. A batholith [3] is a large body of granite with no detectable bottom. A laccolith [4, 7] is a dome-shaped mass which has arched up the rock above. A dike [5] is a vertical sheet-like mass of rock and sill [6] is a horizontal sheet-shaped body of rock. A lopolith [8] is a saucer-shaped mass of rock.

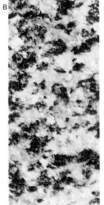

7 Intrusive rocks can often be identified with the naked eye. Granite [A] contains a great deal of free silica in the form of quartz, giving the rock a light colour. Diorite [B] is darker, having less quartz and a quantity of dark minerals. These dark minerals, such as olivine and pyroxine, are more common in gabbro [C]. The light-coloured minerals in this are felspars. Ultrabasic rocks such as dunite [D] consist almost entirely of dark ferro-magnesium minerals.

Sedimentary and metamorphic rocks

The rocks of the earth's surface are of three sorts: igneous (formed from molten magma), sedimentary and metamorphic [Key]. Sedimentary rocks are formed from chemicals, organic materials and fragments produced by the weathering and erosion of older rocks; metamorphic rocks by the heating under pressure of older rocks.

Sedimentary rocks are divided into three types [1]. The first, which is called clastic, is formed by fragments of older rocks; the second is organic, composed of the remains of animals or plants; and the third is chemical, produced by the precipitation of minerals and salts from water. Streams, moving ice and waves, break up older rocks into fragments, some large, like stones or boulders, some about 1mm (0.04in) across, like sand, and some too fine to see, which form mud. Most of these are carried down to the sea by rivers and deposited in deltas or farther out in the sea-bed. Stones too large to be moved by the water remain near the heads of streams or on beaches and are eventually cemented together to form a rock known as conglomerate. Sand is deposited near the coast or on the continental shelf and eventually forms sandstone. Sands are also deposited by wind in desert environments. Mud is often carried far from the shore to become clay or shale.

Plant and animal origins

Organic sedimentary rocks may be made of plant remains, like coal, or from the hard parts of animals; many limestones are made of fossil shells and corals which have extracted lime from seawater to make their skeletons and, dying, have left their remains on the sea-floor. In time the movement of the sea wears the shells into fragments. Over a period of millions of years after burial, the fragments are compacted by weight and cemented to one another by various processes to give limestone. This is called lithification. Accumulation of lime is at present taking place in the Bahamas and the Persian Gulf, but in the past warm seas were much more extensive and limestone was produced over large areas. Chalk is made of countless small shells so minute that they can be seen only with a microscope. Seawater contains large amounts of salts and, if it is evaporated, they are precipitated out as lime is precipitated in a kettle. In tropical areas where hot, dry winds blow over shallow seas, much of the water is evaporated and lime forms on the sea-floor, hardening to a fine-grained limestone [4]. If there is a partially enclosed basin, then not only lime but salts such as gypsum will be precipitated.

Sedimentary rocks are important because they provide oil, natural gas, coal and building stone. They are of great interest, too, because they were formed at the earth's surface and provide much evidence of its nature many millions of years ago. Fine red sandstone [3], for example, indicates the former presence of deserts. The study of ancient environments through the analysis of present-day rocks is called stratigraphy.

New rocks from old

Metamorphic rocks are usually much harder than sedimentary rocks. Some are formed by deep burial, others by the heat of igneous intrusions. Their grains are all interlocking crystals and many, such as slates, schists and gneisses, split easily along certain planes.

1 A

B

C

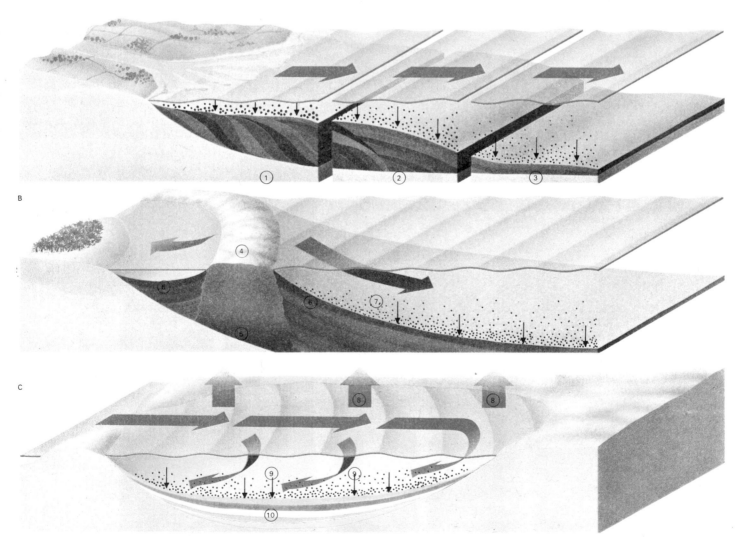

1 The three types of sedimentary rocks are clastic [A], produced by erosion from older rocks; organic [B], formed by the decomposition of living matter; and chemical [C], formed from salts deposited by evaporation. [A] Erosion produces sand and mud which is brought down to the sea by rivers, deposited in deltas [1] and on the sea-floor where it hardens into rock [2]. Large grains are deposited inshore, fine mud [3] farther away – a common origin for clastic rocks. [B] On a coral reef, living coral [4] is found only near the surface. It rests on hundreds of metres of dead coral [5] and on both sides are piles of broken pieces of coral eroded by the waves [6]. The shells of crustaceans also accumulate on the sea-floor [7]. All will form reef limestone, a typical organic rock. [C] Where a partially enclosed basin is found in the tropics the seawater is evaporated [8] and the salts in it deposited [9] forming chemical rocks [10].

Others, such as quartzite and marble, are compact rocks which break in any direction.

When sedimentary rocks are intruded by a molten mass of magma they are altered. This process is a form of metamorphism known as thermal or contact metamorphism. Small intrusions such as dikes and sills merely bake a thin skin of rock and make it harder; large intrusions, such as the Dartmoor (southwest England) granite, alter the rock for several miles around. A large intrusion may heat the rock to 700°C (1,292°F) and take more than a million years to cool, giving time for new minerals to form.

The rocks surrounding an igneous intrusion can be divided into zones, depending on how much they have been altered. Shales will have been changed to slates on the outside and near the intrusion new minerals, such as andalusite, will occur in the slate. Next to the intrusion, hornfels, a hard rock, will form.

Alteration of large areas
Regional (or dynamic) metamorphism [5] occurs where large areas of rock have been buried sufficiently deep for the increase in

temperature and pressure to alter the rocks. The pressure increase is caused by the weight of rocks above and the increase in temperature by the earth's interior heat. Slates are formed by both regional and thermal metamorphism but schists and gneisses are found only in regional metamorphism. Regionally metamorphosed rocks outcrop over a large part of the earth's surface, where old mountain ranges have been eroded away, leaving on the surface rocks that were once deeply buried. Examples are the Canadian Shield and parts of Scotland and Sweden.

A third, rare type of metamorphism is dislocation metamorphism, caused by large areas of rock moving past one another. The pressure shatters the rock and the friction is so great that the rock is partially melted, producing a rock called mylonite. It occurs only in narrow strips, of which the Lizard, in Cornwall, England, is an example. Unlike sedimentary rocks, metamorphic rocks are of no great use to mankind, containing no oil and few useful minerals, and are of little use in building, apart from slate for roofing and marble used in decorative work.

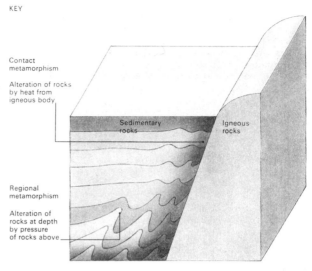

KEY

Contact metamorphism

Alteration of rocks by heat from igneous body

Sedimentary rocks

Igneous rocks

Regional metamorphism

Alteration of rocks at depth by pressure of rocks above

The three groups of rock are igneous, sedimentary and metamorphic. They are seen together

where igneous rock has intruded sedimentary rocks. Its heat has caused the sedimentary rock to

be thermally metamorphosed. Deeply buried sedimentary rock is regionally metamorphosed.

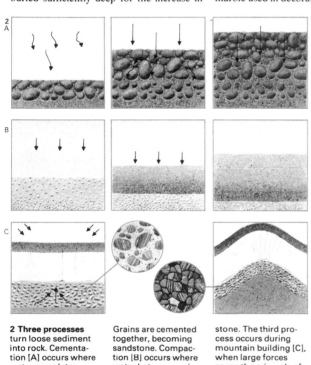

2 Three processes turn loose sediment into rock. Cementation [A] occurs where water percolates between grains, depositing thin layers of iron oxide, calcium carbonate or silica around grains.

Grains are cemented together, becoming sandstone. Compaction [B] occurs where water between grains of sediment is squeezed out by the weight of more sediment. By this means, clay becomes mud-

stone. The third process occurs during mountain building [C], when large forces cause the minerals of rocks to recrystallize in a solid mass leaving no spaces. This is a common occurrence in marbles.

Sandstone

3 Grains of quartz sand cemented together with lime, iron oxide or silica make up sandstone and each grain can easily be seen. Sandstones are usually red, cream or brown, but are sometimes green.

Limestone

4 Limestone is white, grey or cream-coloured rock, often containing many fossils. Limestones are made of calcium carbonate and are formed by the partial evaporation of seawater or from broken shells which are often preserved as fossils.

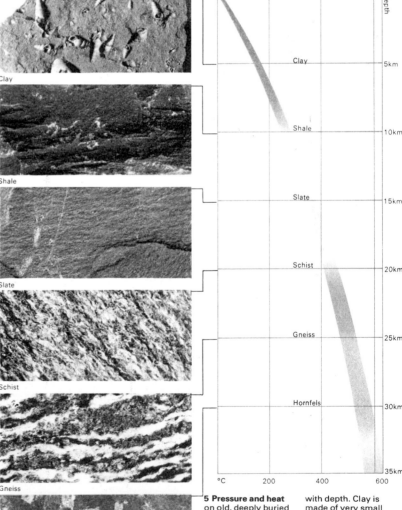

Clay

Shale

Slate

Schist

Gneiss

Hornfels

5 Pressure and heat on old, deeply buried rocks produces regional metamorphism. The temperature and pressure increase with depth of burial, causing new minerals to grow in the rock, and the size of the mineral crystals increases

with depth. Clay is made of very small crystals, but gneiss has 2cm-long (0.75in) crystals. Minerals grow in the direction of least pressure, which means they are aligned and will split easily one way. Hornfels does not show lineations.

depth

Clay — 5km

Shale — 10km

Slate — 15km

Schist — 20km

Gneiss — 25km

Hornfels — 30km

35km

°C   200   400   600

Folds and faults

The earth's mountains and valleys are formed by folds and faults in its ceaselessly changing crust. Folds are rock waves and faults are cracks, and both are caused by the intense pressures of continental drift. They are of major significance to industrial geologists because they often form structural traps for valuable mineral deposits.

How folds and faults form
Folds and faults are usually well developed in both sedimentary and volcanic rocks. They may also form in plutonic rocks such as granite and gabbro. Correct interpretation of their structure is essential in mining. Recumbent folding and reverse faulting can cause beds of coal, for example, to be repeated vertically, while normal faulting can cause a horizontal gap. A coal seam may thus be passed through several times in drilling, or alternatively missed altogether.

Faults that develop above an intrusive granite allow mineralizing fluids to pass into the overlying rocks and there deposit minerals such as lead, tin, zinc and copper ores. Similarly, faults that do not reach the surface may form channels up which oil and gas can rise. In downward folds, where porous sandbeds overlie impermeable clays and shale, collections of water form which can produce artesian springs.

Movement of the massive plates of rock that compose the earth's crust produces intense pressure at the margins of the plates. Where two plates converge, these sometimes throw the rocks up into highly folded and faulted mountain chains. At other plate edges, stretching pulls the rocks apart and forms long depressions bounded by faults, such as the rift valleys of East Africa.

Folds vary greatly in size, from a few millimetres to hundreds of kilometres across. Downward or basin-shaped folds are called synclines and upward folds are called anticlines [Key]. Synclinoria and anticlinoria are the names given to large synclines or anticlines that have smaller folds on their limbs. The Weald of southeast England and parts of the Paris basin, for example, are anticlinoria.

Folds that form at the same time as deposition are known as supratenuous folds. These occur when material that compacts at different rates is deposited at the same time in the same area, as when sand is deposited around coral. Domes are folds in which the beds dip outwards, whereas basins are formed when the beds dip inwards [3].

Classification of folds
There are three main kinds of folds. First true, or flexure, folding forms by the compression of competent (strong) rocks. This may grade into the second type, flow folding, in areas where incompetent (weak) rocks occur [4]. The incompetent rocks behave like a thick paste; they cannot easily transmit pressure and many minor folds usually form. Third, shear folding [5] may occur in brittle rocks by the formation of minute cleavage-like fractures in which thin slices of rock are able to move in relation to each other like a pack of cards pushed in from the side. Except where cut by a fault, all folds eventually die out by closure, the shape of the fold resembling a half basin or dome.

Simple folds usually occur in young rocks like those of the Tertiary and Quaternary eras. Complex folds are found in older rocks

1 Compression creates folds in the earth's crust. First, a simple fold may be created, probably a symmetric anticline [A]. But if there is a continuation of pressure, the fold may become uneven and develop into an asymmetric anticline [B]. At a later stage, a recumbent fold may develop [C]. The anticline is then lying on top of the syncline and the layers of rock on one side of the anticline are inverted. If pressure continues to be exerted, these layers will thin and eventually break to produce an overthrust fold [D]. When these layers disappear due to stretching and fracture, a nappe is formed [E]. Over a long period this nappe may be pushed out many kilometres from its original position.

2 A symmetric anticline [1] and syncline [2] have limbs that dip at similar angles on either side of the axial plane of the fold. The position of the axial plane of an asymmetric anticline [3] and of a syncline [4] may be more difficult to establish. Where compression produces a reverse fault [5] one side of the fault (in this case the left) over-rides the horizontal strata on the other side. In the case of a monocline fold [6], rock strata lying at two levels may be separated by a limb that is relatively steep.

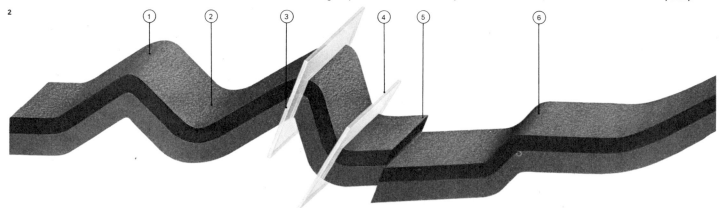

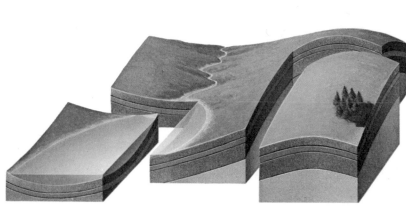

3 Domes and basins are folds that are about as wide as they are long. They are due to complex compressions of the crust. Isolated domes can be due to the subterranean rise of magma or rock-salt.

4 Beds can be competent or incompetent according to their reaction to folding. Competent beds bend and crack [1] without much flowage while incompetent beds shear [2] or form shearing microfolds [3] that alter the thickness of the bed.

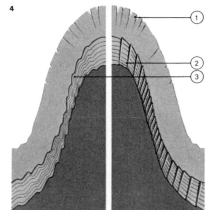

which have been exposed to earth movements for a longer period and which have often been deeply buried within the earth's crust. Very old rocks, such as the Precambrian of Norway, have been refolded many times with the development of structures such as boudinage, mullion and cleavage [6, 7]. These ancient rocks have also been considerably altered by heat and pressure from igneous intrusions and deep burial. Platy minerals, such as micas, then develop parallel to each other and the rock tends to split easily along thin planes. Rocks with this property are known as schists.

With increasing distance from the source of pressure that causes folding, the folds gradually die out both in horizontal and vertical directions. This is well displayed in the Alps where the folds become less complex to the north and also to the west.

Faults and refaulting
When rocks can no longer bend under pressure they crack and a fault is formed [Key]. If the rocks are pulled apart a normal fault forms [10A], while if they are com-

pressed reverse and thrust faults form [10B]. Due to movement along the fault plane, grooves and scratches are ground out on adjacent walls. These scratches allow geologists to measure the relative lateral and vertical movements of faults, and tell, for example, whether the movement was linear or rotational. Faults, which are often associated with earthquakes, are well expressed at the surface as fault scarps and rift valleys such as the San Andreas fault and the Rhine rift valley.

As they are produced by the same pressures, faults are frequently associated with folded areas. Sometimes the surface strata may crack into a complex mosaic of blocks by renewed movement along an existing buried fault. Reactivation of such a buried fault is believed to have been responsible for the disastrous 1966 Tashkent earthquake. Refaulting occurs in many areas where new and different stress fields are superposed upon ancient ones. Some regions have been refaulted and refolded several times, as in the complex Precambrian areas of Finland and Canada.

Fold structures
[1] Trace of the axial plane of a syncline
[2] Trace of the axial plane of an anticline
[3] The crest of the fold
[4] The limb of the fold
[5] Anticline
[6] Dip of the rock strata
[7] Trough between folds
[8] Syncline

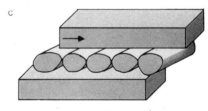

Fault structures
[1] Downthrown block
[2] Angle of dip
[3] Fault plane
[4] Nett slip
[5] Hade
[6] Upthrown block
[7] Hanging wall
[8] Foot wall
[9] Horizontal dip slip (known as heave)
[10] Vertical slip (throw)

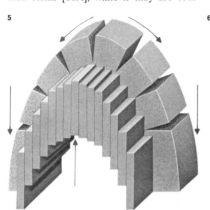

5 Rocks can break instead of bending. Coarse-grained rocks cleave on planes perpendicular to bedding. When the space between fractures exceeds a few centimetres, they are called joints.

Fractures form at the tops of anticlines where weak beds are pulled apart during folding. Finer-grained rocks split by close-spaced faults into slices parallel to the pressure direction.

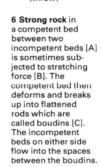

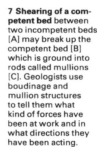

6 Strong rock in a competent bed between two incompetent beds [A] is sometimes subjected to stretching force [B]. The competent bed then deforms and breaks up into flattened rods which are called boudins [C]. The incompetent beds on either side flow into the spaces between the boudins.

7 Shearing of a competent bed between two incompetent beds [A] may break up the competent bed [B] which is ground into rods called mullions [C]. Geologists use boudinage and mullion structures to tell them what kind of forces have been at work and in what directions they have been acting.

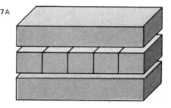

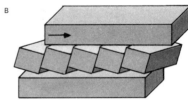

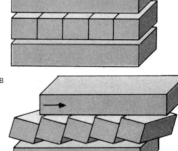

8 Lateral pressure, when applied to a recumbent fold, can produce a low-angle crack [1] along which the overturned limb of the fold [2] may slide. This type of crack in a rock structure is called a thrust fault.

9 Vertical displacement may be more or less equal in some types of block faulting. Where one block is lower relative to those on either side, a graben [A] is formed and where one is raised, a horst [B] is formed.

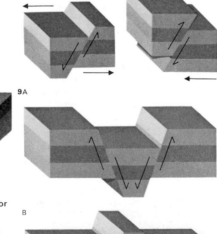

10 Stretching can produce a normal fault [A], compression a reversed fault [B], shearing a strike-slip fault [C], slumping a hinge fault [D] and twisting a rotational fault [E].

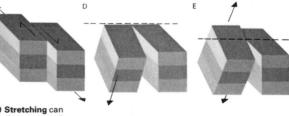

11 Strike-slip faults that move to the right [A] are dextral faults while movement to the left [B] produces sinistral faults. Transform faults are a special kind of strike-slip fault linking major earth structures.

Life and death of mountains

A true mountain is more than just a piece of high ground. It also has underneath it specific geological formations such as strongly folded and faulted rocks, ancient volcanic deposits or large igneous masses such as granite intrusion. Conversely, layers of sedimentary rocks that barely rise from the horizontal should not strictly be described as mountains.

Types of mountains

There are four main types of mountains: fold, block, dome and volcanic. Fold mountains can vary widely in complexity but still conform to the basic type. The Alps [10], Carpathians and Himalayas form the world's largest fold mountain chain. The rocks have been compressed and crumpled in extremely complex ways, with intrusions of molten rock, widespread metamorphism (changes in the rocks) and faulting. The numerous earthquakes in Turkey and Iran indicate that mountains there are still moving.

Block mountains are large-scale faulted structures. Internally a block mountain is usually highly folded and faulted and may have been created either by a deep fault or by an exceptionally large horst (block of raised strata) which was then shaped by erosion. Many block mountains – for example, in the Basin and Range province of Nevada – rise abruptly above the surrounding lowland.

Domes are formed by the lifting of strata, as when granitic magma is intruded. As the lifting increases the surface is worn away by erosion and underlying granite is exposed. When such domes are large and high they constitute true dome mountains, such as the Black Hills of Dakota.

Volcanic mountains differ from others in that they grow visibly during eruptions [4]. When their last growth was recent, their shape is relatively unaffected by erosion. As more eruptions take place on the same site, so the successive outflows of ash and lava increase the height of the volcano. Volcanic mountains in continental interiors are comparatively rare. They are mostly submarine or island features and can form island arcs several thousands of kilometres long; one such arc is the Aleutian Island chain.

Fold mountains are by far the most important because they form very large ranges thousands of kilometres long. Fold mountains are often associated with block-faulted mountains and with volcanic mountains because the forces causing the folding of the rocks are the same that produce faulting and promote vulcanism. The mechanism of the large horizontal compressions leading to the crumpling and folding of the sedimentary cover of the earth's crust was poorly understood before the plate tectonics theory.

According to plate tectonics theory, fold mountains are formed by the movements and collisions of large plates that make up the earth's crust. These plates are usually enormous and may underlie and carry whole continents. When two plates collide the more resistant one slides beneath the other, squeezing upwards the sediment deposited in the geosyncline [6], or trough, between them. The great folds formed in the compressed sediment eventually break out above the surrounding region as mountains.

If the initial clash involves a fast-moving continental plate, the folds may be thrown even higher forming much larger mountain ranges. A continental plate thrust under

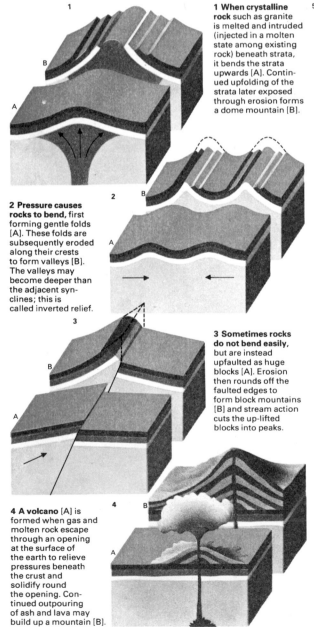

1 When crystalline rock such as granite is melted and intruded (injected in a molten state among existing rock) beneath strata, it bends the strata upwards [A]. Continued upfolding of the strata later exposed through erosion forms a dome mountain [B].

2 Pressure causes rocks to bend, first forming gentle folds [A]. These folds are subsequently eroded along their crests to form valleys [B]. The valleys may become deeper than the adjacent synclines; this is called inverted relief.

3 Sometimes rocks do not bend easily, but are instead upfaulted as huge blocks [A]. Erosion then rounds off the faulted edges to form block mountains [B] and stream action cuts the up-lifted blocks into peaks.

4 A volcano [A] is formed when gas and molten rock escape through an opening at the surface of the earth to relieve pressures beneath the crust and solidify round the opening. Continued outpouring of ash and lava may build up a mountain [B].

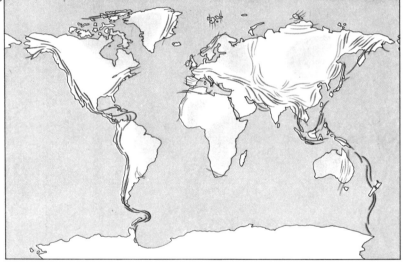

5 Continental areas of the world consist of stable shields surrounded by mobile belts. Between the shields material has been crushed up into mountain chains by collision between plates and continents. The Ural, Alpine and Himalaya mountains were formed by continental collisions, while the American cordillera was formed by collision between a continent and a mobile plate. The East African rift valley indicates that the shield is splitting up to form new oceanic areas.

Cenozoic mobile belts	
Mesozoic mobile belts	
Upper Palaeozoic mobile belts	
Lower Palaeozoic mobile belts	
Precambrian shield areas	

6 Geosynclines are the birthplaces of mountains. They are large troughs where thick layers of sediments can accumulate [A]. Where geosynclines develop between two colliding crustal plates [B] the sediments can be squeezed up as broad ridges known as geanticlines [C]. Further compression creates mountain ranges [D]. The whole process is usually accompanied by pressure-induced recrystallization or melting, which then forms metamorphic, plutonic and volcanic rocks; examples of each of these are gneisses, granites and rhyolites.

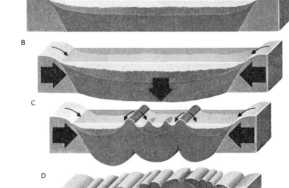

another tends to maintain an upward pressure, rather like a submerged cork seeking to regain the surface: in time the stationary plate is levered upwards and the attached fold mountains move with the plate. The Himalayas were formed when the northern edge of the Indian continental plate collided with and slid under the Asian plate; the Asian plate was then lifted and the world's highest mountain range was created.

Death of mountains
Mountains are sculptured and destroyed by the climatic forces of frost, water (in the form of snow, ice and rain) and wind. Frost may shatter and break up rocks to form screes (masses of debris at a cliff base) and snow and glaciers gouge out rock debris and transport it down the mountainside, leaving the debris as an elongated moraine at the tip of the glacier. Lower down, rivers cut into the mountainside and form zigzag valleys with interlocking spurs. These spurs may in turn be sliced off by glaciers making their way to lower levels down the mountain. In short the erosion of mountains is the continuing story

of the breakup of rocks and their gradual descent under the influence of gravity.

In time, weathering and erosion destroy mountains by lowering them so much that they are eventually transformed into broad plains cut by slowly meandering rivers. In arid climates wind erosion may finish the work by sand-blasting the remaining hills into a bare desert, leaving a surface known as a peneplain [Key] – that is, almost a plain. This stage is rarely reached; more commonly, renewed earth movements uplift the area again, so beginning a new geological phase.

The study of mountains
Mountains help geologists to understand plate structures and to learn more about how rocks behave when they are compressed by moving continents. Mountains also mark the positions of ancient plate boundaries in, for example, Mesozoic-Cenozoic times when great ranges such as the Himalayas were being formed. Similarly, the study of ancient mountain ranges also reveals the sites of ancient oceans, enabling scientists to reconstruct the past geography of the planet.

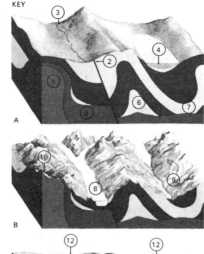

KEY

Three stages in the life of a mountain are shown here. [A] Idealized young complex mountain: [1] granite batholith; [2] major fault offsetting strata; [3] formation of a young stream; [4] sea-level; [5] metamorphic rocks; [6] anticline of upfolded strata; [7] syncline of downfolded strata. [B] Mature complex mountain: [8] glacier scouring U-shaped valley; [9] glacial meltwater forming active stream; [10] erosional "Matterhorn" peak – top of granite batholith exposed by erosion. [C] Peneplain of old complex mountain: [11] peneplain due to total erosion of mountains; [12] rivers reworking sediments of the peneplain; [13] remnant of eroded mountain.

7 The Mont Blanc massif, a lofty mountain range in the French Alps, is typical of the popular conception of mountains. The cold climate due to the high altitude allows frost to split the rocks and, with the aid of glaciers, to carve the mountains into serrated ranges of jagged peaks.

8 This peneplain in the Northern Territory of Australia was formed when a mountain range was eroded to an almost flat surface. Monadnocks rise above the plain showing the former positions of peaks or hard rocks. The surface is scoured by wind and this forms a sandy desert.

9 The Canadian Rockies, in their western part, consist of intensely metamorphosed strata [1]. High pressures here melted granites. These granites, expanding with heat, became lighter than the overlying rocks and rose up through them as intrusions [2]. The uplift sheared the Palaeozoic strata [3] to the east along low-angle faults [4] which also separate these strata from the underlying crystalline basement [5]. The piling-up of these slabs by thrust-faulting finally led to a considerable thickness of sedimentary rocks.

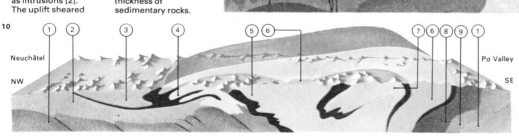

10 The highly folded strata of the western Alps have not only been crumpled and folded but also shoved great distances northwards as nappes. Where pressure and heat were sufficient the sedimentary strata were also transformed into metamorphic rocks such as gneiss and schist [5, 6, 7, 8]. The areas shown here are [1] basement; [2] flysch zone; [3] Pre-Alps; [4] Helvetic nappes; [5] Dent Blanche nappe; [6] Mont Rosa nappe; [7] Ivrée zone; and [9] Dinaric Alps.

Earth's water supply

Water is essential to all life on earth. The study of the earth's water supply, called hydrology, investigates the distribution of water, how it is used by man and how it circulates from the oceans to land areas and back again in the hydrologic or water cycle.

The water cycle – from oceans to land
About 97 per cent of the world's available water is in the oceans [Key]. Oceanic water is salty and unsuitable for drinking or for farming. In some desert regions, where fresh water is in short supply, seawater is desalinated to make fresh water. But most of the world is constantly supplied with fresh water by the natural process of the water cycle [1] which relies on the action of two factors: the sun's heat and gravity.

Over the oceans, which cover about 71 per cent of the earth's surface, the sun's heat causes evaporation. Water vapour, an invisible gas, rises on air currents and winds. Some of this water vapour condenses and returns directly to the oceans as rain. But because of the circulation of the atmosphere, air bearing large amounts of water vapour is carried over

land where it falls as rain or snow (precipitation).

Much of this precipitation is quickly re-evaporated by the sun. Some soaks into the soil where it is absorbed by plants and partly returned to the air through transpiration. Some water flows over the land surface as run-off, which collects into rills and flows into streams and rivers. Some rain and melted snow seeps through the soil into the rocks beneath to form ground water.

In polar and high mountainous regions most precipitation is in the form of snow. There it is compacted into ice, forming ice sheets and glaciers. The force of gravity causes these bodies of ice to move downwards and outwards and they may eventually return to the oceans where chunks of ice break off at the coastline to form icebergs. Thus all the water that does not return directly to the atmosphere gradually returns to the sea to complete the water cycle. This continual movement of water and ice plays a major part in the erosion of land areas.

Of the total water on land, more than 75 per cent is frozen in ice sheets and glaciers as

in Greenland and Antarctica [Key]. Most of the rest (about 22 per cent) is water collected below the earth's surface and is called ground water. Comparatively small quantities are in lakes, rivers and in the soil. Water that is held in the soil and that nourishes plant growth is called capillary water. It is retained in the upper few metres by molecular attraction between the water and soil particles.

Ground water and the water-table
Ground water [4] enters permeable rocks through what is called the zone of intermittent saturation. This layer may retain ground water after continued rain but soon dries up. Beneath this lies a rock zone where the pores or crevices are filled with water. It is called the zone of saturation and usually begins within 30m (98ft) of the surface, extending downwards until it reaches impermeable rock through which water cannot percolate. This impermeable rock layer, lying below the water-holding layer, or aquifer, is called a ground water dam.

The top of the saturated zone is called the water-table. This is not a level surface. It is

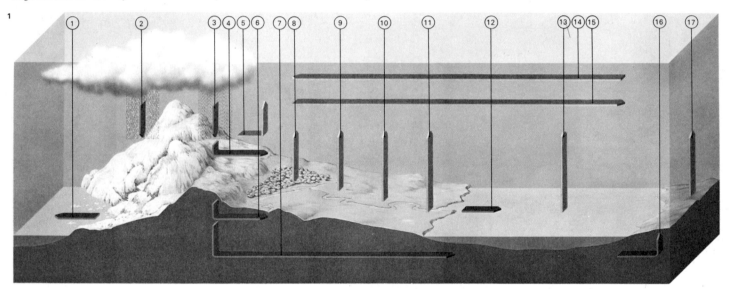

1 **The hydrological or water cycle** is the process whereby water, in some form, circulates from the oceans to land areas and back again. Fresh water is present on the earth as water vapour in the atmosphere, as ice and as liquid water. The elements of the cycle are precipitation as rain [3]; surface run-off [4]; evaporation of rain in falling [5]; ground water flow to rivers and streams [6]; ground water flow to the ocean [7]; transpiration from plants [8]; evaporation from lakes and ponds [9]; evaporation from the soil [10]; evaporation from rivers and streams [11]; evap- oration from the oceans [13]; flow of rivers and streams to the oceans [12]; ground water flow from the ocean to arid land [16]; intense evaporation from arid land [17]; movement of moist air from the oceans [14] and to them [15]; precipitation as snow [2]; ice flow into the sea [1].

2 Sandstone (shown here in cross-section) is a highly porous rock through which water percolates easily.

3 Limestone is a permeable but non-porous rock. Water can percolate only through the joints and the fissures.

4 Ground water seeps through the zone of intermittent saturation [1] until it reaches an impermeable layer above which it forms the zone of saturation or aquifer [2, 10]. The upper surface of the aquifer forms the water-table [3, 13], above which is the capillary fringe [6]. Wells [7] must

be sunk to the water-table because the capillary fringe is not saturated. Impermeable dikes [8] block the flow of ground water. In uniform material the water follows paths [4] that curve down and up again towards the nearest stream. If an aquifer is part of a series of strata including several impermeable layers [11] a perched water-table [12] may result. If it lies between two impermeable strata it is said to be confined [14]. Its recharge area [15] is where water enters the confined aquifer. A stream below the water-table is called a gaining stream [5] while a stream flowing above it is known as a losing stream [9] because it loses water by seepage.

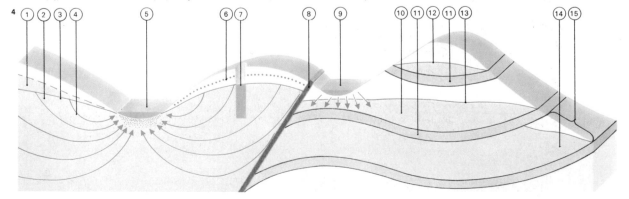

often arched under hills, but beneath plains it generally lies closer to the surface. The water-table also varies in level during the year, depending on the amount of rainfall.

In some places the water-table intersects the surface, forming such features as oases [6] in desert hollows, swamps, lakes and springs. Springs [5] are gushes or seepages of water that may occur along the base of a hillside or in a valley in the hills. They are found where the water-table or an aquifer appears at the surface or where the aquifer is blocked by an impermeable rock such as a volcanic dike. Spring water is usually fresh and clean because it passes through the fine pores of rocks such as sandstones [2] where impurities are filtered out in much the same way as domestic water is purified by sand filtration.

Limestone is not a porous rock but it is permeable – that is, ground water can seep through the maze of fissures, joints and caves in the rock [3]. These apertures are enlarged by rainwater containing dissolved carbon dioxide – a weak carbonic acid that dissolves limestone. In limestone ground water is not filtered in the same way as in porous rocks. In

the late 1800s epidemics of cholera and typhoid often occurred in France in areas where springs emerged from limestone areas. It was finally established that the spring water had been contaminated miles away by rubbish thrown into pot-holes.

Some springs contain so much mineral substances in solution that their water is used for medicinal purposes and spa towns have grown up around them. Occasionally these springs are thermal.

Water from artesian wells

The lowest level of the water-table, reached at the driest time of year, is called the permanent water-table. Wells must be drilled to this level if they are to supply water throughout the year. In artesian wells [7] water is forced to the surface by hydrostatic pressure – this results from the rim of the well being below the level of the water-table in the catchment area. Artesian water is obtained from porous sandstone aquifers that underlie the Great Artesian Basin of Australia. These aquifers are supplied with water from the rain that falls on the Eastern Highlands.

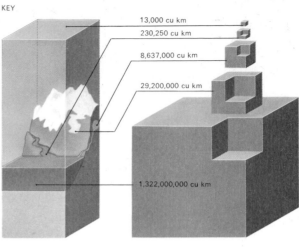

13,000 cu km
230,250 cu km
8,637,000 cu km
29,200,000 cu km
1,322,000,000 cu km

The total water supply of the world is estimated to be about 1,360,000,000 cubic kilometres, and 97.2 per cent of it forms the oceans. Of the remainder, 2.15 per cent is frozen in ice caps and glaciers, and most of the rest is in rivers and lakes (0.0171 per cent) or under land areas as ground water (0.625 per cent). Water vapour represents only 0.001 per cent but this quantity is vital: without it there would be no life on land.

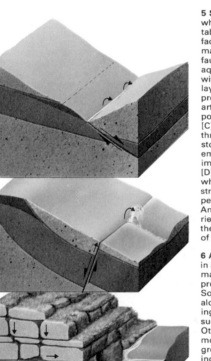

5 Springs appear where the water-table meets the surface. [A] Springs may occur where a fault brings an aquifer into contact with an impermeable layer. [B] Water pressure creates artesian springs at points of weakness. [C] Water seeps through jointed limestone until it emerges above an impermeable layer. [D] Springs form where permeable strata overlay impermeable rock. [E] An impermeable barrier may lead to the formation of a spring line.

6 An oasis is an area in a desert that is made fertile by the presence of water. Some oases are found along rivers crossing the deserts, such as the Nile. Others owe their moisture to underground waters reaching the surface or near-surface. Wadis are intermittent streams that flow only after heavy rainfall but they often have a hidden flow under their beds which can reach the surface to create oases. Aquifers with recharge areas outside the desert can "pipe" water to oases under long stretches of arid desert. These recharge areas are usually mountains suitably sited for catching rain. The natural flow can be increased by pumping the ground water but if the rate of pumping exceeds the water flow into the aquifer in the recharge area the wells will dry up.

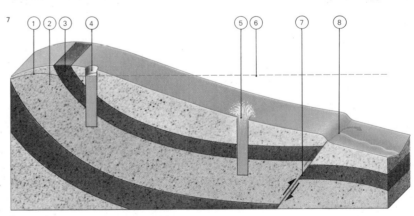

7 Artesian springs and wells are found where ground water is under pressure. The water-table [1] in the confined aquifer [2] lies near the top of the dipping layers. A well [4] drilled through the top impervious layer [3] is not an artesian well because the head of hydrostatic pressure [6] is not sufficient to force water to the surface. In such wells the water must be pumped or drawn to the surface. The top of an artesian well [5] lies below the level of the head of hydrostatic pressure and so water gushes to the surface. Artesian springs [8] may occur along joints or faults [7] where the head of hydrostatic pressure is sufficient to force the water up along the fault.

Areas with artesian wells are called artesian basins. In the London and Paris artesian basins the water has been so heavily tapped that the water level has dropped below the level of the well heads.

Caves and underground water

Most of the earth's surface has been mapped, but in many areas vast networks of caves, largely unexplored, lie beneath the ground. There are several kinds of caves, including coastal caves, ice caves and lava caves. The largest cave systems occur in carbonate rocks (limestone and dolomite), most of them forming in massive layers of limestone.

Formation of caves

Limestone is a fairly hard rock formed from calcium carbonate. Although insoluble in pure water, limestone is dissolved by rainwater containing carbon dioxide from the air and from the soil. Rainwater reacts chemically with limestone and converts it to soluble calcium bicarbonate. Limestone is riven by joints (vertical cracks) and by bedding planes, which are usually horizontal. When limestone is exposed on the surface, rainwater widens the joints into "grikes", dividing the limestone into blocks called clints. This broken pavement surface is a feature of karst scenery, named after the limestone Karst district of the Dinaric Alps in western Yugoslavia

Some authorities suggest that limestone caves are formed when rainwater slowly enlarges the joints and bedding planes as it seeps down to the water-table. Eventually, streams flow into the enlarged joints which form sink-holes or swallow-holes. Such streams may flow underground for many kilometres, dissolving vertical chimneys and horizontal galleries.

However, other authorities do not consider that this explanation accounts for cave networks that have underground chambers with high roofs. Such caves, they argue, must have been formed when the land surface was far higher than it is now and when the limestone was completely saturated with ground water [1]. They believe that, under pressure, the ground water seeped through the rock, until it finally emerged at the surface as a spring. Eventually, the forces of erosion planed down the land surface, the watertable dropped and air entered the dissolved caves. Sink-holes might have been formed when the roofs of caves collapsed.

The Mammoth Cave National Park in Kentucky, USA [Key], is the site of the world's most extensive cave network, with a total mapped passageway of 231km (144 miles), linking it with the Flint Ridge cave system. One of the deepest-known caves is the Gouffre de la Pierre St Martin in the western Pyrenees in France, which drops 1,174m (3,850ft). The largest underground chamber is the Big Room in the Carlsbad Caverns, New Mexico. At a depth of 400m (1,320ft), the Big Room is 1,300m (4,270ft) long, 100m (328ft) high and 200m (656ft) wide.

Features of caves

Limestone caves contain many features formed from deposits of calcium carbonate, including icicle-like stalactites [6] and pillar-like stalagmites [5]. Stalactites develop when water that is highly charged with dissolved calcium bicarbonate seeps through holes in the roofs of caves. Drops of water that hang on the roof are partly evaporated and a tiny quantity of calcium carbonate is precipitated and sticks to the roof. Another drop of water deposits a second film of calcium carbonate in the same place and, in this way, stalactites slowly develop.

1A
B
C

1 As rain falls, it dissolves carbon dioxide from the atmosphere and becomes a weak carbonic acid that attacks carbonate rock (limestone and dolomite) by transforming it into the soluble bicarbonate. Carbonate rocks are criss-crossed by vertical cracks and horizontal breaks along bedding planes [A]. Some geologists believe the caves were formed when the rock was saturated by water. Others believe they formed gradually by solution [B] into a major cave network [C].

2 Limestone surfaces are often eroded into blocks called clints [1]. Surface streams flow into dissolved sink-holes [2], that lead to a deep chimney [3]. Pot-holes [7] are dry chimneys. Gours [4] are ridges formed as carbonate is precipitated from turbulent water. Streams flow at the lowest level of the galleries [17]. Abandoned galleries [13] are common. A siphon [12] occurs where the roof is below water-level. Streams reappear at resurgences [20]. Abandoned resurgences [19] may provide entrances to caves. Stalactites [5] include macaroni stalactites [6], curtain stalactites or drapes [11] and eccentric stalactites [16], formed by water being blown sideways. Stalagmites [14] sometimes have a fir-cone shape [15] caused by splashing, or resemble stacked plates [8]. Stalactites and stalagmites may merge to form columns [10]. Signs of ancient man [18] have been found in caves and blind white fish live in the pools [9].

Drops of water that fall on the floor may also be partly evaporated, leaving small deposits of calcium carbonate that grow upwards into stalagmites. Often it is the impact of the drop hitting the floor that forces the carbonate out of solution. The splashing of the water can give rise to stalagmites that resemble stacks of saucers. Stalactites and stalagmites sometimes meet to form a continuous column [6].

The growth of stalactites and stalagmites is usually extremely slow. Some take 4,000 years to increase by only 2.5cm (1in) in length. However, stalactites in Ingleborough Cave, Yorkshire, have been known to increase by 7.6cm (3in) in ten years.

Another deposit, caused by water seeping through a long crack in the roof of a cave, is a wavy band of calcium carbonate which grows across the ceiling like a fringed curtain. Water flowing down a wall or across a floor of a cave may build up a flowstone. Delicate thread- or finger-like formations called helictites sometimes jut out from a stalactite. Their origin is the subject of dispute. On the roofs of some caves are anthodites, which are branching, flower-like formations. In its pure state, calcium carbonate is transparent or white, but these and other cave features are often coloured by impurities.

Life in caves

Caves harbour a variety of animal life specially adapted to the dark environment, including blind, colourless, almost transparent shrimps, worms, mites, insects and sightless newts, often called blind fish. These creatures live permanently in caves. Bats, also common in cave systems, have weak eyes and depend mainly on their sonar systems to guide them through dark tunnels. Every night hundreds of thousands of bats emerge from the Carlsbad Caverns in New Mexico. Within 15 minutes' flight of the caverns is the Pecos valley, where the bats feed on insects, returning to the caves shortly before dawn.

In prehistoric times the most important inhabitant of caves was man. Archaeologists have found many traces of man's occupation – tools, bones, hearths and, usually well inside the caves, rock paintings which may have had ritual or magical significance.

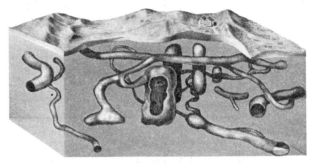

The Mammoth Caves in Kentucky comprise the world's largest underground cave network. The Mammoth Cave National Park consists of a limestone plateau, whose surface is pitted by more than 60,000 sinkor swallow-holes. Surface water drains into the sink-holes that link the caves to the surface. Some sinkholes are connected to the caves by vertical chimneys. The underground caves are interlinked by a maze of passages. The Great Mammoth Cave has more than 48km (30 miles) of continuous passages. In the caves, water seeping through the limestone rock collects into rivers, which finally emerge into the open at the base of the plateau, in the Echo River valley. This system is typical of the arrangement of galleries, caverns and pot-holes found in many limestone areas where acidic water has seeped into the rock and dissolved it.

3

4

5

3 Gours are formed when carbonate-rich waters flow over an irregular surface. The turbulence deposits calcite on the irregularities which grow into a series of ridges perpetuating the process

4 Balcony stalactites are formed by water dripping from the side of a cave wall. They are called stalactites because they grow downwards, but ordinary stalactites hang from the roof of a cave.

5 Stalagmites build upwards from the floor of a cave. They are generally shorter and thicker than stalactites. The tallest known stalagmite is 29m (95ft) high, in the Aven Armand Cave, in Lozère, France.

6

6 Stalactites, stalagmites and columns of calcium carbonate are present in this cave. The columns are formed when stalactites and stalagmites meet. Stalactites are fragile structures and, as they easily break off, do not usually grow to great lengths. The longest known stalactite is supported by a wall in the Cueva de Nerja, near Málaga in Spain. It is 59m (195ft) long and extends from the roof down to the floor.

7 A pot-holer climbs down a wire ladder into a cave. He wears a protective helmet with a calcium carbide lamp. All his equipment must be collapsible to enable him to transport it through the confined spaces that he will encounter.

7

Rivers and lakes

When rain falls on the ground it is either absorbed in the soil or runs downhill over the surface in small temporary gullies called rills. These unite to form a stream. Other streams start from springs, where water that has sunk into the ground comes to the surface, or from melting glaciers. Streams and rivers usually begin in mountains or hills and the downwards pull of gravity gives them energy to cut away the land and form valleys.

Erosion and transportation

The stones and sand formed by erosion of the rock are transported downstream and are finally deposited at the mouth of the river. Erosion, transportation and deposition are the main work of a river and most rivers can be divided into three sections: an upper course in which erosion dominates; a middle one where transportation occurs; and a lower one where deposition takes place [1].

Stream water erodes in two ways: chemically and physically. Weak acids such as carbonic and humic acids in the water help to decompose limestone and other rocks. The ability of a stream to erode mechanically is

closely related to its speed. During normal flow little physical erosion takes place, but during flood the movement of water becomes turbulent and this causes eddies which in turn cause rapid changes in the pressure on the rocks. Sometimes the pressure is so low that a vacuum is formed on a small part of the stream bed; as the eddy changes this vacuum implodes (collapses inwards). Much of the babble of a brook is the sound of implosions. Repeated implosions cause part of the rock to be sucked into the stream and carried away. Erosion mainly takes place at this stage by stones banging into the stream bed and sides and so wearing them away. During the process the stones are broken up into smaller pebbles, so that the boulders in the upper course of the stream provide the sand grains that are present in the lower course.

The faster the stream flows the larger the fragments it can carry. It can also carry more of them. This is why most erosion and transportation occurs during floods. The finest particles are carried in suspension, kept up by the turbulent motion of the water. Eddies bounce the sand from the bottom and

it is carried downstream a small distance by the current before it falls to the bottom again. Coarser material is rolled along the bed.

Deposition of sediment

As the river enters more gentle slopes, some of its sediment is dropped. Where there is a sudden change in gradient and therefore water speed, as when a river leaves the mountains and runs out onto a plain, nearly all the sediment will be dropped, forming an alluvial fan [2]. More usually the material is deposited *en route* as the river current slows up. The coarsest sediment is dropped first.

During a flood, however, river water moves at different speeds. In the river channel the current is fast moving, but where the river spreads over its banks on to the surrounding land (the flood plain) the current slows down and mud and very fine sand are deposited as the water leaves its channel. This forms a ridge or levee along each bank.

The long profile of a river [Key] – the plot of the elevation of the river against distance travelled with a suitable vertical exaggeration to show significant features – is theoretically

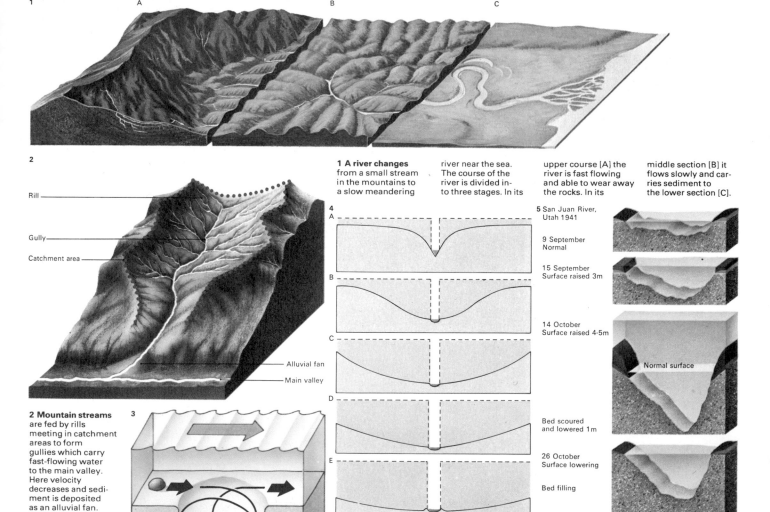

1 A river changes from a small stream in the mountains to a slow meandering river near the sea. The course of the river is divided into three stages. In its upper course [A] the river is fast flowing and able to wear away the rocks. In its middle section [B] it flows slowly and carries sediment to the lower section [C].

Rill

Gully

Catchment area

Alluvial fan

Main valley

2 Mountain streams are fed by rills meeting in catchment areas to form gullies which carry fast-flowing water to the main valley. Here velocity decreases and sediment is deposited as an alluvial fan.

3 Pot-holes occur in the beds of swift rivers or streams. If a small depression is formed in the stream bed a pebble may be caught in it and swirled around by the water, enlarging the depression into a circular pot-hole.

4 A valley is formed by two processes. The river cuts downwards, taking out a narrow slice of rock immediately below its bed to form a V-shape [A]. Weathering widens the valley by changing the rocks forming the sides to soil [B]. As the velocity of water decreases, lateral erosion widens the valley floor [C, D]. In its advanced stage [E] the river flows slowly through a flat plain with deposited material forming levees or dikes.

5 San Juan River, Utah 1941

9 September Normal

15 September Surface raised 3m

14 October Surface raised 4·5m

Normal surface

Bed scoured and lowered 1m

26 October Surface lowering

Bed filling

5 Rivers in their lower courses run over deep channels cut in the bedrock. These channels are normally filled with sand and the river runs in a shallow channel on top. During floods the river deepens its channel by moving the sand below it. Only during the largest flood is the river able to scour the rock bottom. In a large flood the river may be ten times deeper and carry 100 times more water.

a part of a hyperbola, being steepest at the source and flattening at the mouth. This is an equilibrium curve towards which the stream tends to adjust its gradient, digging into its bed and removing material from the upper course and depositing it as the speed drops in the lower. However, this is highly idealized and in practice any number of factors can affect it – differences in rock types in the river bed and the addition of water from tributaries, for example, may produce many irregularities in the hyperbola profile.

The course of a river

Stream beds in their upper section are often bare rock patchily covered by pebbles. Here the stream has greatest capacity to erode and transport farther downstream all but the largest stones. The valley in the upper course has steep sides and a V-shaped cross-section and most pools, rapids, waterfalls [6] and pot-holes [3] occur here, caused by the stream wearing away softer rock more quickly than hard rock. This results in rapids such as the cataracts of the Nile, and where a river flows from a hard bed of rock to a soft

one the latter will be eroded away and a waterfall will be formed as a result.

In the middle section most of the irregularities have been worn away, allowing the river to flow freely in a fairly flat channel. The current is just strong enough to carry most of the sediment supplied to it from higher up. It does not erode downwards and most of the time runs on its own sediment.

In the lower section the river has a very low gradient, often less than 10cm per kilometre (2in per mile). It flows across a broad floodplain. Where the river is flowing slowly, it cannot move stones, even in flood, but because it is large it is able to move a huge amount of fine material. The Mississippi carries about 500 million tonnes of fine sand and mud past New Orleans each year. The river there meanders over a thick layer of its own sediment [7].

When the river reaches the sea the sediment it is carrying is deposited. In some areas tidal currents are strong enough to remove it and the river ends in an estuary. Where more sediment is brought down than can be removed by the sea a delta is formed [10].

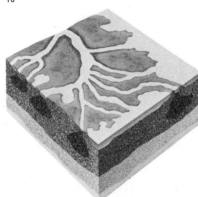

Natural obstruction renewing the graded profile

A river conforms roughly to a convex upward curve that is nearly flat near the sea and gets steeper and more curved inland. This shape is called a graded profile. Waterfalls, lakes and deltas may vary the shape of the stream bed without fundamentally altering the profile.

6

6 Pools and waterfalls are both caused by hard bands of rock spanning the river bed. The softer rocks below a pool have been eroded away leaving a hollow and the hard rock stands up like a dam. Lakes are usually caused by landslides blocking the course of the river or by ice (during the Ice Age) scraping deep hollows. The lakes in the English Lake District and the Great Lakes of America are hollows left by the ice. Other large lakes such as those of East Africa were caused by earth movements. Water flowing over a hard bed erodes the softer beds below, causing a waterfall with a plunge pool beneath. Over time, erosion causes the face of the waterfall to retreat, leaving a gorge downstream of it. Niagara Falls is formed from a hard bed of nearly level rock and has a gorge 10.4km (6.5 miles) long below it.

7

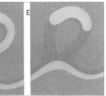

7 Meanders occur where the slope is shallow. In a river bend, the water flows more slowly along the inner bank, depositing sediments and building up the bank, but flows faster along the outer bank, eroding it away. Thus the meander becomes more pronounced [A, B, C] until the arms intersect, allowing the flow to take a shorter route [D]. The abandoned arm silts up [D], forming an oxbow lake [E].

8 In its middle stage a river flows through gently sloping areas. Its eroding and transporting powers are considerably reduced and it runs over a broad flat valley bottom formed by its own deposits of alluvium. Erosion takes place only during floods. The river meanders [2] and the beginnings of floodplains [1] and levees [3] are evident. An oxbow is shown in the process of formation [5] by the river cutting through a meander [4].

8

9

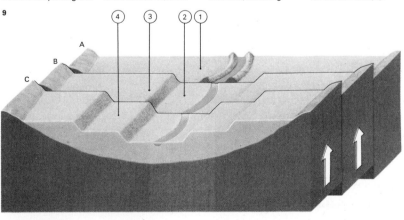

9 A terrace is a flat strip of land along the valley side just above the floodplain. A terrace is formed when the land is uplifted or the sea level drops [B] and the river begins to cut into its floodplain [1] and forms a new one [2] at a lower level. The old floodplain becomes a terrace [3]. Another uplift [C] would cause a new terrace [4]. [A] represents the river valley before uplift.

10

10 A delta is formed where a river enters the sea or a lake. Here all the sediment is dropped, forming a huge, gently sloping mound on the sea-floor. This builds up, causing the river to flow over it to get to the sea. The river branches into separate streams called distributaries. Deltas are found at the mouths of such rivers as the Nile, Mississippi and Ganges. Some rivers have no deltas as sea currents carry away the rivers' sediments.

Land sculptured by rivers

Heavy and prolonged rain may make level ground waterlogged. But once the rain has stopped, the ground will dry out as the water sinks into it. In hot weather standing water will evaporate and plants will absorb water through their roots, transpiring it from their leaves. Sloping ground drains quickly, for the water that cannot sink into the ground flows downhill in rills, then in streams and finally in rivers. That part of the rain that has percolated into the ground will emerge later, at a lower level in the terrain, as a spring and flow away as a stream or river.

Erosion of the land

Water moving downhill will carry with it any particles that it can move. So moving water wears away – erodes – the ground over which it flows. In the course of time rivers have sculptured out their valleys in this way.

In some areas man's activities have greatly increased the erosive effects of rainfall. Too intensive cultivation of southern areas of the United States in the 1700s broke up the protective cover of vegetation that the settlers found there. Heavy rains, falling on the cleared ground, ripped out rills that quickly widened and deepened into a mosaic of gullies. Strong winds, blowing away the soil, hastened the development of such areas, known as "badlands" [5].

Landforms and drainage pattern

As soon as an area of the earth's crust is uplifted above sea-level, the process of erosion begins. The rain falling on it will develop a river system. The rivers will deepen and widen their valleys until in the course of time the whole area is reduced to a low surface – assuming, that is, that there has been no further uplift to rejuvenate the drainage and start a new episode of vigorous downcutting. The inner gorge or canyon of the Colorado River was cut into a much wider, older valley. The drainage pattern and the landforms produced are determined by the composition and disposition (structure) of the underlying rocks [10].

Rivers will quickly emphasize any differences in the hardness of the rocks over which they flow. In their upper reaches, the more resistant bands of rock form waterfalls and rapids in the narrower parts of the valley. If the rocks are lying horizontally, the topography developed is characterized by flat-topped hills [7]. But if the beds are tilted, scarpland topography is produced, in which the more resistant layers form cuestas whose steeper sides face up the inclination (dip) of the rocks and vales are worn out on the outcrop (strike) of the softer beds [8]. The trellised drainage pattern may undergo minor changes. A particular river, perhaps because it has more powerful springs at its source, or greater runoff from the valley sides, or a shorter course to the sea, may cut down the level of its valley floor more quickly than its neighbour and eventually capture it [11].

In areas of gently folded rocks, inverted relief may develop, the river valleys being eroded along the line of the upfolds (anticlines), while downfolds (synclines) underlie the higher ground [9]. Snowdon in North Wales is an example of a synclinal mountain.

Where the beds are more tightly folded, or where near-vertical bodies of igneous rock have been intruded into gently dipping strata, hogsback ridges, steep on both sides, will be

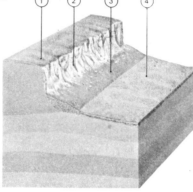

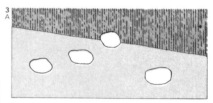

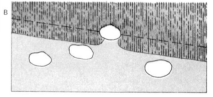

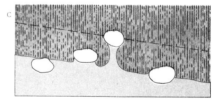

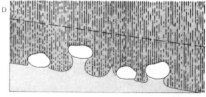

1 The rock formation of a hillside will be gradually broken down into stones and finally soil by water, wind, chemicals and changing temperatures. This loose material will move downhill under the force of gravity. Slopes often show signs of such soil creep, the commonest indication being terracettes [1]. Some slopes have countless little steps that look like sheep tracks across them. Other signs are leaning walls [2], trees with bent trunks [3], a much higher level of soil on the uphill side of a wall [4] and vertical strata curled over where it has been exposed [5].

2 Many slopes have a characteristic shape consisting of a waxing slope [1], the free face [2] where bare rock outcrops, scree slope [3] where debris is piled, and waning slope [4], resulting from erosion.

3 Earth pillars are formed where large rocks occur in the soil [A]. These shelter the underlying soil from erosion and form pillars [B, C]. Once the stone has fallen [D] the soil is easily washed away.

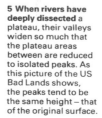

4 The river erosion of an area involves several stages. A newly raised plateau is usually quite flat; the rivers cut into it to form deep gorges. The picture shows the Blue Nile, which is cutting downwards through the African plateau.

5 When rivers have deeply dissected a plateau, their valleys widen so much that the plateau areas between are reduced to isolated peaks. As this picture of the US Bad Lands shows, the peaks tend to be the same height – that of the original surface.

6 The ultimate stage in river erosion is the peneplain – a flat area of land from which most traces of the original plateau have disappeared. In the state of Utah in the USA the desert floor is a good example of a well-eroded peneplain.

produced, while the rivers will erode belts of weaker strata or the line of faults. The Great Glen cut through the Highlands of Scotland from Fort William to Inverness is an example of such a fault-guided valley, but glacial erosion has greatly deepened the valley that had been cut by rivers in pre-glacial times.

Superimposed drainage

Not all river systems are clearly related to the geological structure of the area across which they are now flowing. The drainage system of the English Lake District is clearly radial in plan, but the strike of the lower Palaeozoic rocks (570–395 million years old) runs southwest to northeast. Surrounding the Lake District is a ring of gently outwardly dipping upper Palaeozoic (395–225 million years old) strata. The present drainage system must have originated when these upper Palaeozoic rocks were uplifted to form a dome. Millions of years of erosion have removed all trace of these rocks and the drainage of the Lake District is now superimposed on the lower Palaeozoic rocks of different structure. In the future, the rivers will

gradually change and adjust to this structure.

More extreme superimposition, sometimes called antecedent drainage, is found in India, where the River Brahmaputra has flowed from the Asian plateau to the Indian Ocean since early Tertiary times (about 60 million years ago), before the formation of the Himalayan mountain chains. But their rate of uplift was slow enough for the river to maintain its course across the rising mountains and now it flows through them in stupendous gorges.

In many limestone areas, including chalk downlands, there is a complete valley system, but most of the valleys are now dry with no flowing streams in them. Limestone is a highly permeable rock, so that any rain quickly seeps into it to add to the ground water at depth. That is the position under the present climatic conditions, but in the past rainfall may have been much greater. The level of the ground water would then rise and springs break out higher up the valley sides. During glacial episodes, rainfall or meltwater could not seep into the frozen ground, but must have flowed away, carving the valleys.

Landforms are the result of two conflicting processes. Movement deep within the earth may uplift areas of the crust, while weathering and erosion continually sculpture the surface of the land, wearing it down again. The shapes of individ- ual hills depends on the climate, the structure of the rock and the rate of the lateral and also the longitudinal erosion.

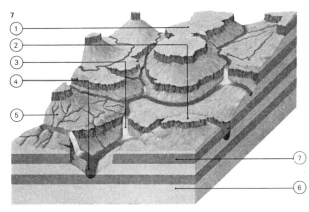

7 In an area underlain by horizontally bedded rocks, rivers follow a dendritic pattern. Their valleys are often steep sided but stepped where erosion has had greater effect on weak strata than on resistant beds. Mesas – isolated tablelands – may form, which may then be eroded to narrower buttes. Landscapes of horizontally bedded rocks are more distinctive in arid regions where rain falls in sharp bursts causing the rivers to swell to raging torrents. Features of such a landscape are: [1] mesa; [2] butte; [3] waterfall; [4] canyon; [5] badlands; [6] weak strata; and [7] more resistant strata.

8 Sedimentary rocks laid down in horizontal layers are often tilted by later earth movements. Main rivers flow down the slope (dip) of the beds and erosion etches out the difference in hardness of the rocks to produce scarpland topography. Tributary rivers flow along the strike vales (running at right-angles to the dip of the rocks) on the outcrop of softer beds [1], while harder rocks [2] are weathered to form features called cuestas [3] with a steep scarp face and a gentle dip slope parallel to the dip of the beds. An intrusion of steeply dipping resistant rocks forms a hogsback [4].

9 In folded-rock areas erosion attacks the raised anticlines [1] more readily than the trough-like synclines [2] because anticlinal flexing of rocks tends to form cracks open to the weather. If this process goes far enough, the result is an inverted relief where the deeper valleys follow the anticlines [3] and the former troughs form the summits [4].

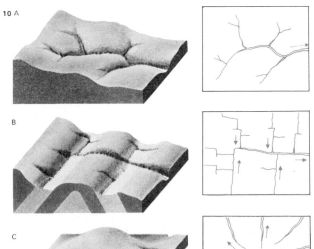

10 The pattern of a river and its tributaries is related to the rocks on which it formed or now flows. On rocks of equal resistance, a dendritic drainage pattern [A] develops. In areas of alternating hard and soft rock, the stream follows the soft rock, forming a trellis [B]. A radial river pattern forms on volcanoes and rock domes [C].

11 River capture is the result of one stream [1] eroding the land at its source. In the process this stream eats into the catchment area of a lesser stream [2] and eventually drains it completely. This leaves a large stream with a sharp elbow of capture and a small "misfit" stream running through a large valley [3].

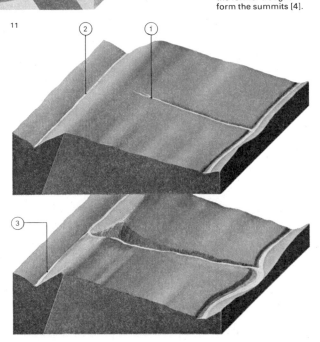

Rivers of ice

Ten per cent of the earth's land surface is covered by glaciers, the relentless and irresistible rivers of ice that are the sculptors of dramatic landscape – the peaks and valleys of the high mountains, the fiords and sea lochs of northwestern Europe, of Greenland, Canada, Chile and New Zealand. Many existing landforms were created by the action of ice (which both destroys old features and creates new ones) during the ice age of the Pleistocene, when as much as 30 per cent of the land surface was glaciated.

Glaciers are formed wherever there is perpetual snow; in other words, they are found in polar regions and on high mountains. As the snow accumulates year after year the older layers are compressed into a granular mass called névé, which later becomes firn when all air is expelled from it. Under the force of gravity this mass starts to move down the slope. As it does so it becomes further compacted into clear, compressed glacier ice.

There are three main types of glaciers: the mountain or valley glaciers, which have their sources in the mountains above the snow line; the piedmont glaciers, formed by the joining of valley glaciers as they spread out at the foot of the mountains; and finally the ice caps, which spread over their source area.

The movement of mountain glaciers

In 1788 the Swiss physicist Horace de Saussure (1740–99) lost an iron ladder on an Alpine glacier. It was found, 44 years later, 4,350m (14,250ft) lower down, thus demonstrating glacial movement.

Ice is a crystalline solid, but it can deform and flow when subjected to a sustained pressure. In glaciers this occurs by slippage of the ice crystals, which are lubricated along their boundaries by a thin layer of liquid water melted by the pressure. The downward motion [2] of the glacier can be seen at its very top, where it is separated from the permanent snow by a deep crevasse known as the bergschrund. Lower down, the movement can be observed by taking sights from fixed points on the mountainside along rows of stakes planted across the glacier. These also show the differential movement of the ice, for a glacier moves faster in its centre

than it does along its edges, where it is slowed by friction. Along a vertical section the speed is fastest on the surface slab, which behaves in a rigid fashion (it breaks, forming crevasses) [4], and the speed decreases towards the bottom. Longitudinal crevasses appear in the surface slab owing to the increasing rate of flow towards the axis of the glacier tongue or owing to the widening of the glacier; transverse crevasses are formed where the slope suddenly increases. Where transverse and longitudinal crevasses intersect, a spectacular ice topography of blocks or pinnacles of ice known as séracs is created.

The rate of movement of a glacier varies considerably and is dependent on the slope, thickness, cross-sectional area, roughness of the bottom and the temperature. Rates can vary from a few centimetres a day to several hundred – 66m (216ft) in the case of an Alaskan glacier.

A glacier can be divided into an upper section, where the temperature prevents melting and more ice is formed, and a lower section where the temperature is higher and ice is lost through melting. A steady rate is

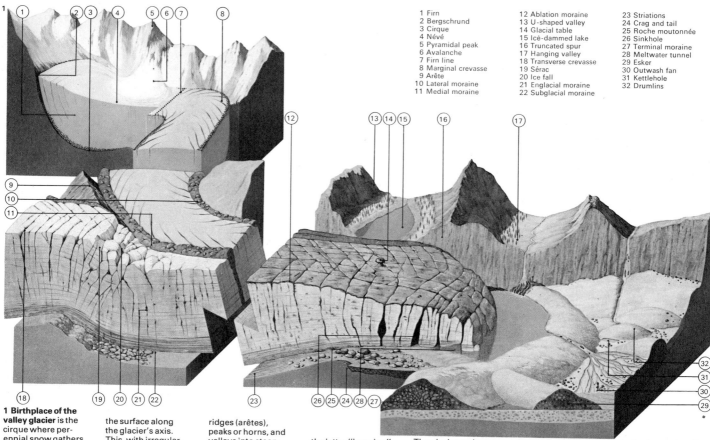

1 Firn	12 Ablation moraine
2 Bergschrund	13 U-shaped valley
3 Cirque	14 Glacial table
4 Névé	15 Ice-dammed lake
5 Pyramidal peak	16 Truncated spur
6 Avalanche	17 Hanging valley
7 Firn line	18 Transverse crevasse
8 Marginal crevasse	19 Sérac
9 Arête	20 Ice fall
10 Lateral moraine	21 Englacial moraine
11 Medial moraine	22 Subglacial moraine

23 Striations
24 Crag and tail
25 Roche moutonnée
26 Sinkhole
27 Terminal moraine
28 Meltwater tunnel
29 Esker
30 Outwash fan
31 Kettlehole
32 Drumlins

1 Birthplace of the valley glacier is the cirque where perennial snow gathers as névé and is compressed to firn. Pulling away from the valley head, the glacier forms a crevasse, the bergschrund. The ice flows fastest at the surface along the glacier's axis. This, with irregularities of the glacier bed, creates crevasses; where these intersect séracs are formed. Glaciers carve the mountains into ridges (arêtes), peaks or horns, and valleys into steep-sided troughs. U-shaped valleys, where glaciers once flowed, have floors that are deeper than those of tributary valleys, leaving the latter "hanging" and often draining by a waterfall. The load of moraine (rock debris) carried away by the glacier deposited at its snout is called till. The glacier melts on the surface along its lower section. The amount of melting can be judged from the height of the glacier tables – unmelted ice pinnacles shaped by a moraine boulder. Meltwaters form subglacial streams which deposit long, winding piles of rubble called eskers under the snout. Other material under the ice forms drumlins and terminal moraines are deposited by retreating glaciers while stationary.

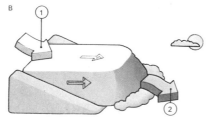

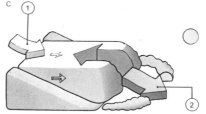

2 The material in a glacier moves constantly downhill. The position of the glacial snout, however, may move downhill [A], remain stationary [B] or move uphill [C] depending on the rate of melting of the ice [2] compared with the rate at which it accretes [1].

achieved when the accretion of ice in the upper section roughly balances that lost lower down. In these conditions the foot of the glacier is stationary. If the climate becomes cooler, the foot of the glacier advances until a new state of equilibrium is reached; under warmer conditions the foot of the glacier retreats to an equilibrium.

Erosion and transport
A glacier is one of the most powerful agents of erosion. Its ice erodes by abrasion and by plucking away at the bedrock. Blocks embedded in the ice are scraped along the bottom, producing grooved (striated) rocks, and resistant rocks are polished into roches moutonnées. The source area is enlarged into an amphitheatre known as a cirque or corrie, and where two such cirques meet they are separated by a sharp ridge called an arête. Three cirques overlapping produce at their centre a pyramidal peak or horn, of which a classic example is the Matterhorn [Key] on the Swiss-Italian border. Mountain glaciers carve their valleys into deep U-shaped troughs; bigger glaciers have deeper valleys than their smaller affluents, giving rise to "hanging" valleys after the glaciers have disappeared.

Glaciers can carry huge loads of debris or moraine [6]. Rocks falling from above on to the sides of a glacier form lateral moraines and where two glaciers converge the inner lateral moraines merge to form a medial moraine. Some debris falls into crevasses to form an englacial moraine and can work its way down to the rocks plucked off the bed and become part of the subglacial moraine.

Glacial deposits
The glacier's debris is eventually deposited at its foot, forming the terminal moraine which is made of totally ungraded material ranging from clay to huge boulders. If the glacier retreats, the abandoned frontal moraine often makes a dam retaining a lake and other lakes appear in the hard-rock depressions carved by the glacier. Rapidly retreating glaciers dump their loads as they go, leaving large rocks as clues to their former size; they also give characteristic and valuable information about former ice ages.

Europe's most photogenic mountain, the Matterhorn, was carved by glaciers into its pyramidal shape.

3 One of Europe's biggest glaciers is the Mer de Glace in the Mont Blanc massif. It is 13km (8 miles) long and 2km (1.2 miles) wide, with a thickness of 150m (500ft). It is formed by the joining of the Talèfre, Leschaux and Géant glaciers, which in turn have several smaller tributaries. Crevasses and surface moraines are conspicuous in this picture, plus a small cirque (with its névé) in the background.

5 Ice caves in glaciers may be formed by incompletely closed crevasses, by the margins of the glacier when it skirts around an obstruction or by meltwaters. Ice melting on the surface drains into crevasses. When a crevasse closes through ice movement, the drain hole is maintained by the water and forms a smooth-sided well. Meltwaters running beneath the glacier can form a network of caves and tunnels.

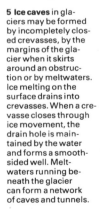

6 Moraine is glacier-borne debris – the rocks, gravel and silt carried by the rivers of ice. It is also used to describe the material once deposited by the melting ice. The terminal moraine at the snout of the glacier illustrated shows the large volume of ungraded matter which ranges in size from huge boulders to fine powders produced by rocks grinding together. This lack of grading distinguishes glacial deposits from those of rivers.

4 The great mass of a glacier flows in a plastic manner, but its surface layers are always rigid and brittle. As a consequence, whenever a glacier flows round a corner or over a hump, or changes its speed, cracks called crevasses appear on the surface at points of tension and wrinkles or pressure ridges are seen at points of compression. The alignment of these depends on the direction in which the pressure acts; they appear in parallel swarms. Two different sets of pressures may produce intersecting swarms, leaving tall pinnacles of ice-séracs between them.

7 Fiords are characteristic of recently glaciated coasts such as those of western Scotland, Norway, southern Chile, British Columbia, southern New Zealand and Greenland. They are long and narrow inlets, steep-sided and often very deep. The deepest in the world is in Chile, with a depth of 1,288m (4,225ft); the Sogne fiord in Norway is the deepest in Europe measuring 1,210m (3,969ft). Shown here is Hardanger fiord, also in Norway. The fiords were the sites of large valley glaciers during the Ice Age. The reason they have been gouged out to such great depths is that glaciers descended to the sea-level which was then very much lower than at present owing to the large amount of water locked into the ice caps.

99

Ice caps and ice ages

The polar ice caps hold just over two per cent of the earth's water; a small amount compared to the oceans (97.2 per cent) but sufficient to raise the level of the oceans by some 40m (130ft) if they were to melt.

Apart from their size, ice caps differ from mountain glaciers in that they flow outwards in all directions from their centres. The largest ice caps are referred to as ice sheets; only two exist nowadays, in Antarctica [2] and in Greenland.

The polar ice sheets
The Greenland ice sheet occupies 1,740,000 square kilometres (670,000 square miles), 80 per cent of the island's area, and has a volume of 2,800,000 cubic kilometres (672,000 cubic miles). Its average thickness is 1.6km (1 mile) and it reaches as much as 3km (1.9 miles) at the centre.

The Antarctic ice sheet has an area about one and a half times as large as the USA – 13 million square kilometres (5 million square miles), and it holds nine times more ice than the Greenland ice sheet, 25 million cubic kilometres (6 million cubic miles). The ice

thickness reaches up to 4km (2.5 miles). This mass flows north and reaches the sea through outlet glaciers and ice shelves that are floating extensions of the ice sheet. The shorelines of the shelves are constantly moving, shedding huge tabular icebergs that are sometimes known as ice islands.

Successive ice ages
The Greenland and Antarctic ice sheets are the last remnants of an ice age that ended, for the mid-latitudes, about 12,000 years ago. Features such as vast amounts of coarse sediments (now referred to as drift), erratic boulders, river terraces and raised beaches had been noted by the early geologists but they were ascribed to the biblical Flood ("Diluvian" deposits). It was not until the mid-nineteenth century that there was widespread belief in the Ice Age.

During the past two million years there have been five major glacial advances and five glacial retreats, the last of these being our present period, the Holocene [1].

Large ice sheets covered the northern continents: most of the British Isles, the

North Sea, The Netherlands, northern Germany and Russia were part of an ice sheet centred on Scandinavia and the Baltic, while mountain glaciers descended from the Alps and the Pyrenees. Siberia and Kamchatka were glaciated, as well as mountains to the south, and in North America the sheet reached Montana, Illinois and New Jersey, and the Rockies had extensive mountain glaciers. There was also an ice sheet covering Argentina up to a latitude of 40°S, large glaciers over the Andes and an ice cap over New Zealand.

The chronology of the periods of glacial advance and retreat is established by the study of periglacial lake sediments (forming annual layers known as varves), of fossil pollens of plants (showing the climatic conditions), of fossil soils between two glacial layers, and of ancient beaches and river terraces which reflect former sea-levels. Other dating techniques involve radio-isotopes and tree rings, while micro-fossils in deep-sea sediments and oxygen isotopic ratios from marine fossils provide clues to the then prevailing temperatures.

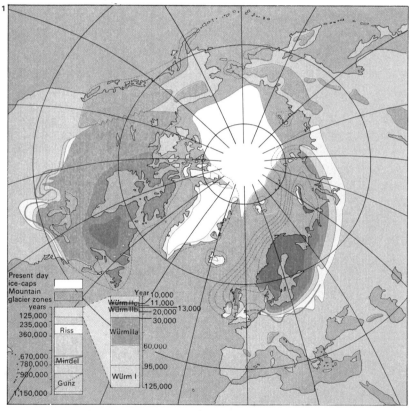

Present day ice-caps
Mountain glacier zones

years		Year
125,000		10,000
235,000		Würm IIc 11,000
360,000	Riss	Würm IIb 20,000 13,000
		30,000
.670,000	Mindel	WürmIIa
.780,000		60,000
.900,000		95,000
1,150,000	Günz	Würm I 125,000

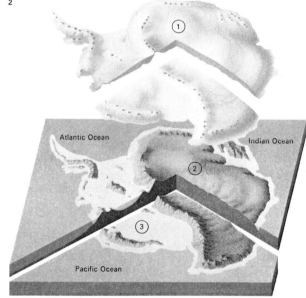

Atlantic Ocean

Indian Ocean

Pacific Ocean

2 Continental ice sheets are now found only in Antarctica and Greenland. In Antarctica the ice [1] covers not only the land [2] but also permanently frozen sea [3]. Beneath the ice the terrain is rugged and variable in height. Because of the weight of the ice, about 40% of the land is depressed below sea-level. If the ice were to melt, there would be a gradual rising of the land, just as the Baltic area is now rising to compensate for the loss of its ice sheet some 12,000 years ago. Because of the melt water, the sea would at first rise faster than the land, drowning much of Antarctica.

1 The last ice age, the Pleistocene, consisted of several periods of glaciation separated by interglacial periods of mild climates. The earliest traces of the glacial advance have been found in Europe in sediments 2,500,000 years old, and represent the Donau glacial stage. This was followed by the Günz (equivalent to the Nebraskan in the American system), the Mindel (Kansan), the Riss (Illinoian) and the four glacial stages of the Würm (Winconsin).

3 During the ice ages, much of northern Europe and North America looked like Antarctica today – a frozen and totally inhospitable world. Antarctica contains 90% of the world's ice and is the only continent without an indigenous human population. It is protected from land grabs both by its climate and by international treaties. The only human beings are found in scattered scientific stations provisioned and relieved from the outside.

Glacial deposits and ice-grooved and polished rock have also been identified in older geological formations, leading to the discovery of former ice ages. Three are known to have occurred during the late Precambrian (940, 770 and 615 million years ago), one during the Devonian (nearly 400 million years ago) and one during the Permo-Carboniferous (295 million years ago).

Origin of ice ages
Some 60 or 70 theories have been put forward to account for the origin of ice ages. Those based on purely terrestrial phenomena call for a predisposed position of the land masses such as the present positions of Antarctica and of the landlocked Arctic Sea, which prevent the temperature-evening effects of the sea from reaching the poles; or else they presuppose changes in the atmosphere, such as a decrease in carbon dioxide content (allowing a faster rate of heat loss to outer space) or an increase in atmospheric dust due to paroxysmal volcanic eruptions, so preventing the warming effect of some of the sun's rays from reaching the earth.

Other hypotheses are astronomical. They propose variations in the sun's output and changes in the sun-earth relationship. One such hypothesis relates the glaciations to the passage of the Solar System through the dust clouds of the two spiral arms of the galaxy: this implies an ice age lasting a few million years every 250 million years. Scientific evidence supports this theory except for the time about 250 million years ago when no ice age occurred but there was, nevertheless, a distinct cooling of the climate as evidenced by fossil faunal changes.

According to the latter hypothesis, we should now be moving out of the last ice age although there is currently much talk of an impending renewal of glaciation. This is based on a southward shift, over the last ten years or so, of the Northern Hemisphere's climatic belts, leading to less sunny summers in the temperate latitudes and to droughts in the Sahel and in Ethiopia and Somalia. But the study of the climate over the past 10,000 years shows many such fluctuations and the present state of knowledge about the origin of ice ages makes forecasting difficult.

KEY

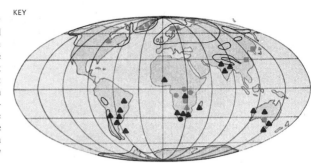

☐ Area of Pleistocene glaciation	● Devonian tillite	● Precambrian 2 tillite (770 million years)
▲ Permo-Carboniferous tillite	■ Precambrian 3 tillite (615 million years)	▲ Precambrian 1 tillite (940 million years)

Ice ages have several times swept over various parts of the earth and, although of short duration by geological standards, have left a durable impression on its crust. The map shows the limits reached by the ice sheets during the last ice age in the Pleistocene (2 million to 12,000 years ago). Evidence for other ice ages comes from tillites, which are consolidated glacial deposits. Also shown are the main locations of Precambrian, Devonian and Permo-Carboniferous tillites. These were laid down in high altitudes but have since been moved out of place by continental drift.

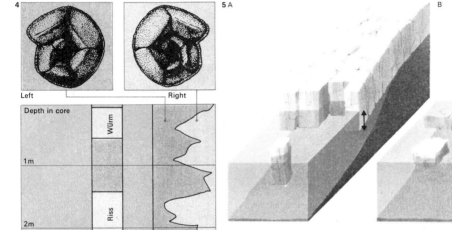

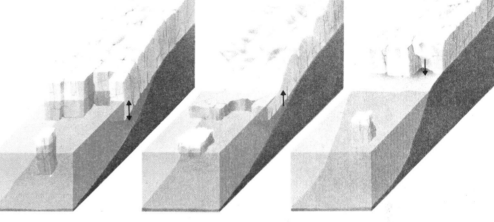

4 The sediments on the ocean floor accumulate very slowly and a few metres can represent millions of years. Microscopic fossils of such animals as Foraminifera can record changes of the climate. The coiling of *Globorotalia truncatulinoides* [top] varies according to the temperature of the water, being predominantly to the left during cold periods and to the right under warm conditions. Analysis of specimens from many cores has provided a good indication of the changes in ocean temperatures. This method is often used with other investigations and particularly with studies on the abundance of other Foraminifera such as *Globorotalia menardii* and *Globigerina pachyderma*, which are also sensitive to changes that affect the sea's temperature.

5 Icebergs form in several ways. When a glacier reaches the sea it floats away from the bed. The movement of waves and tides exerts pressures on this floating ice causing lumps to break away [A]. If the glacier is moving rapidly when it reaches the sea, a projecting shelf of ice forms under the water. The buoyancy of this shelf exerts an upward pressure causing pieces to break off [B]. The snout of the glacier may be above the level of the sea and hence lumps may break off under the force of gravity and fall into the water [C]. The forming of new icebergs is known as "calving". Northern icebergs come from the Greenland ice sheet, but the largest ones originate in Antarctica. The largest iceberg ever seen was 336km (208 miles) long and 97km (60 miles) in width.

6 At periods of maximum glaciation, sea-levels were 180m (590 ft) lower than at the present time because of the large amount of water frozen in the ice. Many of today's islands would be joined to adjacent continental masses – the British Isles, for example, would have been part of Europe. Land bridges appeared, especially in such areas as the Bering Strait. These bridges helped the spread of mankind round the world.

Glacial periods   Coiling ratios

101

Winds and deserts

The most obvious characteristic of the desert is its emptiness for it is almost devoid of plants, animals, mankind and water. Hot deserts are places where the heat of the sun [3] is capable of evaporating all the water that falls as rain; most of them have less than 10cm (4in) of rain a year [2] which falls heavily and in rare showers. Many areas have no rain for years – then a sudden cloudburst causes temporary, fast-flowing streams called flash floods. This water usually drains into shallow lakes that have no outlet to the sea, and there it soon evaporates.

The face of the desert

The hot desert is not all sand; in fact only about 20 per cent is covered with sand. Much is bare rock, often cut by deep wadis (intermittent riverways) [5] or carved into fantastic shapes by winds [10]. The landform of rock deserts is very angular. The rounded hill shapes of more humid lands are missing because there is no steady downwash.

In many desert tracts the sand has been blown away, leaving a surface of boulders [6]. Rock or boulder desert may grade into sand

desert [Key, 4]. At first there are dunes with no sand between them; then these pass into areas where the whole surface is sand-covered and is known as a sand sea.

The geographical locations of most deserts lie within the belts of high air pressure centred on the tropics of Cancer and Capricorn in which the air is always very dry [1]. The deserts of Asia and North America lie in the interior of those continents and are cut off from the rain-bearing winds by surrounding mountain ranges. The world's largest deserts stretch across Africa and great parts of Asia. Europe is the only continent with no large deserts. Almost all deserts, such as the Sahara and the Kalahari, are hot, but a few, such as those in the Arctic and on high mountains, owe their lifelessness to extreme cold.

Weathering, the process by which rock is broken down into sand and clay, takes place very slowly in the hot desert compared with more humid lands. On many days the surface temperature of the rocks varies from about 5°C (41°F) in the cool of the night to about 40°C (104°F) at midday. This results in a daily expansion and contraction of the rock

surface, setting up strains that gradually break it up into sand. The small amount of moisture, mostly in the form of dew, may also cause slow chemical weathering.

Water and wind effects

Water from occasional downpours drains rapidly into the wadis, carrying with it loose stones, sand or mud. It rushes down as a flash flood and the stones it carries erode the sides of the wadis. At the end of the wadi is a cone-shaped pile of stones and sand called an alluvial fan [4]. The water sinks into this, leaving the coarse sediment it is carrying on top, and eventually drains out of the bottom taking with it only the finest material, mostly mud and dissolved salts. It then runs into large, flat areas and forms temporary shallow lakes [4]. Within a few days the water has evaporated, leaving a mixture of salt and mud in what are called salinas.

The main effect of the wind in the desert is to move sand and dust. In humid areas vegetation protects the soil from the wind but in the desert there is no vegetation and moreover the sand and dust are completely

1 Deserts are formed in areas where the rate of water loss by evaporation is greater than the rate of water gain by precipitation. Temperature, as well as rainfall, is very important – forests

grow in cool latitudes in rainfall that would give only scrub and semi-arid conditions in the tropics. Approximately 25 per cent of the earth's surface is characterized by dry climates, and

deserts themselves cover a large proportion of the land between latitudes 10° and 35° north and south. On this map desert areas are red and the regions of semi-arid climates are buff.

2 The rainfall in a desert area such as Cufra, in Libya, is vastly different from that in a wetter area such as Greenwich, in

England. Desert rainfall is usually less than 10cm (4in) a year and is very irregular with cloudbursts and long dry spells.

3 The daily temperature range in a desert is very great due to the lack of an insulating cloud layer. At higher latitudes

maximum temperature is lower but the temperature range is also small since cloud cover tends to contain the heat.

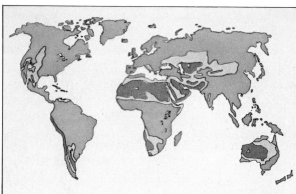

2
| Cufra, Libya | Greenwich, England |

3
| Cufra, Libya | Greenwich, England |

4 The topography of a desert is characterized by the relative absence of chemical weathering. Most erosion takes place mechanically through wind abrasion or the effect of heat. Mesas [1] are large flat-

topped areas with steep sides. The butte [2] is a flat isolated hill also with steep sides. Yardangs [3] are wind-eroded features consisting of tabular masses of resistant rock resting on undercut

pillars of softer material. They are elongated in the direction of the wind. Alluvial fans [5] are deltaic pebble-mounds deposited by flash floods, usually found at the end of wadis [4]. A salt pan

[6] is a temporary lake of brackish water also formed by flash floods. An inselberg [7] is an isolated hill rising abruptly from the plain. A pediment [8] is a gently inclining rock surface.

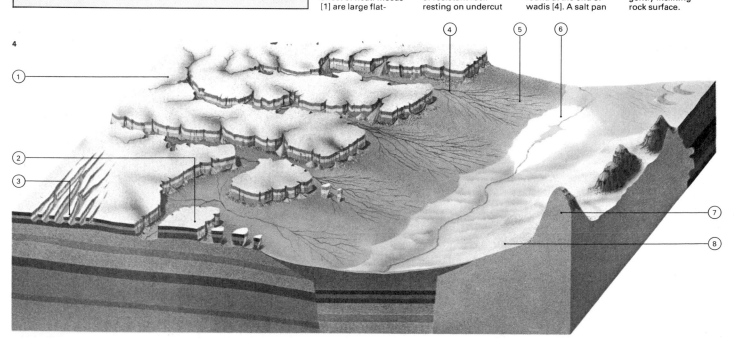

dry and easily moved. The wind takes the sand and dust from the surface of the alluvial fans, plus any sand produced by weathering, and blows it into dunes.

Sand grains are not carried far in the air, but the strongest wind causes the grains to move in series of bounces [10]. Although they are never lifted more than 1m (39in) above the ground, the wind-blown particles "sand blast" any rock or pebbles in their path and polish the surface of any pebble facing the wind. If the direction from which the wind comes varies, the pebble will acquire several flattened surfaces giving it a pyramidal shape. Such a pebble is called a ventifact or a dreikanter. The sand also erodes the solid rock over which it is blown, etching out any softer or weaker parts and leaving the harder rock standing up in ridges called yardangs, or in "rock mushrooms" called zeugens [6].

How sand dunes are formed

There are two main types of sand dunes; barchan and seif dunes. Barchan dunes [9] are usually found on the edge of the desert where there is a relatively small amount of sand and often some scrub vegetation. These dunes are crescent-shaped, with their points facing downwind, and between them there is only gravel or bare rock. The wind blows the sand up the gently sloping windward side of the dune and when the grains reach the top they roll down the steeper leeward side. Therefore the grains at the back of the dune are constantly being brought to the front; in this way the dune slowly advances. Large barchan dunes move extremely slowly, while small barchans may advance 15m (50ft) a year. Where there are many barchan dunes they may line up to form a transverse dune.

Seif or longitudinal dunes [8] cover a much larger area of the desert. They are long ridges of sand separated by strips of rock or stones kept clean of sand by eddies of wind. Barchan and seif dunes merge into areas where all the desert floor is covered with sand and the dunes lose their shape and become part of an irregularly rolling sand surface.

The finest dust may be lifted thousands of metres into the air and carried for hundreds of kilometres and, if blown out of the desert, forms a very fertile soil called loess.

KEY

Deserts are extremely dry areas that support only a much-reduced vegetation and a few nomadic tribes scattered in small encampments such as the Saharan one shown here. A main geological agent in deserts is wind. Its effects are emphasized by the lack of vegetation and of moisture that holds fine-grained particles together. The wind sweeps some areas clean, leaving bare rocks; sand-laden winds sculpture the rocks and the sand is eventually deposited, forming dunes.

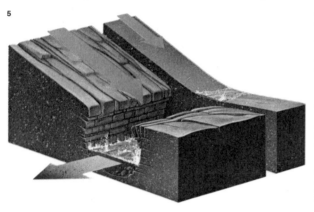

5 Wadis are steep or vertically sided valleys in which water runs only during rare flash floods. They start with random depressions in desert mountain areas or arid plateaus. They are deepened and widened by the floods which, because the water is moving so fast, are able to prise away and move large slabs of rock. During a flood the water may cover the whole width of the wadi.

6 Rocky surfaces are far more common in deserts than sand seas. When loose material containing pebbles or larger stones is exposed to wind, all the fine dust and sand particles are blown away leaving a desert pavement or reg. The surfaces of mesas and larger plateaus are scoured clean by the wind, and form rock deserts called hammadas showing wind-eroded features – yardangs and mushroom-shaped rocks called zeugens.

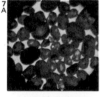

7 Grains of desert sand [A] are largely spherical and appear "frosted" because they have been rounded by countless collisions with other grains. River sand grains [B] are less polished, having suffered fewer collisions. River sand also contains many grains of soft minerals, such as mica, which would have been ground to dust in the desert. Desert sand is more uniform in size than river sand.

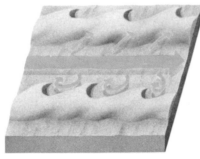

8 Seif dunes are long ridges of sand with bare rock between. Each dune may be up to 40m (130ft) high, 600m (1,960ft) wide and 400km (250 miles) long. The prevailing wind blows parallel to the ridges.

9 Barchans are isolated and crescent-shaped dunes that slowly migrate downwind, horns forward. They occur only in areas such as Turkestan where the wind always blows from the same direction.

10 A pedestal is a large lump of rock supported only by a thin neck. In a sandstorm the wind is only able to make the sand grains bounce up to about 1m (39in) above the ground. When the sand collides with the rock, it sandblasts it and wears it away. The dust and finer particles, which are carried higher, are too light to abrade the rock. Therefore the rock is eroded only at its base, which gives it the appearance of a mushroom.

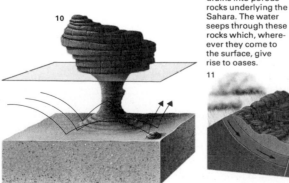

11 Rain falling on the Atlas Mountains drains into porous rocks underlying the Sahara. The water seeps through these rocks which, wherever they come to the surface, give rise to oases.

12 In prehistoric times continuous rivers ran in the Sahara. Their former courses can still be seen from the air. But today it is much drier and habitation is restricted to a few oases.

Coastlines

Coasts are constantly changing [Key], sometimes at a dramatic rate. During a North Sea storm in 1953, powerful waves battered eastern England. Near Lowestoft in Suffolk, the sea undercut an 8m-high (26ft) cliff and removed 11m (36ft) of land in about two hours.

The rate of erosion, which is caused by waves [1], currents and tides, depends on the nature of the rock. Tough outcrops of granite are much more resistant than, for example, the glacial boulder clays, gravels and sands in Massachusetts where erosion of the cliffs of Martha's Vineyard island is taking place at a rate of 1.7m (5.5ft) a year and where a lighthouse has had to be resited three times.

The causes of coastal erosion
The force exerted by waves in the Atlantic has been estimated to be about 9,765kg per square metre (2,000lb per square foot) and this force may be three times as great during severe storms, when blocks of concrete weighing more than 1,000 tonnes have been dislodged. The hydraulic action of water is seen when high waves crash against a rock face. Air compressed by the water in cracks and crevices expands as it is released, sometimes with explosive force, enlarging cracks or shattering rock faces.

Another form of marine erosion is corrosion, when waves are armed with sand, pebbles and, during storms, boulders. The waves lift up these materials and hurl them at the shore, bombarding and undercutting the bases of cliffs. Such action may hollow out sea caves within which erosion continues. Sometimes the roof of a cave collapses to form a small opening or blowhole. When waves pound through the cave, jets of spray spurt through the blowhole.

Because rocks differ in hardness, sea erosion may create a series of bays, cut in relatively soft rock, separated by headlands of fairly hard rock. The exposed headlands are battered from both sides. Sea caves forming on each side of the exposed headland may eventually meet in an arch. When the arch collapses, an offshore pillar of rock, called a stack [2], remains behind. In this way, even headlands of hard rock are finally worn away.

Another form of marine erosion, attrition, occurs when sand, pebbles and rocks collide and are rubbed together by the moving water. Loose, jagged material is smoothed and ground down into finer and finer particles. The sea also erodes land by the solvent action of seawater on some rock.

The movement of eroded material
Eroded material is transported along the coast mainly by wave action. Waves usually strike the shore obliquely. As they move forward, they sweep material diagonally up the beach. As the water recedes, the backwash pulls the loose fragments down the steepest slope at right-angles to the shore. This zigzag movement, called longshore drift [3], moves sand and pebbles along the coast. Currents and tides also contribute to the movement of eroded material.

Because of the importance of coastlines to man, attempts are often made to control longshore drift and erosion. Common methods include the building of groynes [5] (low walls usually at right-angles to the shore) and sea walls to protect the coast against storm waves.

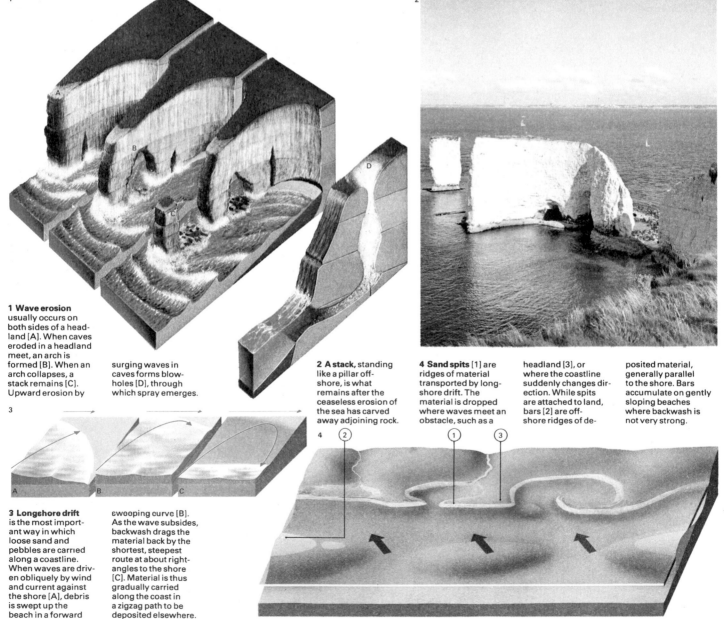

1 Wave erosion usually occurs on both sides of a headland [A]. When caves eroded in a headland meet, an arch is formed [B]. When an arch collapses, a stack remains [C]. Upward erosion by surging waves in caves forms blowholes [D], through which spray emerges.

2 A stack, standing like a pillar offshore, is what remains after the ceaseless erosion of the sea has carved away adjoining rock.

3 Longshore drift is the most important way in which loose sand and pebbles are carried along a coastline. When waves are driven obliquely by wind and current against the shore [A], debris is swept up the beach in a forward swooping curve [B]. As the wave subsides, backwash drags the material back by the shortest, steepest route at about right-angles to the shore [C]. Material is thus gradually carried along the coast in a zigzag path to be deposited elsewhere.

4 Sand spits [1] are ridges of material transported by longshore drift. The material is dropped where waves meet an obstacle, such as a headland [3], or where the coastline suddenly changes direction. While spits are attached to land, bars [2] are offshore ridges of deposited material, generally parallel to the shore. Bars accumulate on gently sloping beaches where backwash is not very strong.

When material moved by longshore drift meets an obstacle, such as a headland, or where the coast abruptly changes direction, the transport of material may slow down and it may pile up in narrow ridges called spits [4]. Spits often curve part of the way across bays and estuaries. Baymouth bars are spits that seal off a bay completely. Other bars, unlike spits, are not attached to land. They are formed in the sea and run roughly parallel to the coast. Similar features are tombolos – natural bridges joining an island to the mainland or linking one island to another.

Other characteristic coastlines

Since the end of the Pleistocene ice age, melted ice has increased the volume of the oceans and many coastlines have been flooded [7]. These coasts of submergence include flooded river valleys, called rias, and flooded glaciated valleys, called fiords. Other coasts have been raised up by earth movements. Coasts of emergence can be identified by such features as raised beaches and former sea cliffs that are now inland.

Some coastlines have a special character

related to the geological structure of the coast. The two main kinds of coastlines in this category are concordant or longitudinal coastlines and discordant or transverse coastlines. A concordant coastline occurs in Yugoslavia along the Adriatic Sea, where the geological structures parallel the coast. Following submergence, the sea has occupied former valleys while former mountain ranges have become offshore islands. Discordant coastlines occur where the coast cuts across the direction of the geological structures, as in the ria coastline of southwest Ireland.

A special feature of coastlines in tropical seas results from the growth of coral. Coral polyps live in warm water with plenty of sunlight and cannot grow in depths greater than 45m (150ft). Fringing coral reefs develop in shallow water near the shore. Barrier reefs lie some distance away from the shore. They may be built on a non-coral foundation or they may have increased in depth as the depth of the sea increased. The most intriguing coral features are atolls [8], circular or horseshoe-shaped groups of coral islands in mid-ocean.

KEY

Coastlines are shaped by erosion and deposition which are the result of wind, waves, currents and tides interacting with the rocks and sediments of the land. Among common coastal features

are headlands [1] of relatively hard rock, isolated rock pillars called stacks [2], cliffs [4], natural arches [5], caves [7] and blowholes [6] in the roofs of caves. Features resulting

from deposition are beaches [3], tombolos [8], lagoons [9], salt marshes [10], spits [11] and sand dunes [12]. To slow down the drift of eroded material along a coast, groynes [13] are often built.

5

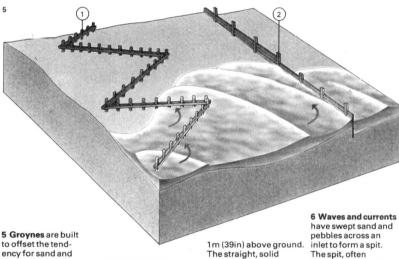

5 Groynes are built to offset the tendency for sand and shingle to be gradually carried sideways along a beach. There are two main kinds of groyne.

The zigzag timber pile type [1] has piles driven 2m (6ft) below the ground and standing

1m (39in) above ground. The straight, solid groyne [2] consists of heavy planks bolted to piles that are also sunk 2m (6.5ft) into the ground

6 Waves and currents have swept sand and pebbles across an inlet to form a spit. The spit, often called a baymouth bar, has cut off the inlet from the sea, leaving behind it an enclosed lagoon.

6

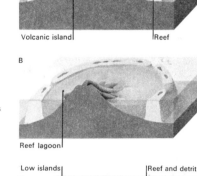

7A

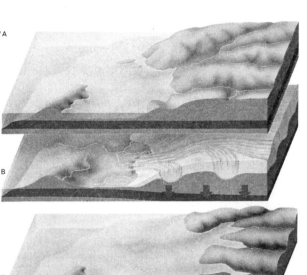

7 Changes in sea-level caused by an increase in the volume of ocean water, or by earth movements, determine the character of some coastlines. When a coastal area unaffected by glaciation [A] is overtaken by an ice age, glaciers and ice caps form on the land [B]. The sea-level drops and the weight of the ice eventually depresses coastal valleys. With the end of the ice age, melted ice returns to the sea. Even though the land begins to rise, recovery is not fast enough to offset a considerable rise in sea-level [C]. Flooded river valleys or fiords (drowned glacial valleys) characterize such a coastline – a coast of submergence.

8A

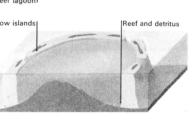

Volcanic island   Reef

B

Reef lagoon

Low islands   Reef and detritus

C

8 Atolls and coral reefs are found only in tropical seas. The most striking coral feature is the atoll, a ring or horseshoe-shaped group of coral islands. Corals grow in warm, fairly shallow water to depths of about 90m (300ft). But the depth of coral in many atolls is much greater than this. One theory is that the coral began to form as a reef in the shallows of a volcanic island [A]. Then the sea-level began to rise and the island slowly sank [B]. But the coral growth kept pace with these gradual changes, leaving an atoll of low islands [C]. In this way, depths of coral to as much as 1,600m (5,250ft) can be explained.

The record in the rocks

The earth's rocks form a tattered and fragmented manuscript of our planet's past. Although sketchy in places, the historical record can be traced nearly 3,800 million years back in time. This date corresponds to the age of the oldest known rocks. The sedimentary strata in particular are ideal signposts through the past since their features identify the circumstances under which they were deposited and made into rocks.

Clues to the past

The record of geological history, as preserved by sedimentary rocks [1], is known as the "stratigraphical column". It refers to the total succession of rocks, from the oldest to the most recent. The study of its distinguishing features is the science of stratigraphy, which deals with the definition and interpretation of stratified sedimentary rocks.

The science of geology was rescued from the futile perusal of biblical texts for clues to the earth's past by the exposition of the principle of "uniformitarianism" by the Scottish geologist James Hutton (1726–97). This was

propounded in Hutton's work, *Theory of the Earth*, published in 1795, and maintained that the nature of present geological processes was fundamentally similar to those of the past and that rock folds and tilts revealed in strata were caused not by violent upheavals, such as earthquakes, but by gradual pressures within the earth. Uniformitarianism implies that the characteristic features of erosion (wearing down of rocks) and the transportation and deposition of sediments produced by erosion are the same throughout history. Since these features can easily be recognized in sedimentary rock laid down millions of years ago, past events are best interpreted in the light of what is known about the present. In Hutton's words, "the present is the key to the past".

Superposition and correlation

The fundamental concept of stratigraphy is the law of "superposition", which states that in any horizontal, undisturbed sedimentary sequence, the lowest rocks are older than those lying above them. This law applies not only to the relative ages of different strata but

also to the minerals and fossils found within a specific layer. Lower-lying ones were deposited before those above them. Superposition is essential to establishing the comparative ages of the various beds in sedimentary formation and is the single most important prerequisite of geological mapping. In archaeology the same principles apply. Artefacts and fossils found in deeper layers of earth predate those in layers above them.

Igneous rocks (formed from molten magma), unlike sedimentary ones, are not laid down in neat successive layers. They can reach their underlying positions only by filtering up through existing formations while still in a molten state. These intrusive rocks, such as granite, gabbro and diorite, are always younger than the rocks that surround them. However, when they reach the surface to form lavas – such as basalt, obsidian and rhyolite (igneous rocks of very fine texture) – they are, as are sedimentary rocks, always younger than the rocks below them.

Since the complete stratigraphical column has never been discovered in any one site (it would have a thickness of many hun-

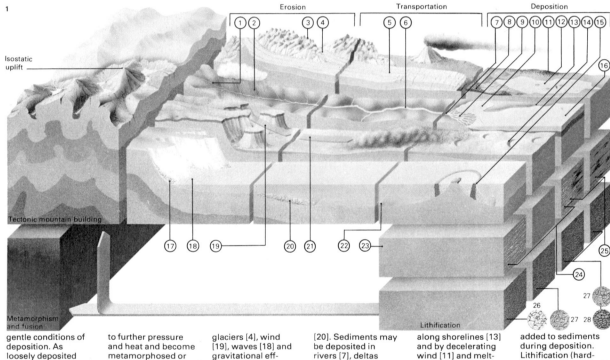

1 The sedimentary cycle begins when sedimentary, metamorphic or igneous rocks are thrust towards the earth's surface, at various times in their history, by mountain building, folding and faulting or the vertical uplift of land freed from the weight of glaciers after an ice age. Rock that becomes exposed to the chemical and mechanical agents of weathering will be rapidly eroded and deposited in new sites by a host of transporting mechanisms. Accumulating sediments possess characteristics that can positively identify the environment and the kind of rock found in their area of origin. They also acquire features that are clues to their environment of deposition, be it desert, swamp, lake bottom or sea-shore. Thus, black shales derived from finely-graded silt and mud can indicate a warm, humid climate and

gentle conditions of deposition. As loosely deposited sediments build up they are transformed into hardened rock. The newly formed rock may be subjected

to further pressure and heat and become metamorphosed or even melted and fused into igneous rock. Agents of erosion include rivers [1], rain [2], frost [3],

glaciers [4], wind [19], waves [18] and gravitational effects [17]. Transportation is performed by glaciers [5], rivers [6], wind [21] and ocean currents

[20]. Sediments may be deposited in rivers [7], deltas [9], lagoons [10], lakes [12], deserts [14], coral reefs [15], shallow and deep seas [16, 22],

along shorelines [13] and by decelerating wind [11] and melting glaciers [8]. Shells [24], plant debris [25] and remnants of other living organisms [23] may be

added to sediments during deposition. Lithification (hardening process) occurs by compaction [28], cementation [27] and recrystallization of fragments [26].

2 The Grand Canyon of Colorado reveals a massive section of the geological history of the earth. Here, the swift-flowing Colorado River, laden with an estimated daily burden of some 500,000 tonnes of debris, has gouged a scar 1.9km (1.2 miles) deep in the surrounding plateau. This erosive activity has been continuous since the Tertiary. The gradual but prolonged uplifting of the area caused the Colorado to cut a deep canyon in order

to maintain its graded profile. In the canyon's plunging walls, hundreds of metres of sedimentary strata are exposed, consisting largely of marine limestones, fresh-water shales and wind-deposited sandstones. The lowest Palaeozoic rocks rest unconformably upon a basement of plutonic and metamorphic Precambrian rock. The granites and schists of this rock are the roots of ancient mountains, their tops long ago eroded

away. Radiometric datings have established these rocks as being some 1,600–1,800 million years old. Even a cursory inspection of the canyon is almost a complete course in palaeogeology. Here can be witnessed the successive ages when submergence, uplift, erosion, deposition and folding and faulting have occurred in the plateau. The fossil record ranges from primitive algae and trilobites through dinosaurs to remains of early camels and horses.

dreds of kilometres), assembling its highly fragmented sections in correct order requires geological detective work to correlate widely scattered beds of rocks.

The most obvious tactic is to follow the layers of a specific outcrop as far as possible. This method is usually only possible over a limited area since erosion, deposition and folding or faulting will tend to interrupt or obliterate rock outcrops [3]. Another method of determining the extent of a formation is by searching for various similarities in the rocks. Various features of deposition, weathering and mineralization all identify rocks that belong to the same formation. Correlations can also be established by comparing vertical sections of rock.

Using fossils as clocks

Fossils are an excellent tool for correlation [2]. The most useful are those that are widely distributed but limited in their vertical range, thus indicating that they flourished for relatively brief periods of time. These are known as index or guide fossils.

As living organisms have always under-

gone continuous evolution, their fossil remains can be used to identify rocks of comparatively similar geological time. The fossil litter within sedimentary rocks enables palaeontologists to recognize different strata of the same age. And it can be logically deduced from the law of superposition that the remains of primitive life forms occur in rocks lying beneath those containing more advanced forms.

Most fossils are the remains of organisms that lived in the same area and at the same time as the rock in which they are found was being deposited. They are excellent guides to the then existing environment. For instance, fossils of reef-building corals [5] are an indication that clear, warm, shallow sea conditions prevailed.

One of the first attempts to relate fossils to the rocks in which they occur was made by the English surveyor William Smith in the late eighteenth century. He established the lateral or horizontal continuity that exists between scattered outcrops of rocks by identifying strata through their fossil content, as well as by their texture, colour and position.

Towering buttes and mesas in Monument Valley, Colorado, reveal the character of the geological ages of the region. Individual beds within these outcrops can be traced throughout the area, although the rock in between is missing, thus demonstrating the use of lateral continuity. The scale of erosion in the Colorado Plateau is matched by few regions in the world. Several thousand metres of rock have been eroded, leaving only isolated, flat-capped outcrops here and there. Not all the outcrops are sedimentary rock for some are the solidified plugs of ancient volcanoes whose sloping flanks have long ago been worn away.

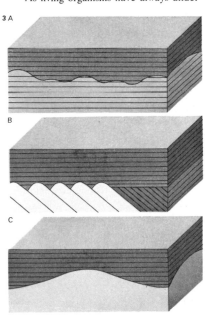

3 A

B

C

3 "Unconformities" occur when there is a break in sedimentation due to erosion. This creates a gap in the geological record of the earth's history. Unconformities are of three varieties. Disconformities [A] are recognizable because the older strata have not been tilted or in any way deformed before younger rock was deposited above them on the same horizontal plane. Angular unconformities [B] occur where the lower-lying strata have been tilted, deformed and eroded before the deposition of other rocks. Where bedded rock layers overlie non-bedded igneous mass, a nonconformity [C] is said to occur.

Rock-forming organisms

Rock-destroying organisms

Rock-accreting organisms

4 Living organisms may both create and destroy rocks. Some rocks are formed when decaying vegetation [1] becomes coal or when the droppings of bird colonies [2] accumulate as phosphate deposits. In marine environments calcareous algae [3] form limestone deposits while fish skeletons [4] may accumulate as beds of phosphate. Corals [5] and tiny globigerina skeletons [6] form limestone sediments while radiolaria [7], which build their hard parts with silica, create siliceous deposits. Tree roots [8] and piddocks [9] hasten rock destruction. Mangrove [10] and dune grass [11] trap loose sediment that may harden.

5

6

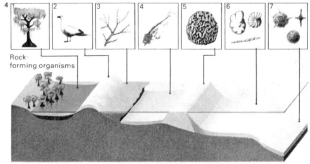

5 Entire islands have been built by small organisms, corals and algae. The wreath-shaped reef and sheltered lagoon of a coral atoll is built upon the crown of a subsiding peak. The symbiotic relationship between certain algae and coral polyps is responsible for the formation of coral islands. Coral itself is too fragile to form a reef unless it is reinforced by the carbonate-producing algae *Zooxanthella* spp. Reef corals thrive in water no deeper than 45m (150ft) or colder than 20°C (68°F). Coral formations in a sedimentary sequence are excellent indicators of the prevailing climatic conditions at the time when the rock was laid down.

6 A delta's sediments are laid down in a specific order that may be endlessly repeated if the region of deposition is sinking. Limestone deposits [4] cover the sea-bed when the delta is too distant to be influential [A]. As the delta encroaches [B], fine-grained muds that will become shale [3] are deposited, followed by coarser, sandstone-forming sediments [2] as the advance continues [C]. As the water shallows, current bedding [D] indicates that sand is being deposited. Once the delta builds above water level [E] it can support swamp vegetation which forms coal [1]. When the region sinks [F] the cycle restarts.

Clues to the past

The earth's rocks are in a state of constant change. Mountains are worn away by wind, rain and frost and the debris formed is transported by rivers, streams, glaciers, wind and sea currents to be deposited on valley floors and sea-beds. There the sediments are buried and subjected to processes that turn them into sedimentary rocks, later to be uplifted as mountains to start the process all over again. One of the tasks of a geologist is to determine the sequence of these events in particular areas and to do this he uses the tell-tale features preserved in the rocks themselves. This study is known as stratigraphy.

The concept of facies
The term "facies" encompasses all the features of a particular rock or stratum of rock that indicate the conditions in which those rocks were formed. Such features include the mineral content, the shapes and sizes of the particles, the sedimentary structures, the fossils, the relationship to the beds above and below, the colour and even the smell – everything that can be described about the rock.

The mineral content can show whether a

sedimentary rock was precipitated out of salts dissolved in seawater or built up from material washed off already existing terrains, and can show the nature of these original terrains. The presence of grains of garnet, for example, show that the original rocks were metamorphic whereas olivine crystals indicate the existence of original rocks that were igneous. The shapes of the constituent particles indicate how far the material has been transported from the source – angular fragments have not travelled far but rounded grains have been carried long distances and have had their corners and edges broken off by the violence of their journey. If a rock consists of particles that are more or less the same size then it can be deduced that the particles have been moved about (or sorted) by currents before coming to rest. A mixture of particle sizes denotes a rapid transportation and dumping of material.

Sedimentary structures give a direct indication of the conditions under which the sediment was accumulated. Ripple marks [7] are formed under shallow water conditions, rain pits [13] and mud cracks show the drying

out of shallow pools, small-scale cross-bedding shows the presence of currents and the direction of the currents can be determined by the attitude of the bedding.

Stories told by fossils
Animals are selective about which environments they inhabit and a recognizable fossil in a rock can be the most important clue a geologist can have to the environment under which the rock was formed [3, 9]. The modern bivalve *Scrobicularia*, for example, lives only buried in oxygen-deficient mud. When a fossil *Scrobicularia* is found in shale it can be inferred that the shale was laid down in an oxygen-free environment. Such organisms are usually very sensitive to environment and when they suddenly disappear in a geological succession it can be deduced that conditions have changed drastically.

The condition of the fossils is also important. If the remains are broken up and the fragments are well sorted any deductions made from them must be fairly suspect. It probably means that the dead bodies have been washed about by currents and in some

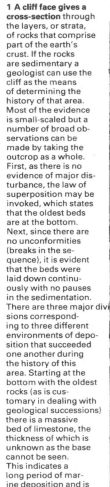

1 A cliff face gives a cross-section through the layers, or strata, of rocks that comprise part of the earth's crust. If the rocks are sedimentary a geologist can use the cliff as the means of determining the history of that area. Most of the evidence is small-scaled but a number of broad observations can be made by taking the outcrop as a whole. First, as there is no evidence of major disturbance, the law of superposition may be invoked, which states that the oldest beds are at the bottom. Next, since there are no unconformities (breaks in the sequence), it is evident that the beds were laid down continuously with no pauses in the sedimentation. There are three major divisions corresponding to three different environments of deposition that succeeded one another during the history of this area. Starting at the bottom with the oldest rocks (as is customary in dealing with geological successions) there is a massive bed of limestone, the thickness of which is unknown as the base cannot be seen. This indicates a long period of marine deposition and is followed by an alternating sequence of shales, sandstones and coal, suggesting a delta environment. A thick deposit of cross-bedded sandstone is found at the top, indicating a desert environment. Closer inspection of individual beds is needed before a detailed history of the sequence can be worked out.

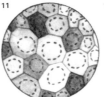

11 The solid mosaic of the sandstone, magnified, reveals the original rounded shapes of each grain within the crystals. This roundness, with the red coloration and constant size, suggests desert sand.

12 The conclusion that a desert existed when the sand was deposited is borne out by the presence of large-scale cross-bedding. This is formed when sand dunes advance over one another, remov-

ing their tops and preserving the bedding on their downwind sides. The red tinge is due to the oxidation of iron – a reaction that takes place under very dry conditions, similar to those found in the deserts of today.

6 Shale, the lowest bed in the next division, is made up of fine mud particles showing that a river was emptying into the sea nearby. The finer debris was carried farther away from the shore.

7 Above the shale is found a bed of sandstone, formed as the river mouth encroached and deposited sand. Samples obtained from the cliff show ripple marks – typical structures

of sands deposited in shallow waters, revealing that the sands were built up almost to sea-level. The ripples are aligned at right-angles to the current and so the direction of the river mouth is determined.

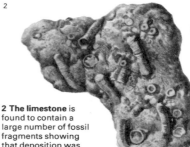

2 The limestone is found to contain a large number of fossil fragments showing that deposition was slow. The broken nature of the fossils shows that constant currents did not allow a dead organism to lie in one place for any length of time.

3 Most of the fossils are of crinoids (sea lilies). These are related to the starfish and are sessile, being anchored to the sea-bed by a flexible stalk. Their presence indicates a shallow sea environment rich in floating organic food particles.

cases they will have been brought into the area from a completely different environment. On the other hand, if the fossil is obviously in its life position, as for example a burrowing creature in its burrow or a sedentary organism still attached to its substratum, then it is quite certain that this is the environment in which it lived and deduction can be made accordingly.

Occasionally a derived fossil may be found. This is a fossil that has been eroded from an original rock and laid down with other rock debris to form the new deposit. Fortunately this occurrence is rare and is unlikely to confuse a trained geologist.

The evidence is put together
After analysing the numerous features of sedimentary formations, a geologist must piece them together painstakingly to form a coherent whole. Some features are confusing and difficult to interpret; others speak for themselves. Thus a cross-section of rock grading from limestone to shale and sandstone [1] is a typical sequence indicating that the sea was encroached on by river sedi-

ments, eventually building the area up to above sea-level. Similarly, periods of glaciation are typified by distinct striations or gouge marks in the rocks where ice sheets, charged with an enormous load of debris, have ground their way across the land. Another feature of glaciation is the random embedding of irregularly shaped broken rock fragments in finer material. This occurs where the glacier has deposited its load and the resulting rock is known as a tillite.

Palaeogeography is the branch of historical geology that is concerned with the past distribution of land and sea. With the relevant items of data obtained from the study of sedimentary formations, a geologist can construct palaeogeographic maps that give a picture of the ancient world. But such maps tend to be somewhat speculative. Information is often sparse and there are enormous difficulties in interpreting the relative ages of outcrops and thus plotting the ancient boundaries between the land and sea. What these maps do reveal with startling effect is the tremendous transformation that every region has undergone.

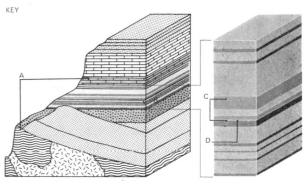

KEY

Rocks can be considered in terms of their stratigraphic units, of which the largest is the group. The Tonto Group of the Grand Canyon [A] is separated by distinct unconformities from the groups directly above and below. It in turn consists of three formations – bodies of rock that share certain generic features. The Bright Angel Formation [B] consists mainly of shales Distinct from the limestone and sandstone formations above and below it. Formations can be subdivided into members such as the dolomite member [C], which are characterized by a distinct lithology. The smallest stratigraphic units of all are beds. The lower dolomite bed [D] is readily identifiable by the division planes between it and its neighbours both above and below. A bed may range in thickness from a few millimetres to several metres and some beds may contain even finer structures.

13 Structures may also show what happened to the sediment immediately after it was laid down. A bed of fine mudstone in the dune-bedded sandstones (itself indicating a temporary flooding in the desert) shows reptile footprints and marks caused by falling rain. Structures such as these provide valuable clues about the climate of the area at the time of the formation of the rocks and give some information about the fauna.

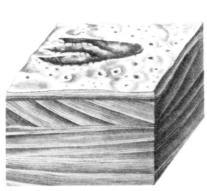

14 A desert region was formed after the area was built up above sea-level by the delta. Rain storms occurred, causing local flooding, and the area was populated by reptiles. By now the volcano would have been eroded to a stump. Conditions such as these were common during the Permian and so the whole cliff face can be said to show a transition from marine to desert conditions in upper Carboniferous and Permian times.

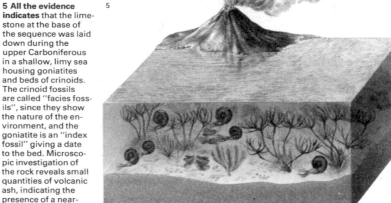

8 Coal, found above some of the beds of sandstone, indicates the presence of thickly forested swamps in which dead vegetable matter accumulated as thick beds of peat. Land had encroached upon the sea.

9 One of the commonest fossils in coal measures is that of a tree stump. The stump and roots keep their shape, being buried in the underlying sand, while the trunk and branches are turned to coal.

10 The sequence of rocks seen in this part of the cliff – shale, sandstone and coal repeated again and again – is characteristic of sediments laid as a delta advances over a marine area. The fact that the sequence is a repeating one indicates that the area was subsiding and the delta was constantly advancing and retreating, building up the sediments. The absence of volcanic material suggests that the volcano was extinct by this time.

4 A fossil goniatite is also found in this limestone. This was a nautilus-like mollusc with most of its body inside a coiled shell. The shell was divided into chambers by zig-zag partitions that differed from species to species. As each species was a free swimmer and common throughout all the seas of the world at different times, whenever a recognizable species is found in a rock, that rock can be dated. This species shows the limestone to be upper Carboniferous.

5 All the evidence indicates that the limestone at the base of the sequence was laid down during the upper Carboniferous in a shallow, limy sea housing goniatites and beds of crinoids. The crinoid fossils are called "facies fossils", since they show the nature of the environment, and the goniatite is an "index fossil" giving a date to the bed. Microscopic investigation of the rock reveals small quantities of volcanic ash, indicating the presence of a nearby active volcano.

Geology in the field

The structure of rock formations is not always immediately apparent, especially where they are hidden beneath overlying layers of soil or are obscured by vegetation. One of the best ways of determining the relationships between rocks and the processes at work within the earth is by mapping. Geological maps therefore provide the key to understanding the geological history of any particular region.

The basis of geological maps
A geological map [2] shows the boundaries, or contacts, between various rock units, as if the topsoil and vegetation had been stripped off. Maps also reveal the size and extent of any rock formation.

Formations are the basic units of geological maps. They can be recognized by their well-defined contrast to surrounding layers and by the fact that they can be readily traced in the field. The basic criterion of a formation is that it must be a rock layer of sufficient importance and of sufficiently distinct an identity for geologists to agree about its characteristics – in other words, it must form a unit which can be mapped.

Where formations have been partly obliterated by erosion, or obscured beneath overlying rock and soil, their shape must be pieced together from isolated and often widely scattered outcrops. A single outcrop is usually insufficient to reveal the complex inter-relations of the various formations in a region. A geologist [6] must make detailed examinations of numerous rock exposures before he can draw a map that assembles his scattered findings into a coherent picture. Such a map reveals the disposition of the rocks and is the basis for understanding a region's structure and history.

The geologist will also draw up cross-sections of the map, showing a vertical slice through the rocks. Canyon walls and coastal cliffs are natural cross-sections of this kind. However, because of their rarity, the geologist must construct his own interpretative section. Cross-sections are derived from interpreting the contours and the attitude of surface outcrops and by making test borings. These sections are essential for determining the commercial importance of ores and in preparing to dig tunnels and mines.

With the knowledge of the fundamental principles that apply to the formation of rocks, a geologist can set off into the field to decipher the structures of a specific region.

Techniques of mapping
There are many techniques for correlating rock formations but the best and most obvious method is to trace a continuous exposure over a distance. In most cases, however, rocks are only sporadically revealed, so the geologist must look for lithological similarities in outcrops. Rocks of the same formation are usually similar in colour, mineral composition and texture although, because most strata change gradually over a distance, other means of identification are also used. Certain characteristics of deposition are especially helpful in identifying separate outcrops as belonging to the same formation. These include ripple marks, formed in sand under very shallow water and later preserved in stone; cross-bedding, which is sand deposited on the underwater slopes of a delta; and graded bedding, beds in

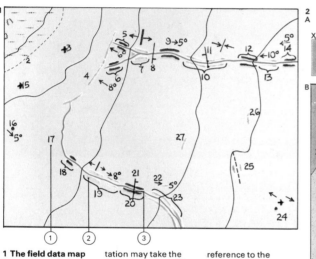

1 The field data map is usually a relief map of the area which the geologist annotates as he works. Such annotation may take the form of numbers [1] referring to an entry in a notebook, colour keying [2] giving a quick visual reference to the rock type, and conventional symbols [3] that describe the folds and faults in the rocks.

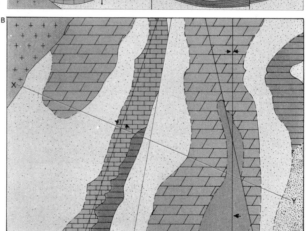

2 Geological maps are interpreted from field maps. They show the surface disposition of the rocks as if the topsoil and the vegetation had been removed [B]. The same area is also shown in cross-section [A]. A granitic intrusion [1] adjoins a basal sandstone [2]. Fossils in a bed [3] identify a Carboniferous formation that grades laterally from limestone to shale and then sandstone. Much of this bed is buried by desert sandstone [4] whereas dolomite [5] and the later shale [6] complete the sequences. The two faults are shown on the map by plain lines. A line with converging arrows is a syncline axis and with diverging arrows an anticline.

3 Facies maps reveal the variations of the rocks within a single formation, which is mapped as if all the overlying rocks were removed. The example shown is taken from bed 3 of map 2. The cross-section [A] shows the present disposition of this formation or bed, the facies map of which [B], shows that it consists of a deep-sea limestone [2] cut by a granite intrusion [1] and grading into reef limestone [3]. Beyond this, the formation shows shallow-water shales [4] and deltaic sandstones [5]. This facies map also shows the thickness of the formation by means of contour lines of equal thickness known as isopachs. These are determined by drilling or by seismological methods.

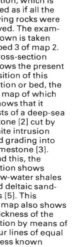
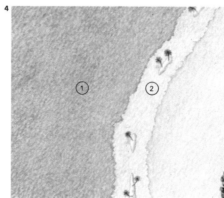

4 A palaeogeographic map is the representation of geographic features at a given geological time. The previous facies map of the formation [3] of map 2, which was deposited during the Carboniferous, can be translated into this map. The shales and sandstone to the SE show the former existence of a land in that direction and of a river flowing from it and building a delta [4] into a shallow sea [3]. Farther out to sea, in waters less than 45m (150ft) deep and more than 20°C (68°F) in temperature, corals and algae built barrier reefs and low-lying islands [2]. In the zone of open water [1] beyond the reef, calcareous plant and animal remains accumulated in deposits of limy mud which, in time, became limestone.

which the coarser material lies at the bottom and the finer material rests on the top.

A highly reliable technique of correlation is that of finding a similarity of sequence. The position of a layer between other readily identifiable layers is an ideal means of correlating scattered outcrops. The fossil contents of rocks are other excellent tools of correlation. Fossils can be characteristic of specific environments and of specific periods in history. They not only identify the formation in which they are found but also help to determine its age.

The structure of an area is important in determining the history of the rocks since their formation. Not all beds are horizontal. Many have been tilted, folded and faulted into a variety of twisted positions. In the field, geologists may notice that the bedding planes of the strata in a particular outcrop slope diagonally into the ground. The acute angle between the plane of this rock and the horizontal surface of the earth is known as the "dip". The angle of dip is measured with a clinometer and is stated in degrees. The "strike" of a rock is the direction in which the

face of its bedding plane lies – this is given as a compass direction. Strike and dip together measure the attitude of a formation. The attitude of a rock provides one of the most reliable indications of the sub-surface structure of a particular region.

Palaeogeographic maps
By interpreting geological maps and examining rocks for clues about the environment in which they were originally deposited, it is possible to piece together clues to the earth's past. This information can be represented in palaeogeographic maps, which portray the surface features of the earth as it existed during any given era in history [4].

Maps can also be constructed so as to show the past distribution of climatic zones. The fossils of organisms that flourished only in specific environmental conditions are an important means of identifying palaeoclimates, but more direct indicators of climate can also be found. These include such features as ice-grooves in erosion surfaces and rain pits in sandstone, each telling their own story of the geological history of the earth.

A geologist coming into an area for the first time is rarely faced with a completely exposed sequence of rocks as in the Grand Canyon. More often the rocks in his area of study are concealed beneath soil and vegetation and exposed only occasionally where the natural covering has been removed by the action of water or the weather. The geologist studies each outcrop and from his notes, and the samples he has collected for further study, he can reconstruct the area's geological history. The different steps in the study of the area shown here are illustrated in maps 1 to 5.

5 The geological history of the area can be unravelled by the study of all the formations shown in map 2A, which are referred to here by the same numbers. The lowest formation [2] is a sandstone deposited in a desert [A]. The sea then advanced [B] producing marine conditions [3]. When the sea withdrew a new desert [C] and sandstone formation [4] occurred. A return of the sea [D] brought calcareous sediments [5] and muds [6]. Later faulting and folding occurred [E] and granite [1] was intruded into the sedimentary layers. Since then erosion produced today's landscape [F]. We can now look at the Key illustration with greater understanding.

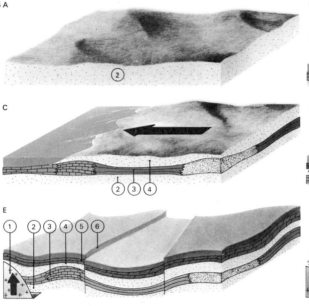

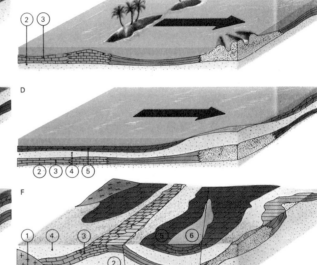

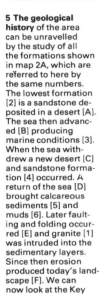

6 The geologist who sets out to do fieldwork must carry with him all the tools and measuring devices that he will need to make his observations. Typically, he will have a compass and clinometer to take the dips and bearings of bedding planes, faults and other features. A hand lens is used to examine details in rocks and a camera is useful to record the attitude and structure of rock outcrops. A hammer is essential for breaking open rocks to examine their mineral composition and to chip off samples that are collected for the specimen bag. Most important is the pen and notebook in which all his observations, rough drawings and maps are recorded.

Right-coiling *Globorotalia*
Left-coiling *Globorotalia*
Tropical forest
Peat bogs
Desert
Ice cap
Limy seas
Salt basin
Coral reefs

Geomagnetic equator

7 Palaeoclimatology is the study of ancient climates through traces left in contemporary rocks. The present-day formations of such preservable climate-related features is shown. The foraminifernan *Globorotalia* is an indicator of sea temperature. It coils right in warm waters and left in cold waters. Coral reefs and major carbonate deposits are both typical of warm, shallow seas. Common to desert environments are evaporite deposits (salt basins) and reddish-hued sandstones. The lush plant life of tropical forests and swamps is the raw material from which coal is formed. Ice sheets groove and scratch the face of rocks and leave characteristic deposits of glacial till, and peat bogs are typical of the tundra environment along the fringes of the ice caps.

Earth's time scale

In the mid-seventeenth century, Archbishop James Ussher (1581–1656) of Ireland reached the conclusion that the earth was created at precisely 9am on 23 October 4004 BC. His findings were arrived at after diligent study of religious texts. Not until well into the nineteenth century did efforts to establish both absolute and relative techniques of geological dating meet with any semblance of success. In 1897, the renowned British physicist William Thomas Kelvin (1824–1907) attempted to deduce the earth's age from the temperature difference between the young molten planet and its present state, assuming that the rate of heat loss was constant. His estimate of 20-40 million years was more than a hundred times lower than current estimates. Radioactivity was then unknown, so Kelvin failed to take into account the fierce heat generated by the decay of radioactive elements within the earth.

The law of superposition
Although early efforts to find an absolute dating system repeatedly failed, a relative time scale proved far easier to develop. Such a system merely seeks to establish the order in which rocks were laid down [1]. It does not make any reference to fixed units of time. The entire sequence of rocks deposited since the beginning of time is known as the geological column. Once the law of superposition (which states that in strata which have remained undisturbed since deposition older rocks lie beneath younger ones) had been elucidated by William Smith (1769–1839) late in the eighteenth century, piecing together the geological column was simply a long, arduous task of identifying and correlating rocks and slotting them into their appropriate order in the stratigraphic sequence. The entire column was subdivided into units based on events that were taken to be natural breaks between one geological era and the next. The major divisions, therefore, are of widely differing lengths of time [5].

The correlation of rock strata was made easier by observing the fossils they contained. Organisms of any particular time in history possess quite distinct characteristics that can be used to identify the widely scattered rocks in which these fossils occur [3]. Strata containing similar fossil assemblages can be assumed to have been deposited during the same period of geological history.

The search for absolute dating
The breakthrough to an absolute time scale was finally achieved with the discovery that radioactive decay proceeds at a constant pace. In 1907, a chemist at Yale University, Bertram Boltwood (1870–1927), found that the decay of radioactive minerals could be thought of as a convenient yardstick of time. He recognized the regular relationship that existed between decay products and their parent elements and that progressively older specimens possessed increasing amounts of stable end products [8].

The most useful concept in radiological chronology is the notion of a half-life, the time it takes for half a given amount of material to decompose, or decay, into a radiogenic product. The half-life of uranium-238, for example, is 4,510 million years. After a lapse of this time, only half an original given quantity of uranium remains, the rest having been transformed into a series of radioactive

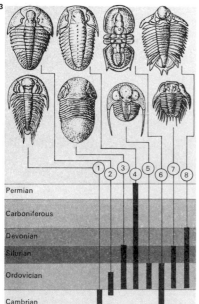

1 The relative ages of rock structures can be understood from clues in the rocks. In this cross-section the oldest formation is of metamorphic basement rock [1]. It was tilted and heavily eroded before being buried by a sedimentary sequence [2] that in turn weathered and was buried by a later sequence [3], shown by fragments of 2 found in 3. Tectonic activity caused a fault [4] to displace earlier rock [3 and 1] followed by an intrusion of magma [5]. Erosion, followed by a sea inundation, deposited a new layer [6]. The most recent structure is an igneous intrusion [7] to the land's surface.

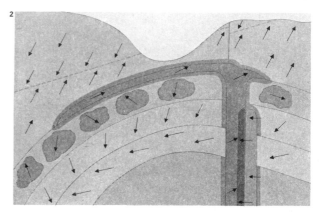

2 The earth's magnetic field can provide a useful tool for the dating of rocks. When a rock is formed, magnetic particles in it align themselves in the direction of the earth's lines of magnetic force acting at the time. If the changes in direction and position of the lines of force are established the ages of the rocks of an undisturbed sequence can be determined by investigation of their magnetic alignment. If the rocks have been disturbed the variations in their alignments indicate the nature of the movements involved. The complex history of the example shown can be interpreted by a study of the alignments of the magnetic particles.

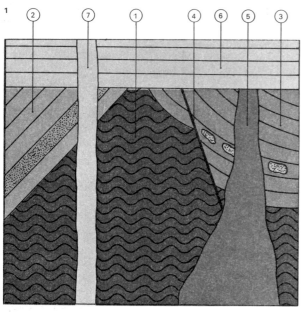

3 Index fossils are useful for determining the ages of rocks. The age ranges of the various families of trilobites are known. If proetid and agnostid trilobites are found in the same rock, it is Ordovician in age.

1 Redlichiida
2 Asphidea
3 Ilanidae
4 Proetidae
5 Trinucleidae
6 Agnostida
7 Odontopleurida
8 Lichida

Permian
Carboniferous
Devonian
Silurian
Ordovician
Cambrian

4 Orogeny is the process of mountain building by folding and thrusting. In the geological past, there were several major orogenic climaxes, which make ideal reference points as they form breaks in the stratigraphic column through an increase of erosion and changes in sedimentation patterns.

isotopes, eventually decaying to the lead isotope Pb-206. Thorium-232 has an even longer half-life, of some 14,100 million years, while that of carbon-14 is of only 5,570 years.

The age of a rock specimen is arrived at by comparing the ratio of decay elements to the remaining amount of parent material. The known half-life of the element in question is then used to calculate the sample's age. This technique has only become reliable since the 1950s when mass spectrometers, instruments that can analyse and measure elements in quantities of only a few millionths of a gramme, were developed.

The process of decay is extremely complex. The disintegration of unstable atoms is spontaneous and has never been shown to be affected by surrounding physical or chemical conditions. This is one of the only processes on earth which can be assumed to have had a constant rate throughout time, making it an ideal standard for the measurement of absolute age.

Absolute dating establishes the age of a specimen from the time it crysallized into a mineral, not the age of the element itself. Once a crystal has crystallized, chemical composition is fixed. The decay products within it are the result of the disintegration of a radioactive parent element.

Finding the age of the earth
Uranium, and its close cousin thorium, are not the only elements that are suitable for absolute dating. Potassium-40, with a half-life of 1,300 million years, occurs throughout the earth's crust in measurable quantities. It decays into argon-40, an inert gas found drifting in the atmosphere. A comparison of the ratio of these two elements in the crust and air yield a figure of some 4,600 million years for the age of the earth. The oldest rocks of the great Precambrian shields of North America, Greenland, Africa and Australia yield dates of up to only 3,500 million years. The discrepancy between the two figures is perfectly plausible since a long cooling period must be allowed for before any major rock systems could have formed a crust. Despite all these up-to-date techniques, many rocks cannot be dated absolutely.

KEY

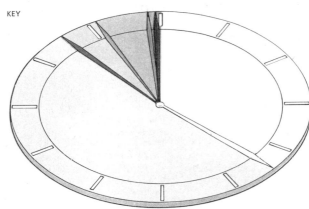

The colossal time-span over which geological processes operate is emphasized if one compresses the 4,600 million years of earth history into 12 hours on a clock face. The first 2 hours 52 minutes are obscure. The earl-

iest rocks occur at about 02.52 hours but the planet remains a lifeless desert until 04.20, when bacterial and algal organisms appear. Aeons of time drag by until just after 10.30 when there is an explosion of invertebrate

life in the seas. Dinosaurs wander the land at 11.25 only to be replaced by birds and mammals 25 minutes later. Hominids arrive about half a minute before noon. The last tenth of a second covers the history of civilization.

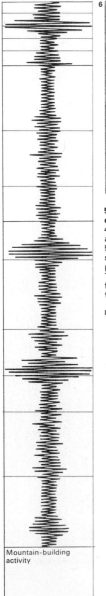

Quaternary	2	Cenozoic
Pliocene		
Miocene		
Oligocene		
Palaeocene and Eocene	65	
Cretaceous	135	Mesozoic
Jurassic	195	
Triassic	225	
Permian	280	Palaeozoic
Carboniferous	345	
Devonian	395	
Silurian	430	
Ordovician	500	
Cambrian	570	
Precambrian	m.y.	

Mountain-building activity

5 The age of the earth is some 4,600 million years, although only the last 570 million years show an abundance of plant and animal life. The most widely found fossil remains from any specific

period are called index fossils and are used to correlate various rock formations of the same age. Mountain building took place mostly during specific periods in the geological time scale.

6 Varves are thin bands of sand, clay and silt deposited as easily recognized annual layers in glacier-fed lakes. Varves can be read to determine the dates of the retreat of the last ice age.

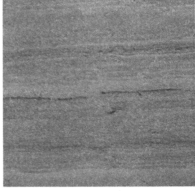

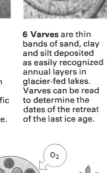

7 Dendrochronology is the use of annual growth rings of trees to measure time. The innermost rings of recent trees can be matched to the outer rings of older trees and a chronology can be set up.

8 N = neutron
P = proton

Normal carbon-12 atom   Nitrogen-14 atom   Carbon-14 atom

O_2

CO_2

Pulses in number of C-14 atoms

5,570 years

11,460 years

Time in years

Carbon-14

β

Nitrogen-14

8 Radiocarbon dating is typical of the techniques that use radioactive decay to estimate age. Carbon (C) posesses two isotopes, C-14 which is radioactive, formed by cosmic ray bombardment of nitrogen-14 (N-14), and C-12 which is not. The C-14 combines with oxygen to form carbon dioxide which is absorbed by living organisms. A constant ratio of C-14 to C-12 is established in each organism during its life. After death no more carbon dioxide is absorbed and the C-14 decays steadily, by emitting beta particles, to N-14, falling to half its original quantity every 5,570 years. The age of organic remains can be estimated by comparing the ratio of C-14 to C-12 in them.

INDEX

Bibliography

General
New Concise Atlas of the Earth; Mitchell Beazley, 1978
Structure of the Earth
Cook, A. H.; *Physics of the Earth and Planets*; Macmillan, 1973
Jacobs, J. A.; *Earth's Core*; Academic Press, 1975
Bott, M. H. P.; *Interior of the Earth*; Arnold, 1971
McElhinny, M. W.; *Palaeo-Magnetism and Plate Tectonics*; Cambridge U.P., 1975
Tarling, D. H. & M. P. Tarling; *Continental Drift*; Penguin, 1972
Calder, N.; *Restless Earth*; B.B.C., 1972
Scientific American; *Continents Adrift and Continents Aground*; W. H. Freeman, 1976
Sullivan, W.; *Continents in Motion: The New Earth Debate*; Macmillan, 1977
Fuchs, V. (Ed.); *Forces of Nature*; Thames & Hudson, 1977
Waltham, T.; *Catastrophe: the Violent Earth*; Macmillan, 1978
Francis, P.; *Volcanoes*; Penguin, 1976
Bullard, F. M.; *Volcanoes of the Earth*; Univ. of Texas, 1976
Jordan, P.; *Expanding Earth: Dirac's Gravitation Hypothesis*; Pergamon, 1971
Hallam, A. (Ed.); *Planet Earth*; Elsevier-Phaidon, 1977
The Earth in Perspective
Robinson, A. H. & R. D. Sale; *Elements of Cartography*; Wiley, 1969
Roblin, H. S.; *Map Projections*; Arnold, 1969
Tooley, R. V.; *Maps and Map-Makers*; Batsford, 1978
Dury, G. H.; *British Isles*; Heinemann Educ., 1973
Stamp, L. D.; *Britain's Structure and Scenery*; Collins (New Naturalist Series), 1970
Church, R. J. H.; *Advanced Geography of Northern and Western Europe*; Hulton, 1968
Monkhouse, F. J.; *Regional Geography of Western Europe*; Longman, 1974
Clarke, F. I. et al.; *Advanced Geography of Africa*; Hulton, 1975
Brice, W. C.; *South West Asia*; Univ. of London Press, 1966
Cole, J. P.; *Latin America*; Butterworth, 1975
Robinson, H.; *Latin America*; Macdonald & Evans, 1977
Weather
Bodin, S.; *Weather and Climate*; Blandford, 1978
Calder, N.; *The Weather Machine*; B.B.C., 1974
Sutton, G.; *Weather*; Teach Yourself Books, 1974
Scorer, P. R.; *Clouds of the World*; David & Charles, 1972
Harvey, J. G.; *Atmosphere and Ocean*; Artemis Press, 1976
Watts, A.; *Instant Weather Forecasting*; Adlard-Coles, 1968, Hart-Davis Educ., 1968
Griffiths, J. F.; *Climate and the Environment*; Elek, 1976
Seas and Oceans
Anikouchine, W. A. & R. W. Sternberg; *World Ocean*; Prentice, 1973
Atlas of the Oceans; Mitchell Beazley, 1977
Bhatt, J. J.; *Oceanography: Exploring the Planet Ocean*; Van Nost. Reinhold, 1978
Perry, A. H. & J. M. Walker; *Ocean-Atmosphere System*; Longman, 1977

Bellamy, D.; *Life-giving Sea*; Hamish Hamilton, 1975
Shepard, F. P.; *Earth Beneath the Sea*; Johns Hopkins, 1968
Shepard, F. P.; *Submarine Geology*; Harper & Row, 1973
Cotter, C. H.; *Atlantic Ocean*; Brown, Son & Ferguson, 1964
Menard, H. W.; *Marine Geology of the Pacific*; McGraw-Hill, 1964
Toussaint, A.; *History of the Indian Ocean*; Routledge, 1966
Maury, M. F.; *Physical Geography of the Sea*; Harvard U.P., 1972
Deacon, G. E. R. (Ed.); *Oceans*; Hamlyn, 1968
Sweeney, J. B.; *Pictorial History of Oceanographic Submersibles*; Hale, 1972
Penzias, W. & M. W. Goodman; *Man beneath the Sea*; Wiley, 1973
Geology
Buerger, M. J.; *Contemporary Crystallography*; McGraw-Hill, 1970
Buerger, M. J.; *Elementary Crystallography*; Wiley, 1963
Glasser, L. S. D.; *Crystallography and its Applications*; Van Nost, Reinhold, 1977
Fraser, R.; *Understanding the Earth*; Penguin, 1967
Robinson, H.; *Physical Geography*; Macdonald & Evans, 1977
Bank, H.; *Precious Stones and Minerals*; Warne, 1970
Sparks, B. W.; *Rocks and Relief*; Longman, 1971
Carmichael, I. S. E.; *Igneous Petrology*; McGraw-Hill, 1974
Hatch, F. H. & R. H. Rastall; *Petrology of Sedimentary Rocks*; Murby, 1971
Miyashiro, A.; *Metamorphism and Metamorphic Belts*; Allen & Unwin, 1973
Carson, M. A. & M. J. Kirkby; *Hillslope Form and Process*; Cambridge U.P., 1972
Moore, W. G.; *Mountains and Plateaux*; Hutchinson, 1970
Young, A.; *Slopes*; Oliver & Boyd, 1972
Edwards, R. W. & D. J. Garrod; *Conservation and Productivity of Natural Waters*; Academic Press, 1972
Waltham, T.; *Caves*; Macmillan, 1974
Crickmay, C. H.; *Work of the River*; Macmillan, 1974
Dury, G. H.; *Rivers and River Terraces*; Macmillan, 1970
Sugden, D. E. & B. S. John; *Glaciers and Landscape*; Arnold, 1976
John, B. S.; *Ice Age*; Collins, 1977
Cornwall, I. W.; *Ice Ages: Nature and Effects*; Baker, 1970
Cooke, R. U. & A. Warren; *Geomorphology in Deserts*; Batsford, 1973
Steers, J. A.; *Coastline of England and Wales*; Cambridge U.P., 1964
Steers, J. A.; *Coastline of Scotland*; Cambridge U.P., 1973
King, C. A. M.; *Beaches and Coasts*; Arnold, 1972
Ager, D. V.; *Nature of the Stratigraphical Record*; Macmillan, 1973
Seyfert, C. K. & L. A. Sirkin; *Earth History and Plate Tectonics*; Harper & Row
Kummel, B.; *History of the Earth*; W.H. Freeman, 1970
Tank, R.; *Focus on Environmental Geology*; Oxford U.P., 1976
Ager, D. V.; *Introducing Geology: Earth's Crust as History*; Faber, 1975

Fabian Acker CEng, MIEE, MIMarE; Professor Leslie Alcock; Professor H. C. Allen MC; Leonard Amey OBE; Neil Ardley BSc; Professor H. R. V. Arnstein DSc, PhD, FIBiol; Russell Ash BA (Dunelm), FRAI; Norman Ashford PhD, CEng, MICE, MASCE, MCIT; Professor Robert Ashton; B. W. Atkinson BSc, PhD; Anthony Atmore BA; Professor Philip S. Bagwell BSc(Econ), PhD; Peter Ball MA; Edwin Banks MIOP; Professor Michael Banton; Dulan Barber; Harry Barrett; Professor J. P. Barron MA, DPhil, FSA; Professor W. G. Beasley FBA; Alan Bender PhD, MSc, DIC, ARCS; Lionel Bender BSc; Israel Berkovitch PhD, FRIC, MIChemE; David Berry MA; M. L. Bierbrier PhD; A. T. E. Binsted FBBI (Dipl); David Black; Maurice E. F. Block BA, PhD(Cantab); Richard H. Bomback BSc (London), FRPS; Basil Booth BSc (Hons), PhD, FGS, FRGS; J. Harry Bowen MA(Cantab), PhD(London); Mary Briggs MPS, FLS; John Brodrick BSc(Econ); J. M. Bruce ISO, MA, FRHistS, MRAeS; Professer D. A. Bullough MA, FSA, FRHistS; Tony Buzan BA(Hons) UBC; Dr Alan R. Cane; Dr J. G. de Casparis; Dr Jeremy Catto MA; Denis Chamberlain; E. W. Chanter MA; Professor Colin Cherry DSc(Eng), MIEE; A. H. Christie MA, FRAI, FRAS; Dr Anthony W. Clare MPhil(London), MB, BCh, MRCPI, MRCPsych; Professor Aidan Clarke MA, PhD, FTCD; Sonia Cole; John R. Collis MA, PhD; Professor Gordon Connell-Smith BA, PhD, FRHistS; Dr A. H. Cook FRS; Professor A. H. Cook FRS; J. A. L. Cooke MA, DPhil; R. W. Cooke BSc, CEng, MICE; B. K. Cooper; Penelope J. Corfield MA; Robin Cormack MA, PhD, FSA; Nona Coxhead; Patricia Crone BA, PhD; Geoffrey P. Crow BSc(Eng), MICE, MIMunE, MInstHE, DIPTE; J. G. Crowther; Professor R. B. Cundall FRIC; Noel Currer-Briggs MA, FSG; Christopher Cviic BA(Zagreb), BSc(Econ, London); Gordon Daniels BSc(Econ, London), DPhil(Oxon); George Darby BA; G. J. Darwin; Dr David Delvin; Robin Denselow BA; Professor Bernard L. Diamond; John Dickson; Paul Dinnage MA; M. L. Dockrill BSc(Econ), MA, PhD; Patricia Dodd BA; James Dowdall; Anne Dowson MA(Cantab); Peter M. Driver BSc, PhD, MIBiol; Rev Professor C.

W. Dugmore DD; Herbert L. Edlin BSc, Dip in Forestry; Pamela Egan MA(Oxon); Major S. R. Elliot CD, BComm; Professor H. J. Eysenck PhD, DSc; Dr Peter Fenwick BA, MB, BChir, DPM, MRCPsych; Jim Flegg BSc, PhD, ARCS, MBOU; Andrew M. Fleming MA; Professor Antony Flew MA(Oxon), DLitt (Keele); Wyn K. Ford FRHistS; Paul Freeman DSc(London); G. S. P. Freeman-Grenville DPhil, FSA, FRAS, G. E. Fussell DLitt, FRHistS; Kenneth W. Gatland FRAS, FBIS; Norman Gelb BA; John Gilbert BA(Hons, London); Professor A. C. Gimson; John Glaves-Smith BA; David Glen; Professor S. J. Goldsack BSc, PhD, FInstP, FBCS; Richard Gombrich MA, DPhil; A. F. Gomm; Professor A. Goodwin MA; William Gould BA(Wales); Professor J. R. Gray; Christopher Green PhD; Bill Gunston; Professor A. Rupert Hall DLitt; Richard Halsey BA(Hons, UEA); Lynette K. Hamblin BSc; Norman Hammond; Peter Harbison MA, DPhil; Professor Thomas G. Harding PhD; Professor D. W. Harkness; Richard Harris; Dr Randall P. Harrison; Cyril Hart MA, PhD, FRICS, FIFor; Anthony P. Harvey; Nigel Hawkes BA(Oxon); F. P. Heath; Peter Hebblethwaite MA (Oxon), LicTheol; Frances Mary Heidensohn BA; Dr Alan Hill MC, FRCP; Robert Hillenbrand MA, DPhil; Catherine Hills PhD; Professor F. H. Hinsley; Dr Richard Hitchcock; Dorothy Hollingsworth OBE, BSc, FRIC, FIBiol, FIFST, SRD; H. P. Hope BSc(Hons, Agric); Antony Hopkins CBE, FRCM, LRAM, FRSA; Brian Hook; Peter Howell BPhil, MA(Oxon); Brigadier K. Hunt; Peter Hurst BDS, FDS, LDS, RSCEd, MSc(London); Anthony Hyman MA, PhD; Professor R. S. Illingworth MD, FRCP, DPH, DCH; Oliver Impey MA, DPhil; D. E. G. Irvine PhD; L. M. Irvine BSc; E. W. Ives BA, PhD; Anne Jamieson cand mag(Copenhagen), MSc (London); Michael A. Janson BSc; G. H. Jenkins PhD; Professor P. A. Jewell BSc (Agric), MA, PhD, FIBiol; Hugh Johnson; Commander I. E. Johnston RN; I. P. Jolliffe BSc, MSc, PhD, ComplCE, FGS; Dr D. E. H. Jones ARCS, FCS; R. H. Jones PhD, BSc, CEng, MICE, FGS, MASCE, Hugh Kay; Dr Janet Kear; Sam Keen; D. R. C. Kempe BSc, DPhil, FGS; Alan

Kendall MA(Cantab); Michael Kenward; John R. King BSc(Eng), DIC, CEng, MIProdE; D. G. King-Hele FRS; Professor J. F. Kirkaldy DSc; Malcolm Kitch; Michael Kitson MA; B. C. Lamb BSc, PhD; Nick Landon; Major J. C. Larminie QDG, Retd; Diana Leat BSc(Econ), PhD; Roger Lewin BSc, PhD; Harold K. Lipset; Norman Longmate MA(Oxon); John Lowry; Kenneth E. Lowther MA; Diana Lucas BA(Hons); Keith Lye BA, FRGS; Dr Peter Lyon; Dr Martin McCauley; Sean McConville BSc; D. F. M. McGregor BSc, PhD(Edin); Jean Macqueen PhD; William Baird MacQuitty MA(Hons), FRGS, FRPS; Professor Rev F. X. Martin OSA; Jonathan Martin MA; Rev Cannon E. L. Mascall DD; Christopher Maynard MSc, DTh; Professor A. J. Meadows; Dr T. B. Millar; John Miller MA, PhD, J. S. G. Miller MA, DPhil, BM, BCh; Alaric Millington BSc, DipEd, FIMA; Rosalind Mitchison MA, FRHistS; Peter L. Moldon; Patrick Moore OBE; Robin Mowat MA, DPhil; J. Michael Mullin BSc; Alistair Munroe BSc, ARCS; Professor Jacob Needleman, John Newman MA, FSA; Professor Donald M. Nicol MA PhD; Gerald Norris; Professor F. S. Northedge PhD; Caroline E. Oakman BA(Hons, Chinese); S. O'Connell MA(Cantab), MInstP; Dr Robert Orr; Michael Overman; Di Owen BSc; A. R. D. Pagden MA, FRHistS; Professor E. J. Pagel PhD; Liam de Paor MA; Carol Parker BA(Econ), MA (Internat. Aff.); Derek Parker; Julia Parker DFAstrolS; Dr Stanley Parker; Dr Colin Murray Parkes MD, FRC(Psych), DPM; Professor Geoffrey Parrinder MA, PhD, DD(London), DLitt(Lancaster); Moira Paterson; Walter C. Patterson MSc; Sir John H. Peel KCVO, MA, DM, FRCP, FRCS, FRCOG; D. J. Penn; Basil Peters MA, MInstP, FBIS; D. L. Phillips FRCR, MRCOG; B. T. Pickering PhD, DSc; John Picton; Susan Pinkus; Dr C. S. Pitcher MA, DM, FRCPath; Alfred Plaut FRCPsych; A. S. Playfair MRCS, LRCP, DObst, RCOG; Dr Antony Polonsky; Joyce Pope BA; B. L. Potter NDA, MRAC, CertEd; Paulette Pratt; Antony Preston; Frank J. Pycroft; Margaret Quass; Dr John Reckless; Trevor Reese BA, PhD, FRHistS; M. M. Reese MA (Oxon); Derek A. Reid BSc, PhD; Clyde Reynolds BSc; John

Rivers; Peter Roberts; Colin A. Ronan MSc, FRAS; Professor Richard Rose BA(Johns Hopkins), DPhil (Oxon); Harold Rosenthal; T. G. Rosenthal MA(Cantab); Anne Ross MA, MA(Hons, Celtic Studies), PhD, (Archaeol and Celtic Studies, Edin); Georgina Russell MA; Dr Charles Rycroft BA (Cantab), MB(London), FRCPsych; Susan Saunders MSc(Econ); Robert Schell PhD; Anil Seal MA, PhD(Cantab); Michael Sedgwick MA(Oxon); Martin Seymour-Smith BA(Oxon), MA(Oxon); Professor John Shearman; Dr Martin Sherwood; A. C. Simpson BSc; Nigel Sitwell; Dr Alan Sked; Julie and Kenneth Slavin FRGS, FRAI; Professor T. C. Smout; Alec Xavier Snobel BSc(Econ); Terry Snow BA, ATCL; Rodney Steel; Charles S. Steinger MA, PhD; Geoffrey Stern BSc(Econ); Maryanne Stevens BA(Cantab), MA(London); John Stevenson DPhil, MA; D. Michael Stoddart BSc, PhD; Bernard Stonehouse DPhil, MA, BSc, MInst Biol; Anthony Storr FRCP, FRCPsych; Richard Storry; Charles Stuart-Jervis; Professor John Taylor; John W. R. Taylor FRHistS, MRAeS, FSLAET; R. B. Taylor BSc(Hons, Microbiol); J. David Thomas MA, PhD; D. Thompson BSc(Econ); Harvey Tilker PhD; Don Tills PhD, MPhil, MIBiol, FIMLS; Jon Tinker; M. Tregear MA; R. W. Trender; David Trump MA, PhD, FSA; M. F. Tuke PhD; Christopher Tunney MA; Laurence Urdang Associates (authentication and fact check); Sally Walters BSc; Christopher Wardle; Dr D. Washbrook; David Watkins; George Watkins MSc; J. W. N. Watkins; Anthony J. Watts; Dr Geoff Watts; Melvyn Westlake; Anthony White MA(Oxon), MAPhil(Columbia); Dr Ruth D. Whitehouse; P. J. S. Whitmore MBE, PhD; Professor G. R. Wilkinson; Rev H. A. Williams CR; Christopher Wilson BA; Professor David M. Wilson; John B. Wilson BSc, PhD, FGS, FLS; Philip Windsor BA, DPhil(Oxon), Roy Wolfe BSc(Econ), MSc; Donald Wood MA PhD; Dr David Woodings MA, MRCP, MRCPath; Bernard Yallop PhD, BSc, ARCS, FRAS Professor John Yudkin MA, MD, PhD(Cantab), FRIC, FIBiol, FRCP.